Fred Bear's Field Notes

Fred Bear

THE FRED BEAR SPORTS CLUB PRESS
GAINESVILLE, FLORIDA

By Fred Bear

FRED BEAR'S FIELD NOTES

THE ARCHER'S BIBLE

FRED BEAR'S WORLD OF ARCHERY

Fred Bear's
Field Notes

ISBN 0-9619480-0-0
Library of Congress Catalog Card Number 76-2752
Copyright © 1976
Reprinted 1987
Reprinted 1991
Reprinted 1994
All Rights Reserved
Printed in the United States of America

Lovingly dedicated to my wife, Henrietta,
who painstakingly interpreted and put in order
the contents of my many weather-worn
and battered notebooks

PREFACE

In publishing this diary of fifteen of my hunts, I hope to share with you the exhilaration of time spent in the wild—leaving man's first footprint, perhaps, in some remote area. Or simply to enjoy the peace and solitude of sitting with your back against a tree in the forest.

Alfred Pease wrote in his *Book of the Lion:* "The most and best is known to the man who quits his bed before sunrise . . . who spends his days on the mountains and forests . . . who bears the heat and cold and hunger and thirst . . . for the love of nature . . . to visit the utmost refuges of beast and bird."

I have done such things. My youth was spent on a farm in Pennsylvania. I was taught to hunt and love the out-of-doors by my father. School was interesting to me but the yearning to be afield was so strong that classes eventually lost the battle and had to be made up in night school after I left home and went to Michigan.

It has been my good fortune over the years to enjoy many great hunts in almost all parts of the world. I kept a diary on each hunt and from these dog-eared, rain-soaked pages evolved the chapters of this book.

» «

At the time most of these notes were written, ecology was not the household word it is today. Few people spoke of endangered species and the population explosion, with its resultant loss of wildlife habitat, was not generally understood.

Progress was defined in terms of land cleared, highways built, and Gross National Product. Saving our wilderness was of concern to only a few. Ecology now has become an all-important concept and is everybody's business.

Just a few years ago it was legal to locate polar bears by airplane. It was also legal to hunt grizzlies by baiting. Today, through the efforts of those who hunt and enjoy the outdoors, fair-chase laws have been created and many other conservation problems solved, almost wholly by the sportsman. His license fees and 11 per cent excise tax on guns, ammunition, and archery equipment, in addition to the 10 per cent tax on fishing tackle, raises millions of dollars each year for wildlife projects.

There are, unfortunately, some individuals and organizations who would outlaw hunting. Ignoring biological facts, this faction thinks that nature can cure all the problems our wildlife faces. They condemn, while munching a lamb chop, the killing of wild animals. These people have two standards, holding that domestic animals are born to be slaughtered but that wild animals are sacred. A cut of meat, nicely packaged in the food market, has no more emotional effect on the housewife than a bunch of carrots. Yet it was, just a few days before, a living animal. She is paying the butcher to do her killing.

The hunter does the job himself. Not in a slaughterhouse where the animal has no sporting chance, but in fair chase, matching wits with wild animals in their own terrain.

It must be recognized that the world of wildlife has altered considerably since the days of the market hunter. The buffalo is gone. The plow is turning the prairies to feed our overpopulated world. Elk, sheep, and goats have taken refuge in the mountains. In the lower forty-eight states, grizzly bears exist for the most part only in parks. But almost all other animals have increased to greater numbers than ever before.

Early in this century, hunters began to realize that game laws and bag limits were needed and they set about to establish regulations. Today, millions of their dollars are fed into these projects each year. On the other hand, those who would curtail hunting spend great sums on propaganda and lobbying against hunting but very little to benefit the very wildlife they hope to preserve. The majority of this group is sincere in its beliefs, although trained wildlife biologists could tell them that wildlife can be "preserved" into extinction. That game cannot be stockpiled. If a herd of deer, for instance, is not managed, it can destroy itself, the forests, and other species as well.

I do not mean to say that the hunter is entirely without blame. There is work to be done in this field, also. We must teach more respect and appreciation for the outdoors, more respect and understanding for fair-chase rules, and we must encourage the proper use of gun or archery equipment so that kills will be done as humanely as possible.

Just a few years ago as many as fifty thousand deer died yearly of starvation and cold in Michigan. Many northern states had the same problem. Overpopulation and no food. Hunters were then used by biologists to reduce the herds to the carrying capacity of their range. There is no other practical way to manage wildlife.

Wildlife habitat is being reduced by thirty-five hundred acres a day in our country. Our world problem is population control. There could soon be no place for wildlife, or people.

» «

Theodore Roosevelt once wrote: "I wish that members of the Boone & Crockett Club, and big game hunters generally, would make it a point of putting down all their experiences with game or with any other mark-worthy beast or bird . . . noting any change of habits and any causes that tend to make them decrease in number. . . ."

I have tried to do that in this book which is concerned with my sixty-five years of hunting, the last forty with the bow and arrow. The chapters will take you to most of the places in the world where big game is found and my wish is that you, too, may someday experience the thrill of such trips, with honorable regard for the rules of Fair Chase and the laws of conservation.

CONTENTS

INTRODUCTION: THE EARLY YEARS

My interest in archery and bowhunting began in 1925 after seeing a film of Arthur Young hunting with a bow in Alaska. Later I had the pleasure of knowing Art Young and in shooting with him during the two years he lived in Detroit where we spent many happy hours making bows and arrows in my workshop. A hobby that was to become my life's work.

During the early days of bowhunting we struggled to find acceptance for this sport by the public. But by the early forties it was well seated, not only in Michigan and Wisconsin, but in Pennsylvania, California, and many other states. Today there are more than 1,250,000 bowhunters in the United States alone.

For a few years my hunting was confined to the state of Michigan, with occasional jaunts to Wisconsin, but by 1942 I ventured into Canada for moose and bear. This led to other trips into northwestern Ontario and then to an invasion of the West. First, to try my bow on antelope, mule deer, and elk in Wyoming. Then, elk and bighorn sheep in Montana. British Columbia beckoned and I left footprints in Alberta.

In 1955 I made my first trip to Africa. Success in terms of trophies was not spectacular, but it was a great adventure. Africa is a beautiful and interesting continent and like most hunting areas, the first trip is often exploratory. Finding out what not to do the next time.

My story starts with this hunt.

Chapter 1

AFRICA - 1955

Air France Flight ⚡462 left New York at 6 P.M. on the evening of March 2, 1955. On board was a small group of bowhunters making up the first organized safari to hunt with bow and arrow in Africa.

With me on the expedition were Joe Woodard and Steilson Ferris of Michigan; Al Vander Kogel, Ken Lockridge, John Smith, and Frank Travins, New York; and Cliff Wiseman from New Jersey.

My notes were made on this trip under an assortment of conditions—usually at dinner while I forgot the quinine tablet beside my plate. Or perhaps in the branches of a fever tree overlooking a water hole or leaning on the sizzling hood of one of the hunting cars. . . .

Our White Hunter was Jean Gerin, a Frenchman who did not speak English nor did we speak French. In spite of this we hunted together for more than a month, accomplishing many of the things we set out to do, Gerin having learned no English and we having learned no French.

FORT ARCHAMBAULT, AFRICA, MARCH 4, 1955

After our enthusiastic send-off in New York, we arrived in Paris the following morning. The party scattered for a day in the city while I, accompanied by the three photographers with the group—Don Redinger, Telesports, Pittsburgh, (assigned to make a film of the hunt), Bob Halmi and Bill Holman, New York—went to the Air France offices to arrange for additional flights around hunting territories in Africa.

At 6 P.M. we were on our way again, dropping down for gas at Tunis, the first stop on the African continent, and then on to Fort Lamy where we made a second stop. Since we were not allowed to leave the plane in Tunis because of some political troubles, we got our first glimpse of Africans at Lamy. Some of them, the women in brightly colored clothes, boarded the plane and traveled with us to Fort Archambault. This is a city of twenty thousand blacks and some one thousand whites. The only industry is the cotton gin. Cotton is raised on small plots in the many native villages nearby and is processed, baled, and shipped to market in France.

We were met here by our white hunter, Jean Gerin, and his two assistants, Mike and Noah. Noah can speak just enough English to assure our escape from the jaws of hippos and lions. Gerin and Mike can speak none. This is a complicating situation but through Noah we manage to communicate somehow, perplexing as it is.

Gerin's equipment is excellent—three hunting cars and a five-ton truck and utility trailer, both loaded to the top with safari equipment, luggage, and hunting gear, demijohns of French table wine, and several black men who speak nothing but Sango. The hunting cars are war surplus weapons carriers that have been fitted with special bodies. The wide front seats hold four men.

Three of the natives are trackers and gunbearers. The rest hold titles commensurate with their duties. The mechanic is supposed to keep the cars running and spends all of his days and half his nights under the hoods of the fleet with little or no effect on the performance of the motors. There is also a laundry worker, two who serve as waiters and wash the dishes, one looks after the beds, and several are in charge of skinning, drying, and the care of trophies. Some have no title at all and are simply along for whatever job might turn up. Labor is not costly in Africa and safaris go out well manned.

N'Gokotou is the tracker assigned to my group, a man with an enviable reputation and well known in hunting circles throughout this part of Africa. Ours are the first modern bows and arrows these natives have ever seen and even in Sango we understood what they thought of our weapons. . . .

Saturday, March 5—We left Fort Archambault at noon today, glad to climb into the hunting cars shaded from the blazing sun. After crossing the Auk River on a ferry propelled by a gasoline engine made in Michigan and operated by several natives, we drove for several miles through the bush before crossing the river for a second time. The ferry this time was made of surplus army pontoons and zigzagged across, manipulating the current for power. Sometimes we wondered if the current wouldn't suddenly take over and send us all to the bottom with the hippos.

We made camp at Golongosso, a small native village, about 9 P.M. This was to be our hunting headquarters from which the group went out into the different areas for game.

"Camp" consists of a long dining table set up in the middle of an open space. Arranged along either side are single iron beds covered with canopies of mosquito netting. A straw mat, three by six feet, was laid on the ground beside each bed and a metal trunk for personal belongings completes our home. There are no tents of any kind since this is the dry season and no rain is expected for at least a month.

Had a shot at a hartebeest today. Our first sight of African game. No luck.

Sunday, March 6—We started hunting at 6 A.M. At a small lake we saw many large water birds and later ran into baboons and wart hogs. The latter were too fast for us and at 10 A.M. we went back to camp.

We visited the native village near our camp. Must get used to women wearing nothing but a G string of bright beads. . . . I did manage to notice they were weaving mats and pounding meal, however.

It is hot. We hunted again from four to six this afternoon. Saw all kinds of game but no shots. Had our first indication that African game is going to be difficult to approach within bow range. No trouble at all to get up to within 100 to 150 yards, but to get closer is quite a problem. All split-hoof animals are the prey of lions and leopards and it keeps them constantly on the lookout.

Just finished dinner! Anything you've heard about French cuisine was not exaggerated. Even out here in the bush—five courses complete with five changes of china and silver. Excellent food, nicely served, and tapering off with dessert and tea or coffee, not to mention the bottle of wine always on the table.

At lunch today, I thought of some of the hunting camps I've seen in the States. Out with a guide who carries an old frying pan tied to his saddle, a piece of bacon in his saddlebag, and a loaf of dry bread. The paying guest hauls in the water and firewood while the guide cooks the bacon and hands you the frying pan to scour out when he's through. . . . In Africa if you so much as lay hands on the pitcher to pour yourself another glass of water, the white hunter's eyebrows intimate that gentlemen leave such things to the help.

Drums are beating.

9:30 P.M.—Just returned from watching the natives dance in the village. Terrific!

Monday, March 7—Sitting in a blind some of the natives helped me build. Nothing has come by but we will wait a little longer. I shot a reedbuck this morning. He was feeding near the water in quite tall grass. It took thirty minutes or more to get close enough to him, crouching down in the grass and trying to move forward at the same time. He was an adult buck about the size of our white-tailed deer. Had horns about eight inches long.

This was our first bow kill and a start in the difficult job of bagging African game with a bow.

There are lion tracks in front of this blind. Fresh ones.

Tuesday, March 8—We built a new blind late yesterday afternoon and stayed out all night. Hoped to get shots at animals coming to a natural salt lick. Nothing happened until midnight when two doe antelope came by.

Sometime later a lion came to the river to drink. I could hear him lapping up the water. He padded across the opening directly in front of our blind.

The original purpose of this trip was to try the bow only on smaller African game. It was not intended to attempt kills on lions or elephants. A bow is deadly with good hits on animals of any size but it is not a stopper when quick kills are necessary if facing a charge.

Our blind last night was on the ground under heavy foliage. In spite of our resolutions concerning larger game, if we had been in a tree, I believe I would have shot. The moon was full and straight overhead. The opening before us was flooded with light, when a lion walked across thirty yards away. My tracker picked up the rifle to try the sights but the darkness under the tree blanked out even the end of the barrel. With the gun useless for an emergency, it seemed wise to forgo action, although a bow can be shot with great accuracy in darkness.

A hyena followed the lion at some distance. Both prowled the area until daylight, the lion moaning and groaning. Nothing else came near us.

I had a couple of long shots at antelope this afternoon. Took a nap and a swim in the river and am about to have dinner. A native wearing a white jacket is setting the table with freshly laundered cloth and napkins. There is wine with all the meals. Making me strong. My bow feels light.

Leaving for a temporary camp in the morning to be gone two or three days.

Friday, March 11—We're back from a three-day hunt. Several shots but too long range. Leaving this afternoon for area farther on. Four lions were seen down by our blind here last night.

Saturday, March 12, 7 P.M.—In the new camp. We were on the road most of the day. Don took many pictures. We came across a village of what we thought at first were Ubangies. Gerin says they are not Ubangi, however, but members of the Chad tribe. I always thought plate-lipped women were Ubangi. That's what they always told us at the circus.

Plate-lipped women of the Chad tribe.

It was not a pleasant sight. These women—most of them old now—disfigured themselves in their youth, we were told, to discourage capture by bands of raiding Arabs. After seeing their hardship trying to eat and drink with those plate lips, we wondered if it wouldn't have been better to go with the Arabs. They allowed us to photograph them (for a franc note) and they also put on a dance for us. (More franc notes.)

I mailed a letter home from Kyabe today. It was the first opportunity to send mail out. Kyabe is a typical small African town. The houses are made of mud and straw. It is hot here, too. One of the stores had a refrigerator with cold beer. A rare treat after ten days of drinking lukewarm water. We saw little game except four giraffe.

Planned to swim this evening but the river is full of crocodiles. Took a shower instead. Our makeshift camp showers, although adequate, are not nearly so refreshing as a swim.

There is an abundance of guinea fowl here. A little wild for the bow but easy to get with a shotgun. They are excellent eating and our French-trained cook knows how to fix them. He also knows how to prepare antelope meat. The white hunters shoot some each day for the table and for the natives and their families. The natives are not allowed to have guns and we never saw them with a bow of any kind. Consequently they do not have much meat except what the white hunters get for them. They live for the most part on fish taken with spears, and vegetables they grow in their little garden plots. The soil is so rich that a seed dropped in the ground springs up like Jack's beanstalk and several crops are harvested each year.

The missionaries carry rifles and when they visit a village they are more sure of a welcome with a good-sized carcass in the back of the truck. Preaching and teaching first, then meat, as a reward for good behavior and close attention.

Monday, March 14—No shooting yesterday. We spent the day looking over territory. Found a place where many trails led from the bush down to tall, green grass growing at the edge of a lake. I made several stalks on waterbucks, kob, and reedbuck but without success.

Last night was spent in a tree blind near a buffalo trail. Shooting platforms are commonly used here for three reasons: (1) when off the ground, human scent is not so likely to alarm animals; (2) animals seldom look up for danger; (3) it's safer.

The natives helped me build a blind.

The natives helped me build the blind about ten feet off the ground and some thirty yards from a promising game trail. We spent the night and most of the morning in the blind but saw nothing but giraffe and ten wart hogs. I went down for a shot at one of the wart hogs and got within twenty yards, only to find it was a sow with piglets. We learned that wart hogs do not have the curiosity of antelopes who usually stand a moment if one does not move. The wart hog looked up, saw me through the brush, and was off, tail straight in the air, the whole family after her.

At daybreak this morning, three natives walked past my tree. They noticed the tracks of our blind makers and signs of limbs dragged across the ground, etc. This caused considerable confusion among them—chattering and gesticulating— but it never occurred to them to look up at my blind just a few feet above their heads. After much consultation and a closer inspection of the ground, they finally moved off, the riddle unsolved.

There were a great many night sounds during our vigil in the tree, eerie night birds and of course the hippos. Radar, our name for the native who goes out with me on expeditions of this kind, slept most of the night unmindful of the mosquitoes and other bugs crawling around. For my part I hoped that I had not ignored my quinine tablet too often. Radar is no doubt infected with malaria and the same mosquito biting him and then me could result in trouble. I did not sleep well in the blind, needless to say.

There were fresh elephant tracks in the area this morning and I made a good stalk on a waterbuck. One fine buck in a group of six or seven meandering here and there, feeding on their way to the lake. I managed to work in ahead of them for a shot. Just as the first one stepped out onto the trail road, Gerin came around the bend to pick me up and the whole herd wheeled in a wide circle immediately out of bow range.

I found some satisfaction in swearing in English while smiling at Gerin in French.

Tuesday, March 15—Unbearable heat! Our drinking water is from the river, run through a filter and served warm. A whole glass does nothing to quench one's thirst. We drink two or three gallons a day.

9 P.M.—It is cooler now. We stopped at a village today. Not a soul was in sight, although several small fires were smoking. We stood around a few minutes before eyes began to peek out of the bush. One by one the inhabitants came back, half afraid and yet curious to see us at close range. The little ones were cute but very shy and reticent about getting close to us. One little fellow kept smiling at me though and I finally got him to accept a piece of chewing gum. From then on he was my boy, walking beside me whenever I took a step and looking mighty important about the whole thing.

We took pictures of some of them with a Polaroid camera and this sent them into fits of laughter. Sometimes they looked at their pictures upside down but they still laughed. One of the men was not pleased with his picture. He gave us unfriendly looks, muttered, and shook his head. We wondered if he had imagined himself handsomer than the picture showed.

The men around these villages do none of the work. Women carry all the water, take care of the gardens, gather reeds to make mats, et cetera, while the men sit around on the ground playing games. One of the games is similar to Chinese checkers. They make small depressions in the ground and move colored beans or nuts from one to the other. It seemed to be an absorbing business. We could not figure out what the rules might be.

Wednesday, March 16—It is about 10:30 A.M. I am alone at the dining table out in the open, although sheltered from the sun by a small piece of canvas.

No hunting this morning. When I woke up at 8 A.M. with a headache and sat up in my iron bed with its net canopy, immediately there was coffee, bread, and jam beside me. This little breakfast appears on the spot whether one wakes up at 5 A.M. or 8 A.M. It is always delicious and hot.

The hot bread served at camp is made from flour bought from the natives. They pound the grain in an upended log with mahogany rams about three or four inches in diameter and perhaps six feet long. Two women with naked, flopping breasts do this work while the men sit on the ground playing checkers.

The bread is baked in a shallow hole in the sand filled with hot embers. Top of the stove cooking is done on a piece of sheet iron supported by stones over a fire.

The natives do not seem to mind the sun at all. They are out there now, ironing, chopping and drying meat, and preparing the usual five-course luncheon. They have been laughing and joking all morning.

We put on an archery exhibition at one of the villages yesterday and tried to get the natives to show us their skill with the spear. Most of them carry long spears but seldom kill anything with them. Only one man showed up. He threw it halfheartedly at the mark with disappointing results. The best part of his performance was when the spear glanced off a rock and bent the point and he simply wrapped his big, wide toe around it and bent it straight again.

Our bows and arrows fill them with wonder. The men wanted to try shooting them but could not muster the strength to do so. Each unsuccessful effort, however, was accompanied by an amazed expression and a prolonged "a-a-ah-h."

This is difficult bow country. With a gun, a hunter can go out at daylight, make several kills by 8 A.M., and come back to camp and rest in the shade. With a bow, he must spend most of the day at the job and the excessive heat takes the will out of a man.

Game is hard enough to approach when one is alone but because of safari rules it is only on rare occasions that I can slip away without at least one black following me.

Almost all game is in herds of from ten to thirty—sometimes hundreds—usually in the open with little cover. Even the bush isn't too dense and animals can see at much greater distances than one can reach with an arrow.

9 P.M.—I went out with Gerin for an evening hunt. More could be accomplished on this trip if communication were not so exasperating. To make plans for a hunt I talk English to Noah, Noah talks French to Gerin, Gerin talks French and Sango to N'Gokotou, N'Gokotou talks Sango to natives, natives make sign language to me, and our plans usually go awry.

Friday—I think—We stopped off to watch and photograph some natives butchering an elephant today. One of the photographers shot it with Gerin's gun and the custom is to employ natives to take out the tusks in exchange for the meat.

To speed up the work the job is let out to men from two different villages. This sets up a rivalry for the meat and knives fly furiously without regard for fingers and toes.

By the time we came along, the great carcass was alive with natives—under, on, and *in* it. Every bit of the colossal animal is salvaged by the meat-hungry blacks. We moved off when fires were lit under the drying racks. . . . A bit reminiscent of the Chicago stockyards in the twenties.

Saturday, March 19—About 8 A.M. Sitting in a blind at a salt lick with Radar. We gave him this name because he rides on the fender of our hunting car, guiding the driver through the bush with a wave of his arm.

I have been thinking about that elephant carcass. I shot an arrow into it to see what penetration was possible. The arrow disappeared entirely. Might be able to kill one at very close range if the arrow did not hit a rib. Elephant ribs are one and a half inches thick and four or five inches wide.

It is very hot. Radar is dozing, his face turned up in the sun. It will always bemuse me how these natives can endure this sun. Back in camp one of the men wears an old World War II army overcoat all day long. I have wondered why but by the time my question ran through our communication system the coat would be worn out.

We named him "Radar." He sat on a fender and directed us through the bush.

A few days ago one of the villages agreed to stage a dance for the cameras in daylight. (Their dances usually take place at night.) The terms: three antelope.

We arrived on the scene in the middle of the day when the light was best for pictures. The natives had rigged themselves out in all their trappings—lion skins, leopard skins, yards of bright cloth, head scarves, et cetera. The drummer wore an olive-drab army overcoat.

Little girls, big girls, small boys and grown men, and even a half dozen plate-lipped women took part.

As the frenzy mounted, so did the dust. Clouds of it whirled around our heads —sweat, old hides, and sand. The dancers seemed oblivious to our discomfort as they leapt and bowed and stomped out the ritual.

On a mat in front of one of the huts were the three antelope, skinned and quartered. Terms of the contract specified that the dance came before the feast. For most of the afternoon, the meat laid there in the sun subject to flies, sniffing dogs, and curious children. By the time it was turned over to the natives, it could not be called fresh by any bounds of imagination. We inquired if they actually liked food in this odoriferous state and our interpreter replied that "they don't eat the smell, they eat the meat."

6 P.M.—Hiked around with Radar until late this afternoon. Shot a five-foot iguana with my bow. Radar discovered it under a matting of thick, dry grass. He parted the grass with a stick so I could see it and motioned frantically for me to shoot. I thought it was a python when I shot.

Sunday, March 20—Spent the morning with Radar. We saw five waterbucks and several large monkeys. No shots.

A letter came from my wife today. The first mail since we landed. It enclosed an illustrated letter from seven-year-old granddaughter, Hannah, portraying Papa Bear encircled by a herd of attacking, sway-backed zebras. I am apparently saved from this fate, however, by a group of natives bristling with shields and spears. The letter came the last twenty kilometers by foot.

The evening hunt was very quiet. Hot. Nothing moved except black gnats swarming about my face.

Drums in the village until midnight last night. Booming again tonight. May have to buy them to get some sleep.

Tuesday, March 22—We went out on the plains this morning to take pictures and saw a lioness at five hundred yards. I am sitting in my blind now, tortured by gnats. They love the mosquito repellent we use.

Thursday, March 24—We went to the plains for pictures again today. Got back in the blind at 4 P.M. I shot another reedbuck. He dropped at four hundred yards. This is the last hunting day in this territory.

We are putting on a dance for the *natives* tonight. Will leave for Fort Archambault tomorrow. Most of the party will leave for home from there.

Friday, March 25—The natives laughed themselves sick over our efforts to entertain them with a North American Indian war dance last night. We have started packing. It is raining today.

1 P.M.—Have just had lunch. It rained for only two hours but is a cloudy day

and chilly for the first time. The luncheon tables were set up in the sun instead of under the trees.

Saturday, March 26—The trip back to Archambault was uneventful but interesting. We saw many species of game and birds we had not seen before and, for the first time, enjoyed a cool ride.

The planes come in to Fort Archambault twice a week and on these days the Arab traders display their wares to the travelers. There are all kinds of things to buy—ivory carvings, leather goods, beads, etc. Most of them show remarkably fine workmanship and are quite reasonably priced. One has to know about bartering, however. Rule of thumb is never to pay more than a third of asking price.

Arab traders display their wares.

Wednesday, March 30—The photographers and I are down near the Belgian Congo now. Flew down from Fort Archambault and are spending a few days in Brazzaville. Had dinner with the game commissioner of East Africa last night. An interesting and educational evening. Much shopping and sightseeing. Bought a zebra skin for Hannah.

Thursday, March 31—We are 175 miles from Brazzaville tonight. Sleeping in a fine inn with good bed and shower. There was a hard storm last night. Delayed our trip into Pygmy country—roads greasy and fog in the hills. This jungle country is quite different from the dry plains farther north.

Noon—We're having lunch now—french-fried potatoes, omelet, and ripe pineapple. We will start for Pygmy country this afternoon with an escort. There are no mosquitoes here and the climate is pleasant.

5 P.M.—In a village twenty miles from Mouyoundzi. When the truck broke a spring we were conducted to the chief's house for the night and made welcome and comfortable. The villagers have brought offerings of pineapples, avocados, and peanuts. Many hands working on broken-down truck. Hope to be on our way again in the morning.

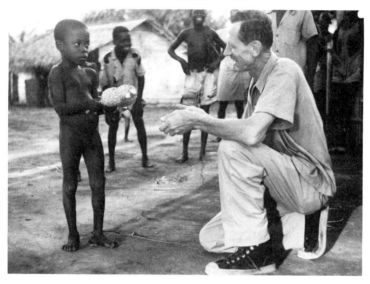

Natives brought offerings.

Friday, April 1—We have reached our destination and are camped in a new, white hospital building. Last night a native in our host village serenaded us far into the wee hours with a homemade guitar. In early morning I swapped a shaving mirror for the guitar.

We sent a runner on ahead yesterday to make arrangements in the Pygmy village for photographing a dance and net hunt. Early this morning they arrived with bows and nets to escort us to their village.

A walk of five miles through steaming jungle seemed long and very hot. The village is in a clearing in thick jungle.

The Pygmies have tiny little bows trimmed with monkey fur. Their arrows are

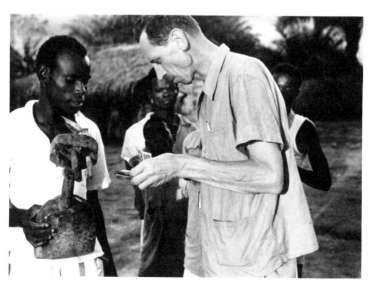

A native guitar is purchased.

fletched with a tough leaf and the deadly little points are dipped in poison which makes them very effective for their size.

Pygmies are not good marksmen but are the best dancers we have seen yet. Even a woman with a baby strapped to her back was full of grace.

It was too dark in the jungle for pictures of the hunt. They brought in a tiny antelope, however, caught in the net, and collected barter for it as promised.

There were beautiful flowers and delicate plants on our trek out through the jungle. Back at our camp by two-thirty for a lunch of sardines, sausage, grapefruit, green tangerines, and wine. Don's ulcer is acting up. Good-by to Babinga country.

Palm Sunday, April 3—Back in Brazzaville. Arrived at midnight last night. A long, hard, rough, tiring trip. We had ham and eggs at the Beach Hotel and then to bed. The lights of Leopoldville across the river twinkled in the dark from the Belgian Congo.

We're at an artists' colony now, buying native watercolors. Beautiful, exotic work by native pupils of a Frenchman, Pierre Lods.

Monday, April 4—There are many bicycles in Brazzaville and small cars. Women (white) take their children to school on bicycles.

It is also man's country down here—the women do all the work. I just watched a native man meet his wife at the ferry. She had a big load of something to carry. They argued a while, then he helped her put part of the load on her head and the rest in her arms while he rode off ahead on the new bicycle she'd brought.

Saturday, April 9—We're on a plane now going back to Archambault. Wearing shorts and white socks like Englishmen.

This has been an interesting side trip. The country is wild and beautiful. I would like to float down one of these rivers someday. Gasoline is a dollar a gallon here.

It is getting warmer as we fly north. I have decided to hunt for two more weeks with Gerin. I would like to kill a lion with the bow. Gerin suggests building a blind in a tree and watching a bait on a moonlit night. I certainly wouldn't tackle it any other way.

Easter Sunday, April 10—I can see my family getting ready for church back home. . . . We have just left Archambault for the last hunt. Several miles out a herd of elephants crossed the road in front of us. Gerin says it is a good omen. I hope so.

3 P.M.—Have only to cross the river once more and then to Golongosso where we will again make camp.

7 P.M.—I am having dinner with two French hunters we met here. The menu consists of young wart hog roasted over hot coals. Wonderful good, as my Pennsylvania ancestors would say.

Monday, April 11—Gerin found a natural salt lick where we will build a platform for lion hunting this p.m.

3 P.M.—Had to change our plans because of a heavy rainstorm. There is a

steady downpour and the wind blows like a hurricane, blowing the kapoc pods off the trees. Gerin says the barren ground will bloom with flowers after the rain.

We are staying in a Government house—small concrete shelters spotted around the country for the use of travelers. There are four good-sized rooms in this one and it has a thatched roof.

This country is beginning to fascinate me. From my tree platform I can expect to see anything from the tiniest antelope to a lumbering elephant. African magpies, pelicans, and countless species of long-legged water birds are everywhere. Buzzards, hawks, and eagles perch in the trees near camp watching their chance to swoop down for tidbits at the meat-processing area.

Radar was happy to see me again. He wears a knife in handsomely decorated sheath on his upper left arm. I hope to buy it from him before I leave.

4 P.M.—The rain is slowing up. In the trees the buzzards, that sit out the rain hunched over and miserable, are now beginning to stretch their wings out along the branches to dry.

"Radar" wears a knife in a handsome sheath on his left arm.

Tuesday, April 12—We built the platform last evening. Gerin shot a kob and dragged it around on the ground for lion-bait scent. I spent the night in the blind but no lion. An oribi going by at dawn with four wart hogs is all the action I saw. A nice kob came in just now—winded me and left.

Gnats have been giving me trouble. I am ten feet up in the tree and except for a few blind spots, I can see a hundred yards each way. This should be a good spot.

8 A.M.—Six waterbucks just came in. I missed the first shot and they all took off. Gerin is coming for me at ten. Camp is five miles away.

7 P.M.—Gerin has decided our lion bait is not good. Too near the salt lick. He made a new blind. After lunch we left for the new location but saw nothing there this evening, although Gerin shot a rabbit on the way. Good luck, he says.

Wednesday, April 13—Hot as blazes today. I left for the salt lick early this morning. Nothing came in, so got uneasy and went down to look for a wart hog. Found one but blundered upwind from him and that was that. Did some still hunting later and had a good stalk on an oribi. Shot him at about thirty yards. He didn't go far. It was an adult buck with beautiful jet-black horns about five inches long. Just a little fellow—weighs about thirty-five pounds. A nice trophy but not much help in rounding out a film.

Thursday, April 14—We stopped in at the river salt lick this morning. There were lion tracks around and I stayed until nine-thirty. Nothing. Shot at another wart hog. Nice lead but under his belly. Saw a hartebeest and two reedbucks from the blind also but too far. Fresh limes help quench our thirst on these long treks around the dry plains.

7:30 P.M.—Had my first shot at a hartebeest this evening. He walked within twenty yards of me and I loosed a nice arrow but he flinched at the sound of the bowstring and the arrow went over his back. Very disappointed. He would have made a nice trophy.

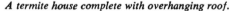

A termite house complete with overhanging roof.

I am beginning to change my mind about stalking game in this country. Under certain conditions it is not quite so impossible as I first thought. At one time today I made a sortie back through the bush. There were about twenty waterbucks near a water hole and possibly a hundred kob and reedbucks, all within sight at one time. If the cover had grown close enough to the water hole for a bowshot, I might easily have had some luck.

The rain chased us into the Government house again tonight. I met a French couple here, François Sommers and his wife who were on their twenty-first trip, photographing African animals. They had a limited knowledge of English— enough so that we could converse a little.

During our visit we discussed at some length the subject of bowshooting in Africa. Mr. Sommers is of the opinion that hunting from a platform or salt lick is not the best way. After the past days of rain chasing us indoors, I am inclined to listen. Employ N'Gokotou, Sommers says. He is one of the best trackers in Africa. Why not use *him* for finding game. Give him your bow and follow him. When he gets within range of game, he will hand you the bow.

Sunday, April 17—I tried Sommers' suggestion today and went out with N'Gokotou. Gerin drove the truck. It took some doing to get near four kob grazing about two hundred yards away. N'Gokotou got off the truck and motioned for me to follow him. Lining up with a tree between us and the animals, we walked straight up to within thirty yards. The trunk of the tree was not quite large enough to cover us and the kob could see us make our approach. Incredulous as it seems they stood there and let us walk toward them. Just as we reached the tree, N'Gokotou handed me the bow and I was ready. In order to shoot, however, it was necessary to move slightly out to one side before raising the bow for a shot and this no animal I have seen in Africa, or anyplace else, will stand for.

We tried N'Gokotou's technique several times but always with the same results. Stepping out from the tree for the draw was the signal for the game to bounce off.

Tuesday, April 19—This was my day.

Sommers invited me to go out with him to some small plains that lie to the south. This area, he said, was the home of large herds of hartebeest and damalisque.

We cruised around in Sommers' truck until we spotted some damalisque at the edge of the plain in more or less rough country. The bush jutted out along the rim in places and the prospect of getting within bow range seemed quite favorable.

It was the last day of my hunt and the sun was extremely hot. We carefully maneuvered the truck behind a rise of ground and from there I made my way down to the edge of the bush.

It seemed even hotter now. Sweat tickled my nose and ran into my eyes during the last few yards, down on my hands and knees inching along through thinning cover—still sixty yards from the large, antelope-type animal. This was as far as I could go. Another move would send the herd crashing out of sight.

Cursing the rain that had spoiled so much of last week's hunting and the deadline compelling me to start home the next day, I knelt, staring at the damalisque. With hopes for a lion gone, this was my last chance to bag a trophy of any size and the outlook for success grew dimmer by the minute.

A native leopard trap is examined.

It was difficult to approach closely in the open country.

A maribou stork waits expectantly.

Then it happened. Something loomed up at the corner of my eye. Another damalisque had appeared from nowhere between me and the herd, grazing along with his head down.

He was near enough and neither saw nor heard me raise up for a shot. The arrow slid into the body cavity while the rest of the herd thundered away to safety.

This was a beautiful trophy, bagged at the eleventh hour. Gerin estimated his weight at around five hundred pounds. Ringed black horns, within two inches of the record, curved back from his head and cameras whirred as four natives carried him off to the truck on a pole over their shoulders.

» «

Monday, April 25—We're on the plane going back to New York. There is time to reminisce over this trip.

Bowhunting in Africa for the first time is not too different from first hunting trips to any new country or territory—the initial trip is likely to be more or less experimental wherein one learns about the animals and terrain and comes back with a wealth of experience and ideas of how he will proceed on the next trip.

I talked with many hunters—none of them bowhunters—but there were things to learn from them. An Englishman, for instance, over there to hunt, included in his equipment a headdress made of the skin of a large black bird that abounds in that country. Hunters strap this gear on their heads, he said, and crawl through the bush. They can get very close by this means. And Elisha Gray, of St. Joseph, Michigan, told me he wore a camouflage suit to great advantage in Africa.

Next time I would use dark make-up on hands and face and hunt almost entirely in the bush near salt licks and water holes. Always on foot and alone, if possible. I would make every effort to make arrangements with the white hunter for permission to go out alone. He, of course, makes this rule for his own protection, but while the native he sends with you has no gun, nor even a spear, the general idea seems to be to keep the hunter from getting lost.

One shouldn't ignore the trackers, however. They have sharp eyes and earn their living outwitting game. We left several archery outfits with them when we left and hope they will try their hand with them. At best, they might learn to appreciate our problems and be better guides for bowhunters another time.

Chapter 2

YUKON TERRITORY - 1956

There's a land where the mountains are nameless,
And the rivers all run God knows where.

There are lives that are erring and aimless,
And deaths that just hang by a hair.

There are hardships that nobody reckons,
There are valleys unpeopled and still.

There's a land—oh, it beckons and beckons,
And I want to go back—and I will.

ROBERT SERVICE

Them Kjar, Yukon Game Commissioner, looks the bow over.

A picturesque country this Yukon Territory, its western boundary hugging the Alaskan line and the Northwest Territories pinching it so narrow that there is only a slight touch on the Arctic Ocean.

Our hunting area was bounded on the east by the Whitehorse-Skagway Railway, on the north by Alaskan Highway, by the Haines Highway on the west and the British Columbia border on the south. West of this area more than half the country is covered by the vast Hubbard Glaciers.

From start to finish our hunting field would measure about sixty miles as the crow flies. By pack train the distance was close to 150 miles and the total miles we actually covered must have been at least 300. There were no inhabitants in this area of approximately 1,500 square miles.

Several years before, a friend of mine had made this trip. He reported many moose and grizzlies there but we found them less plentiful.

Buck, my horse, ate the red berries I stuck in my hat band and together we had a great experience.

YUKON, 1956

DON REDINGER, Photographer   GEORGE JOHN, Guide
ALEX VAN BIBBER, Outfitter   JOE HOUSE, Wrangler
ED MERRIAM, Cook   RON HOLLAWAY, Prehunt Guide
              DR. JUDD GRINDELL, Bowhunter first two weeks

Friday Evening, August 24, 1956—Sitting in camp at the take-off point with rain pattering on the tent. Judd comes in this evening and Alex will meet the plane at Champagne (about fifty miles) and arrive here about noon tomorrow.

Will start the hunt Sunday. We're along the Haines Highway ninety-three miles from the seaport of Haines, Alaska.

The trip so far has been a bust. Them Kjar, the game commissioner of Yukon Territories, met us at the plane with the official Yukon welcome. We went to his office to obtain hunting licenses, have some refreshments and a chat.

A beautiful pair of Dall sheep horns was lying on the floor. I examined them in admiration and Them told me that he had confiscated them. "Took them from a hunter who had bought them from an Indian." He then told the story of large moose antlers he had confiscated also, a few years ago.

Same story. "A hunter had bought them from an Indian. We apprehended the Indian as he had done an illegal act. Were about to put him in jail but learned that he had ten kids and thirteen dogs that we would have to feed while he was serving time.

"So we reprimanded him severely and that ended the issue.

"The antlers remained here in my office for several years. They were beautiful. One day a Boone and Crockett scoring man came along. He measured them and we were amazed to learn that we had a first-place Alaskan-Yukon-record moose. All due to the straight shooting of one of our local people.

"There was great happiness. All of this glory for the Yukon. We had a fine rifle properly engraved, held a banquet and our guest, the Indian, was duly honored."

»«

I had arranged with our outfitter to arrive several days ahead so there would be time to do some fishing in Sockeye Lake. Alex had engaged Ron Hollaway, a Cree Indian with a panel truck, loaded with camping equipment, to take care of us. Them suggested, instead of Sockeye Lake (he had a boat, motor, and trailer), that he would take us to Aishihik Lake where we could catch giant lake trout. Ron went with us. We made arrangements to have a plane pick us up three days later.

We got there late afternoon, fished for two hours, caught nothing, and then a high wind came up, blew for three days, and we could not go out on the lake.

Found a place to catch grayling by the hundreds on flies.

Went out to the highway, flagged a truck taking gas to an army field, and had the army phone for a plane to pick us up Sunday which was a day ahead of schedule.

To make a long story short, Them Kjar left Sunday a.m. thinking we would be picked up. Ron had brought a driver with him who took his car back to Whitehorse.

So we had no car and the plane never came. We were isolated on a windswept, bleak, above timberline, dusty lakeshore. So windy it was almost impossible to cast a fly and no sun for pictures—a total loss.

Ron finally walked out to the military road on Wednesday. After four hours he got a ride to the Alaskan Highway (forty-five miles). Got another ride to Champagne, came back with a pickup, and bailed us out.

We stayed the night at Haines Junction where the Haines Highway takes off from the Alaska Highway southwest to the Alaskan port of Haines.

Alex Van Bibber had returned three days early from a very successful hunt and we met him that evening. A fine-looking fellow, alert and capable.

Next morning we went to the Klukshu Indian village where they catch and smoke salmon. The run was over and the men were all out hunting.

We came on out the Haines Highway to this camp from where we start our hunt. Yesterday we went to Haines looking for a creek with salmon in it to shoot with a bow and for pictures. We found one but it was raining.

Saw a bull moose along the highway. He ran into the bushes. I grunted and he came back to within fifty feet of the car—but that was in Alaska. Farther on, in British Columbia, we saw a mother grizzly and two cubs on a gravel flat about 400 yards away. Mother was digging for something. We watched them for over a half hour from higher ground. Could not get to them because of a fast river, besides, we were in B.C. and my license is for the Yukon.

Again it was raining and no pictures.

Today it looked like it might clear up and this afternoon we went back to Alaska to the salmon river. It was not raining but the light was poor. I shot a thirty-pound salmon and we took pictures.

Judd will be here tomorrow. We will sort gear and take off Sunday morning. First camp is only four and a half hours. I hope for a change of luck. I feel that we will do well as there seems to be plenty of game. Big bear tracks all over. One of our wranglers was chased by a bear while rounding up the horses one morning. It chased him down a steep bank, and he jumped on a horse for a fast getaway only to find that the horse was hobbled. Fortunately, the bear gave up the chase.

We will have twenty-one horses, a good cook who is with us now, two wranglers, and two guides.

Our hunt started from this camp along the Haines Highway.

Sunday, August 26—Just finished dinner here at Blanchard Camp. Rained all morning and then cleared. Got away from the highway at 11:30 A.M. Rode until 2 P.M. and stopped for tea and cold short ribs of moose. Got here at five-thirty—made camp and here we are. All gear wet, but we have a stove now and can dry out.

Saw a great many bear tracks and sighted two bull moose and four cows. The country is quite open. We are just about at timberline. Above this, nothing but willow and buckbrush and above that, rocks. This is a mushroom paradise. Saw many big bolitas, some ten inches in diameter with white meat one-inch thick.

Alex has a good outfit with unusually nice horses. The colts practically live in the house with their owners. During the stop for tea this afternoon one of the pack horses walked into our circle and stopped, wanting his pack taken off. He was very disappointed when it was only tightened. When we reached camp the pack horses nudged us with their heads wanting the packs taken off. Finally freed of their burdens, they rolled on the ground with relief.

Camp is in the brush by a cluster of dead, isolated spruce trees. The cook tent is fourteen-by-sixteen, our tent nine-by-twelve. The guides and wrangler have a nine-by-twelve also.

Blanchard Camp.

Monday, August 27—Judd and George, the Indian guide, went moose hunting. Alex, Don, and I went to look for goats and sheep near Blanchard Lake. We saw eight sheep but could not get close to them. Back in camp at 7 P.M.

Daylight breaks here at 3:30 A.M. and darkness comes about eight-thirty but it is not entirely dark all night. Judd saw two cow moose and several goats across on the other mountain. We will go after them tomorrow.

Tuesday, August 28—Judd and George took bedding and went north after a moose. They plan to stay two days. We went across the mountain after goats. Got up to where they were about 10 A.M. and tried a stalk on a lone billy after taking his picture. Fourteen more watched us from above. Wind crossed us up both on the billy and on the group of fourteen. There were two nice billies in this lot, too. We chased them all over the mountain but had to concede this round to the goats.

Back in camp around 7 P.M. Moose hunters were unsuccessful.

Wednesday, August 29—In camp. It is 7 P.M. and we just had dinner. Dumplings, moose stew, peas, potatoes, lettuce, celery, soup, prunes, freshly baked cake and cookies. Judd and Alex have the spotting scope on a big bull moose across the next mountain. Judd plans to get him tomorrow. He stalked a bull today. Got very close but the brush was too thick.

We went after goats again. Climbed the mountain all the way up but did not find them. We had planned to move to the next camp tomorrow, but will stay now so Judd can hunt the moose and we will go after goats later.

Saw quite a few ptarmigan, hoary marmots (these whistlers warn the goats of our presence), bald eagles, flickers, whisky-jacks, magpies, juncos, ravens, and several birds I do not know.

The country has many parka squirrels. These are about the size of small prairie dogs and look like a young groundhog.

Water very good here. Runs down from glaciers as in B.C.

Don has had a rough day. His saddle came off when he mounted this a.m. A rock fell on his leg up the mountain, and in coming back his horse bogged down in the tundra and willows and they both got muddy.

Thursday, August 30—Had intended to move camp today but Judd's moose was still on the mountain. We decided to take a day off and help him. Our camp is in a valley and the moose was on the mountain facing us. Willows, buckbrush, and alder higher than a man's head make it difficult for a hunter to make progress on foot, so we agreed on a set of signals as we watched the moose with the scope and two binoculars.

Alex took Judd across the river and he went on foot from there. It was 10 A.M. before he came out into an opening and motioned for instructions. We directed him with a towel-flagged stick for several hours, following the moose with the glasses while he ambled over the territory, now stopping to feed, then standing still seemingly looking at nothing, and even lying down once or twice. At 4 P.M. Judd was within twenty-five yards of him but the brush was too thick to shoot. Then the wind changed suddenly and the bull took off over the mountain. It was quite an exciting day. Had intended to wash my clothes but found this far more interesting.

Friday, August 31, 8 P.M.—Friday was not unlucky for me. I shot a grizzly today.

We got packed up and off at nine-thirty to move to the next camp. It was quite a chore to load so much gear on so many horses. The pack train is a fine sight, however, winding along through the mountains, fording streams, etc. Before we started, Judd and I did some practice shooting. We do this every day.

Stopped for tea at 1 P.M. Roast moose, ham, candy bars, and fresh doughnuts. Back on the horses again we saw a black bear come over the mountain ahead and cross in front of us about a half mile away. We watched him for a while and,

The pack train is a beautiful sight, winding through the mountains, fording sreams. . . .

when he went over a knoll in the creek bottom, Judd and I decided that any bear that size was a trophy and we should go after him. All twenty-one horses stopped then, too, to watch the show.

Judd went up over the knoll and I went around the end on the double. When I saw the bear again he was digging for a parka squirrel. There was a rock twenty-five yards from him offering cover and I lost no time getting up to it, pausing to take a good look and plan my shot. I realized, too late, that the bulldog profile of the bear in front of me was that of a grizzly and not a black bear. Alex had decided to sit this one out since he deemed it unnecessary to back his client for a black bear.

My arrow went straight where I was looking, immediately behind the shoulder.

The bear let out a growl, made two jumps toward me, and then turned out of sight over the knoll. When I got there he was down—about seventy-five yards.

Judd had the bear in sight all the time. He said it came over the knoll, went down into the creek bottom, made two small circles, and folded up. It was a breathtaking show. Don says he has it all on film and the rest of the party witnessed the whole thing from about one fourth of a mile away. This was good as we had not yet proved the bow to our guides and wranglers.

It was not a big bear, but a grizzly. Black with silver tips on the head and shoulders. We took pictures in the rain and snow before skinning him out. Going on toward camp (a willow thicket with no wood) we spotted fourteen goats and Alex and Judd and I made a stalk. Got within 100 yards but no closer. We found the cook tent up and the cook trying to get dinner with wet willow wood. Hudson Bay rum made the rounds in celebration of the kill. Raining and snowing off and on. Everything wet down.

It was not a big bear, but a grizzly.

Saturday, September 1, 7:30 A.M.—Breakfast over. Horses being rounded up and dishes done. Still raining but not too cold. Ed has great difficulty cooking. He stuffs pieces of paper into the draft hole to try to get a proper fire. The stove sits on uneven rocks, so pancakes are thick on one side. . . .

Yesterday I gathered a sugar sack full of mushrooms and tied it on the back of my saddle. Traveling in the rain softened and spoiled them beyond use however. A great disappointment to me.

Packing up now. Next camp is base camp where there is a supply of wood. Will have some drying out to do. Alex and I will make another try at the goats on the way. Goats won this round also.

At base camp now. Fine place. Alex had food stored on a high cache.

Sunday, September 2, 7:45 P.M.—Just finished a big dinner. Moose, rice, scalloped potatoes, soup, pie, cake, and stewed dried apricots.

Alex shot a four-year-old ram today for camp meat (moose meat getting low). We ran into about twenty-five ewes and kids with this small ram in the group. Mutton for a few days now. Ate the grizzly heart last night. Supposed to make strong men of us.

Judd and George (Indian) took off for a side camp this a.m. for moose. Will be gone for two or three days.

Saw a red fox and a lynx today. Two bull moose yesterday.

Getting my mountain legs now. Feeling fine. Big appetite. Shot seven arrows at a blue grouse and then he flew away.

Monday, September 3, 6 A.M.—In the cook tent waiting for breakfast. Had four hours of sunshine yesterday. It felt very good. There was frost last night and it is sunny and clear now. George says the frost will kill the berries, start the moose rut and bring the bears out in the open looking for gophers and marmots.

I have a sprig of bright red cranberries in my hat and my horse, Buck, nips at them at every opportunity. There are some blueberries here and also some blackberries. Some man-sized glaciers around and snow on all the high places. When it rains below, it snows up high.

Later—Went down the valley today and stopped frequently to glass the mountains. Didn't see a thing all day except ptarmigan. Sun was out all day and very warm. We had a lazy day. Took a nap on a knoll and rode back to camp about three-thirty to make camp pictures. Sun lasted only another hour and then Judd and George came back from their hunt. They saw no moose but did see three grizzlies. Judd wanted to tackle them with the bow but George would have none of it. He had been mauled by them and is scared to death. Being his last day here, Judd took the Indian's rifle and shot the biggest one.

Alex and George entertained us with bear stories this evening. Have my fanny well broken into the saddle now.

Tuesday, September 4, 6:30 P.M.—Sitting under a tent fly roasting a slab of sheep before a hot fire. I'm in a willow thicket by Devil's Hole Lake, about five miles from base camp.

I hunted up this way. Saw a bear but he saw us first and went off. We climbed up high on horses and ran into snow. When we got down it was raining. Judd is at base camp. Not hunting today. His plane comes in at this lake at noon tomorrow.

Don, my photographer, is having trouble with ulcers and will fly with Judd to Whitehorse for some medicine and then come back.

Had roast mountain sheep last night. It tastes like roast leg of the best lamb. This slab of ribs is beginning to smell good.

We arrived at this camp with two pack horses, a small tent, sleeping bags, and plenty of grub. Really living high. Plenty of candy bars, cookies, oranges. Alex forgot to bring dishes, cups, and silverware! He is now carving wooden spoons. Shot a parka squirrel today.

Wednesday, September 5, 6 A.M.—Snow coming down in the largest wet flakes I have ever seen. About an inch on the ground now. Rained all night. Those heavy tarp bags kept our sleeping bags dry and we had a good cozy sleep.

Took some still pictures of our camp in the snow. Alex says he has seen two feet of snow here in August.

Base camp is just below timberline. Plenty of good dry spruce for wood. Side camps like this are usually above timberline and one has to scrounge for wood.

The next side camp is "Goat Canyon" where we expect to have good goat hunting. Sheep are not so high. Mostly in the buckbrush. Grizzly and moose could be anywhere.

A bad trip for pictures so far, with only one and a half days of sun. Had fair light for the shooting of the grizzly, but rain during close-ups afterward. Don says he got pictures of me shooting the bear and the bear going over the hill.

I forgot to mention the most important part of the notes from this a.m. Those sheep ribs, wow. I ate nothing else except some canned pears.

Snow coming down in the largest wet flakes I have ever seen.

Breakfast is over now. Corn flakes, bacon, and eggs. Sitting under a fly on our bedroll wondering what to do. Visibility zero. No plane today.

10 A.M. the same day—Just had tea and a snack. Very comfortable and warm but the inactivity kills me. I would like to go back to base camp, but Alex says the snow on the willows would bog us down. (Not me with my nylon pants and jacket.) It is still snowing and raining. Fog is about 100 feet up. No plane today. We expect Judd and George any time.

I skinned the parka squirrel and have his hide on a drying board.

3 P.M.—Had a nap after finishing the ribs. Judd and George came in an hour ago and we are all sitting around the fire. Rain has stopped and the sky seems to be clearing. George and I will go back to base camp and turn this one over to Judd and Alex. Will be glad to be doing something.

Thursday, September 6, 4 P.M.—George and I got back last evening. Brought Judd's saddle horse and a mare with cameras and sleeping bags packed on her. George led the saddle horse and I rode on "Freddie." He is the best mount I have had yet. Will do just about anything. Good thing, too, because when we passed our grazing horses across a small lake about two miles from camp, the mare made a break for them. Thanks to Freddie I was able to head her off at the water's edge, or she would have swum the lake and put our cameras out of commission.

Alex, Judd, and Don stayed at the wet willow camp at Devil's Hole Lake hoping for a break in the weather and the plane. Rain off and on last night. No plane yet and I doubt if one will come today. Can't hunt—fog too low. Have been fixing up our tent since early morning. Washed all my dirty clothes. Cleaned and dried cameras. Greased my boots and kept a fire going to dry my laundry.

Ed is a good cook and he is good-natured.

George says all this rain is good. "Moose wash velvet off antlers, then rut starts."

Still feasting on the sheep. It is delicious. Killing time like this, waiting for the weather, is hard on me. Wastes too many days.

I was surprised to hear Alex say that there are wild horses north of here. They live through the fifty to sixty below winters. It is from these wild herds that he gets new blood for his saddle and pack horses.

Between hunting seasons, Alex rents his horses (he has about sixty) to prospectors and mining companies. He also takes out survey groups, using a dog team when the snow is too deep for horses.

It is now 6 P.M. and Ed is cooking something that smells good. He is fifty-six years old, is divorced, and has three grown boys in Vancouver. Not the cleanest cook in the world, but things taste good and he is good-natured.

Alex's father was a Scotsman and his mother an Indian. He is wise in the way of the bush and is slowly grasping the problems of the bowhunter, and appreciates the fact that it is a tough game.

Across this narrow valley from camp are two mountain peaks with snow on them. Between them a glacier-fed stream tumbles recklessly over many waterfalls on its way to the river below us. Whisky-jacks are stuffing themselves with kitchen scraps.

Friday, September 7, 7 A.M.—STILL RAINING. Stella, one of the horses, is high up on the mountain across from us. We thought for a while she was a moose. Just finished breakfast. George is planning to take some food up to the boys in the other camp. Think I'll go with him.

I wonder if I've mentioned Tiger in my notes. He is a young husky, two years old. His father is a wolf. Alex brought him to camp to keep the grizzlies away. He never makes a sound. He wants to be friendly but is held back by some ancestral instinct. As for me, I would like to have a grizzly come in. Last trip here the cook saw two at night and this is the spot where Joe was chased by one. We have been up and down this valley though and have seen no fresh bear signs.

9 A.M.—We are waiting for Joe to bring in the horses. Quite a life—that of a wrangler. Up at 4 A.M. and out shagging after the horses. He never knows where they are. It is a rough and unpleasant task on a cold, frosty morning. They do not have a bad job during the day, however. Nothing to do but sleep, read, and cut wood.

Joe doesn't like to cut wood. Doesn't like to do anything but work with his horses. He quit a two-dollar-an-hour job in a garage to wrangle on this hunt for ten bucks a day.

Ed reads most of the day. The place is well supplied with magazines, mostly men's magazines with snappy stories and pictures. George and Joe sleep in their wet-down tent. No air mattresses and thin sleeping bags. George washed his clothes three days ago and they are still wet.

Horses are here. I hope he has Freddie.

7 P.M.—Went up to Devil's Hole Lake and found the men in better spirits than I expected. Stayed about two hours and came back. Don came with us. He is cold and wet.

Had not been back here long before we saw the plane go in to the lake and then come out. Alex came back and we all had mail. Two letters and a package containing Softi-Pack Life preservers from Mrs. B. Might need them if it doesn't stop raining. Eighteen days of rain so far.

Don't know what the plans are for tomorrow. "Depends on the weather," Alex always says when I ask him, so I won't ask him tonight.

Saturday, September 8, 8:15 P.M.—Camping under the stars tonight on Kluhini River, just before entering Goat Canyon. Got here at dusk, made a fire, ate supper, and am now lying by the fire writing by candlelight. Rained early today but is clear now.

Left camp at eight-thirty this morning. Spent two hours chasing a pair of rams and got here late. The country is beginning to show color.

Sunday, September 9, 7 A.M.—Nice, frosty morning. Sun shining on the white top of Mount Nevin. This is very close to British Columbia. We will hunt close along the edge.

It looks like a good day. There are four goats in view from camp.

Had a good sleep in the open last night. Alex woke me up at midnight to see the northern lights.

Monday, September 10, 6:30 A.M.—Too tired to write last night. We went up into Goat Canyon yesterday morning and started after some goats. Got some good pictures but no trophies. Got back to the horses at 5 P.M. and it was dark when we reached camp in the spruce thicket.

It is a beautiful day. Not a cloud in the sky for the first time. Very hot going up the mountain. Ate many kinds of berries: two kinds of cranberries, soapberries, raspberries, blackberries, etc.

Sometimes we lead the horses.

We are camped at Upper Hendon Lake. The B.C. stake is just fifty yards from camp. The trip was very rough going. Dense willow and alder thickets and piles of rocks. Instead of leading the horses we often let them go ahead of us. Sometimes we held on to their tails going up steep places.

Tuesday, September 11, 6 P.M.—Had a big meal last night. Fried sheep steak, onions, beans, bread and jam, fruit, and always, tea. Had a good night's sleep.

Spotted a billy from camp this morning. We went off after him spending all day up high but he was not for us. Two hundred yards was the closest we could get.

Alex is cooking dinner. After dinner now, stuffed, and writing by flashlight swinging overhead. It is windy and cloudy all over. We hope for the best.

Have a tarp stretched up over my bed in the event of rain.

Wednesday, September 12, 10 A.M.—Perched on a moss-covered bench halfway up the mountain. Three goats are bedded down across a small canyon from us. We can't move until they do. Hope they go the other way so we can cross the canyon and get closer to them. On the mountain across from us now are two more goats, and up the valley are three more.

There does not seem to be much game in this big country. But it is a good place to hunt because it is open and what game there is can be seen. This country should be able to support much more game.

We are looking down on the snaking Hendon River as it flows below. Increasing in size as the many glacial streams, carving canyons on their way down the mountains, join it. Yesterday we came upon a place where a rocky cliff had given way and came down like an avalanche. Rocks were ground to dust and alder groves buried. It was nature at work with her carving tools, reshaping the mountains. Someday this may be a mighty forested area and someone may find the arrow I shot yesterday to scare some goats out of a canyon. . . .

I had my first brush with "devil's-club" [a spiny shrub] this morning in an alder thicket. Bad stuff.

Yesterday the plane dropped supplies for us without benefit of parachutes. Just packaged them well and kicked them out. It was quite a job finding them, George said.

I am not too sure of getting a goat. It is extremely difficult to get close enough, and rain has used up so much time. We will spend two more days here and then will have to move on. I would regret not getting one of these monarchs of the peaks.

Thursday, September 13, 10 A.M.—Just twenty-four hours since I wrote last. We are sitting on the mountain near where I wrote yesterday. Alex and Don are cleaning a big billy goat on a ledge overlooking the canyon.

My spirits were low yesterday when I wrote that I was not sure of getting a goat here. Three hours later I had one.

When I wrote yesterday, we were within 500 yards of the goats as the crow flies but much, much farther on foot. There was a steep canyon between us with a rushing, glacial river tearing down the middle. The goats were bedded down where they could see us if we tried to cross.

They finally got up and fed down into a depression, and we started out in all haste. As soon as we topped over we saw goat horns above a ledge, and I started making my way toward him. The wind was right, the footing was right, and he didn't hear me until I had made some progress. Then he got up and started off. I put an arrow through his ribs at about twenty yards. He was out of sight in seconds.

Straining after him, trying to look under, over, and around the crags where he might be, I suddenly saw him get up not very far away. My arrow found its mark again, going straight through him low behind the front shoulder, and he tumbled off the ledge.

We could reach him only by being lowered with ropes, and since it was getting dark we had to get off the mountain immediately. We had no choice but to leave him and get back to camp.

This morning, armed with ropes, we went back to recover my trophy. Fortunately, he did not break his horns in the fall off the cliff. They were 9½ inches long. He was approximately a two-hundred-pounder, a fine goat for a full mount.

The beautiful billy goat where he fell on a ledge high above the Hendon River.

2 P.M.—Got back to camp at 1 P.M. with the goat. George had a stew waiting. He is now working on the hide, head, and feet of the goat.

It is good to have at least part of a day to loaf and rest up. Goat hunting with a bow and arrow is really rough. I think this will wind up my hunting for these cliff dwellers.

Have some pictures to make tomorrow morning when the sun is on the right side of the mountain. After lunch we plan to start back to base camp.

5 P.M.—Had a good nap. Alex and George have just finished their work on the goat skin. We're sorting gear, sharpening arrows, cleaning cameras, doing small odd jobs, and taking it easy.

Alex is a going concern, always doing something. He told us one night about his childhood in this wild country. In order to attend school at one point, it was necessary to float down the Yukon River, in the company of four of his younger brothers, to spend the winter in Dawson City. They had only their provisions and some blankets and had to fend for themselves on the five-day trip. When the raft got waterlogged, they were obliged to pull in to shore and build a new one. My mind went back to my own childhood when I complained of having to ride five miles to school on my bicycle after a warm breakfast in our cozy kitchen.

It is getting very windy and cloudy again but is still shirt-sleeve weather. On sunny days when the glaciers melt faster, the river in front of the camp rises about six inches. This is a beautiful campsite, but no place for practice shooting. The thin topsoil barely covers solid rock.

Alex just called me to see three goats he has spotted with the scope. There is comfort in knowing that I don't have to climb those mountains again today.

Have a goat hindquarter and two slabs of ribs hanging up. Roast ribs tonight.

On sunny days the glaciers melt faster and the river rises about six inches.

Friday, September 14, 5 P.M.—Farewell to Goat Canyon. It was rugged hunting. I like to hunt goats but that place is not good for hunting with a bow.

We got a break with the sun before we left and spent the morning doing pictures. We should have a fine goat film.

It is cloudy and windy now and looks like rain. The tent is up and goat ribs are roasting. We are now across the river from Goat Canyon. Same nice site we camped at on the way in. It is just a short day back to base camp.

What a pleasure to ride again after our arduous mountain climbing, in spite of the fact that we had to almost swim the swollen river. We will hunt on the way back to base camp.

6:30 P.M.—Dinner is over and I'm sitting by the fire with a cup of tea. The goat ribs were good. Not quite so tasty as sheep, but fine enough.

Nobody knows what time it is. There are four watches in the party and about every other day we set them by the time one of us has. My time was good until the stop-hand button was moved by heavy brush. I have not had the right time since.

There is time to reminisce now. Oddly enough, the first arrows I shot at big game here in the Yukon were kills. These glass arrows have given me great confidence. They perform like the birch ones I used long ago.

Sitting by the fire in Goat Camp.

Saturday, September 15, 6 P.M.—Back at base camp writing at the kitchen table. Got in at 3 P.M. Saw about twenty-five sheep on the way. Alex went after one for camp meat but no luck.

Washed some clothes, took a bath, and rearranged our equipment. We will move base camp tomorrow morning. This place is known as either "Devil's Hole" or "Cache Camp." A cache of groceries is always left here for emergencies, stored on a high platform.

This place is known as "Devil's Hole" or "Cache Camp." A cache of groceries is always left here, stored on a high platform, for emergencies.

Our next camp is two days away. We will look for sheep and maybe see a grizzly or moose en route. Have seen only one grizzly to date and no moose for about ten days. It is about time to run into one.

We found a box that had been dropped by the plane and overlooked before. It contained some medicine for Don's ulcers but he feels fine now. It is good to get some table cooking again. Ed has a cake baked and some cookies in a bowl.

Sunday, September 16, 7:30 P.M.—Camp Archell. Got here a half hour ago. Left Cache Camp at 1 P.M. today. Don took pictures this morning of the pack train coming here. We traveled about fifteen miles and are camped on the edge of a big lake just for the night. Will leave again in the morning for sheep country.

Saw four goats near camp this morning. No game on the way here. We're always amused at the way the horses act up. Cache Camp is the halfway mark, and they know they are headed for home. Has the same effect as a bag of oats just out of reach on a long pole before their noses.

Dinner is being prepared. I hope it is good; I am hungry. Had to retie eleven packs on the way. George salvaged some turnips that leaked out of a torn sack. He rides the rear to check on things that drop off. They had a hard time finding all the horses this morning.

Monday, September 17, 7:30 A.M.—Am sitting under a spruce tree with a steady, drizzling rain coming down. We were up at 5 A.M. Breakfast is over and the boys are packing up. Packing the horses in the rain is quite a mess. It looks like a long rain, too. We can't see the mountains. Another day without pictures. Yesterday was the only time we had sun while the whole pack train was moving. The trip is more than half over and we still have a great deal to do to get a film out of it.

I hope the Razorheads are rolling at the factory now. They are really deadly missiles. The hits on the two animals shot so far have gone entirely through. Those wide razor blades seem to clear the way for easy passage of the arrow.

I asked Alex if he thought the game in this country was holding its own, and he said that he thought it was. But, he also said that not as much game is killed now as twenty years ago. When he was a boy his family would kill twenty to twenty-five moose, every winter—four for themselves and the rest for the sled dogs. Most of the natives we see here now live by their can openers.

The cook tent is down; packing is almost finished. It is still raining but I can see the outline of a mountain now.

Mountain Camp, 3:30 P.M.—We are in the open at timberline. Nothing above but alder, willow, and buckbrush. Sheep, grizzly, and moose are supposed to be here.

The weather cleared around noon with showers off and on. I shot two blue grouse with a blunt arrow I made from one of Alex's 300-magnum cases. Nice big grouse that will taste good. We have a shoulder of goat left. Alex and George and I will go out after camp meat tomorrow.

"Mountain Camp"—we are in the open at timberline.

I shot two blue grouse with a blunt arrow made from one of Alex's 300-magnum cases.

Don is feeling rough again. Wants to rest and try to get well.

So far we have eaten some moose left over from a previous hunt, a sheep, and half a goat. One moose should last the six of us for the rest of the hunt. A sheep would taste better.

Tuesday, September 18, 11:30 A.M.—Nothing much to report. Raining this a.m., and I decided not to go with Alex and George for camp meat. They were back at ten. Weather closed in on them.

Slept until nine and then made two more blunts from 30-06 cases. All set for ptarmigan and blue grouse now. Yesterday's two grouse were all white meat. Ed is going to make a stew. Alex and Don are reading. Joe and George playing cribbage—all here in the fourteen-by-sixteen cook tent.

Another day lost. Almost all of our time to date has been spent on goats. Just a short two weeks left. We are two days from Champagne now. Tomorrow we plan to ride to side camp for sheep. This is also moose and grizzly country.

5 P.M.—Alex and I just got back from a hike to the top of the hill above camp. Looked the country over with glasses. Saw seven sheep about three miles away or one day away by horse.

Cold and windy. George says we will have snow. There is a misty rain falling now. A tipsy three-quarter moon last night. George says the weather will be bad until you can hang a powder horn on the moon.

We are packed up to leave for side camp in the morning. We have plenty of wood cut for our little stove if we can't go. George and Alex are playing cribbage. Joe is reading love stories and Ed making a stew. Don is sleeping.

Alex and I don't agree on the date. One of us has lost a day somewhere. The floor of our cook tent is covered with redolent spruce boughs.

Wednesday, September 19, 7 A.M.—It rained last night and is still coming down. We were up at five-thirty. Breakfast is over and we're all packed up to take off. Joe went after the horses before daybreak and is not back yet.

Hunting deer in Michigan, or almost anywhere, is good in this kind of weather, but not here. One does not just wander around in this country hoping to run into game; it is not that plentiful. We scan the mountains from a high point with glasses. If something is sighted, the scope is zeroed on it to determine sex or whether it is a sheep or goat. Game found in this way is usually miles away and in rain, mist, or fog, visibility is limited to a very short range.

We cannot predict the weather because we can see only to the top of the next mountain. A bad storm can be on us in a few minutes out of what we thought was a clear sky.

8 A.M.—Shaved and trimmed my hair with a battery razor. Joe just came in with the horses. He looks cold, wet, and crabby. These wranglers never put on enough clothes.

Packing up now. Will be gone for a week, depending on our luck.

» «

7 P.M.—Sitting by the fire in a willow thicket overlooking Dezadeash Lake and river. For dinner we had soup, cold roast goat toasted over the coals, spaghetti, peas, jam, peaches, and cake. This is a nice snug side camp. Don and I have an eight-by-ten tent. Alex and George each a lean-to made from a tarp.

Got here at three-thirty and made camp. Light showers on the way. Saw a red fox and flock of ptarmigan. We also saw fresh bear diggins along the way.

After our tent was set up we climbed a knoll and saw an immense bull moose on the slope across from us. He was almost a mile away, but the scope showed wide, broad antlers. At least sixty-inch spread, Alex said.

We had to make a decision—go after him now with no light for pictures, or take a chance of finding him tomorrow and hoping for better light. The majority of opinion was that we leave him. He is too good a trophy to shoot just for camp meat.

I was influenced in my decision by the fact that we are in moose country. Have seen more moose sign here than anywhere.

A gentle slope runs downhill all the way to a wide valley through which the river flows. Up the mountain behind us is sheep country.

I prefer this country to any we have been in and the hunting is certainly easier.

When the decision was made to leave the moose for tomorrow, Alex observed that the combination of the bow and camera was a tough one. "Makes a lot of work for the guides."

Thursday, September 20, 10 A.M.—I am sitting on my horse, Buck, on the mountainside trying to find the big bull. Cloudy again. It rained last night and early this morning. Clouds are right down on us. Woke up at 5 A.M.

Twelve Noon—Huddled on the lee side of a spruce waiting out a snowstorm and for a spot of sunlight that could shine through a hole in the clouds. We think our moose is bedded down about 200 yards from us. Jumped him an hour and a half ago and watched him go to this spot.

1 P.M.—Still here. Two snowstorms have gone through and another coming. Had lunch and tea. I think the moose moved on ahead of us. Two rams are on the mountain ahead.

6 P.M.—Back in camp. The moose gave us the slip with the help of snow squalls. We rode on to a high knoll and looked the country over. Nothing.

Fire going here and a hot rum in my belly. Time is getting short. One and a half hours of sunshine today.

If there was ever moose country, this is it. Flats and fingers of willow running up the draws. I asked Alex why there were not more moose here.

Wolves, he said. Temperatures are extremely low here in winter and the wolves run the moose in deep snow. Breathing violently from the exertion they frost their lungs and die of pneumonia.

When the plane came in to take Judd out, Alex got a letter from his wife saying, among other things, that a wolf had attacked one of the horses and that she had been called upon to sew up a large tear in the skin on his shoulder.

And Alex told us that last winter when the snow was deep and the weather cold, wolves had come in to a trapper's camp at night and killed and eaten his sled dogs who were tied up, unable to escape.

Following our hunt, Alex says he will pull the shoes off the horses and turn them loose. They will fend for themselves during the winter.

Friday, September 21, 10 A.M.—Sitting on a tuft of grass on a mountainside. George and Alex are scanning the country looking for "dingook" (moose). Weather is fair and visibility good, although it would seem that snow is brewing. I put my insulated underwear on this morning for the first time. We need sun, not only for pictures but to be able to see moose and bear. (Buck is trying to eat the tuft of grass I am sitting on.)

A few minutes ago I suggested to Alex that with time running out, we forget about sheep and concentrate on moose. I would rather get a big moose than a sheep. Also, to get an action picture of shooting sheep is no small feat. But with the right setup it would not be difficult on moose. Besides we need meat badly, and what we did not eat we could pack out with us.

We can't hunt sheep anyway in this weather. Just about the time we start a stalk, a cloud settles down on us and the climb has been in vain.

Got a beautiful picture yesterday morning in a short spot of sun. Looking down over Dezadeash Lake with the mist rising from it and a bank of clouds pierced by the snow-capped mountains beyond.

Buck is standing over me now, sleeping. His head overhangs mine. His front legs are my back rest. When we stop for tea we drop the reins so the horses can eat and have catnaps. They are very nice horses, with marked personalities. Each horse has a buddy and care must be taken not to separate pals in selecting horses for a side trip.

Twelve Noon—No moose yet. We're having lunch. Had fun rolling half-ton boulders down the mountains.

4:30 P.M.—Back in camp. All we saw today were four sheep far away.

A remarkable sight this afternoon—a fiery ball in the sky. George said it is a planet called the sun. The sun was out all afternoon, but we had nothing to pho-

Camp overlooked Dezadeash Lake in the distance.

tograph. A very cold wind almost blew us off our horses. We rode about fifteen miles today. Not enough moose sign to justify hunting further here.

Eating the last of the goat and badly in need of red meat. We will try with the bow and, if we can't get close enough, Alex will take one with the rifle. I can taste those ribs now.

Saturday, September 22, 5:30 A.M.—Huddled by a smoking fire. Breakfast finished. George just went for the horses. It is cloudy again, although the sun could break through with the proper arrangement of clouds. With no photo light we plan to ride at the lower edge of the mountain and try to find a moose. Went to bed at five-thirty last night to get out of the wind. The days are much shorter now. Daylight at 5 A.M. and dark at 7 P.M.

6:30 P.M.—We're camped in a willow thicket again. Have been in the saddle all day. Saw a cow moose and a fox. Shot two ptarmigan. I broiled one over the fire and ate him. No sun all day. Snowflakes in the high wind. It is snowing hard now, about an inch on the ground. Snow blurs the ink on my notebook. I'm going to bed.

Sunday, September 23, 6 A.M.—It stopped snowing after we went to bed. The sun is shining on the peaks this morning. Has not reached us yet. Alex watched a hawk catch a ptarmigan earlier. A fox was after them. Maybe this snow will change our luck.

The ink freezes in my pen. Have to thaw it out every so often.

5:30 P.M.—Just got back to base camp. We've been in the saddle all day. There was snow in the air almost constantly. This cut down visibility and we saw nothing.

Five days of traveling and camping wherever we were at nightfall. Looking over valley after valley, seeing nothing but one big bull moose and a cow. I shot two ptarmigan today. These are different from the ones I shot before. Today's birds are rust brown and white which George says are the true ptarmigan, while the others were gray and white rock ptarmigan.

I have not seen a rabbit but saw tracks in the snow. Alex says they are snowshoe rabbits. There is also a smaller one here called the rock rabbit.

A bull moose came down to within 200 yards of camp last night. We saw his tracks this morning. Alex says the moose saw the horses and came down to investigate. Thought they were moose. Saw many wolverine tracks also.

Monday, September 24, 6 A.M.—Waiting for Ed to make pancakes. It snowed again last night. A cold moon lit up the area before we went to bed. It is very cold this morning. Ed slept with the potatoes to keep them from freezing.

Alex says he has made up his mind now. . . . George and Joe will go up the mountain to get a ram for meat. He and I will take a tent and stove and go to Jo Jo Lake to see if we can find a moose and catch a few fish to eat. The upper end of this lake is about three hours from here.

After Joe and George come back from the sheep hunt, they will move camp to lower Jo Jo Lake and we will join them there in three to five days.

Our tent was half blown down when we came back last night. I had words with the lazy wrangler, Joe.

9:30 A.M.—Just about all packed up. Trouble finding the horses again.

6 P.M.—Camp made and Alex frying grayling in our snug tent. We caught the fish on Jo Jo River about two miles down from the lake. The river runs through a big flat covered with buckbrush and willow. It is almost a mile wide and five miles long, a real moosey looking place.

Just before dark I climbed the hill back of camp and saw a cow moose about half a mile out in the willows. We plan to hunt this area for several days on the theory that the moose have left the high country. We are lower here and there is no snow. The sun was out all afternoon.

A red squirrel has a nest in the spruce our tent leans against. He's been scolding us for trespassing.

Tuesday, September 25, 11:30 A.M.—On a hillside waiting for lunch. Saw a young bull moose standing in the willow meadow looking at us this morning. Made a stalk and Alex missed him three times with his rifle at about three hundred yards.

Snowflakes in the air and no sun today.

3:30 P.M.—Back in camp. Rode all over the mountainside but saw nothing. Saw many old signs and some fresh, but no moose. Looked for bear, too, but they are practically nonexistent.

5:30 P.M.—Have just finished dinner. Glassed the willow meadow twice since we came in. Nothing but snowflakes. Have decided to abandon this area and forget about moose unless we just happen to run on to one.

Tomorrow we will pack up and move halfway down on Jo Jo Lake. Maybe we can still get a film by including some fishing. May have a try at sheep there, too, and there is always a chance of running into a bear.

It seems to me that the hunt is about over. A good, hot shower would be damn welcome.

Wednesday, September 26, 6:30 A.M.—Just had breakfast. Alex is washing dishes. The horses must have sensed the move down Jo Jo (toward home). They came in an hour ago. It is storming again. Snow all over above us. Could see base camp from high ground yesterday. Snow up there and snow where George went for sheep. If he did not get one the day he left us, he will have trouble and we will go off canned meat and on to a fish diet—assuming we can find fish.

Am well broken to the saddle now and Buck and I get along very well. After an all-day ride in the wind and snow with no game sighted we both get a little cranky. But when we ride into the base camp, the horses whinnying at each other, the warm cook tent looks inviting and Buck rubs his nose against my shoulder as if to say "I know I started up too fast after you got off to shoot that ptarmigan, and that I was sleepy on the trail, but we are home now. . . ."

I was heavy on the bit, too, but Buck didn't deserve it. These horses are not like any I've ever seen before. In camp the hands spend most of their time talking about them and always refer to them affectionately by name—Buck, Pal, Ole, Skeezix, Indian, Ol' Blue, Freddie, etc.

5:30 P.M.—We have a camp set up now, halfway down Jo Jo Lake. I am sitting by an outdoor fire while Alex gets dinner on the stove in our nine-by-twelve tent. No job to get firewood here. Plenty of dry down spruce. Just push a tree over and it is good for a hot blaze for an hour or two.

Still cloudy and still spitting snow occasionally, although it does not stay on the ground. We would feel the cold more but, with the exercise one gets on a hunt like this and the wonderful warmth of padded nylon undersuits, we are quite comfortable leaning against our saddles around the fire. The horses are hobbled and feeding nearby. Their bells tinkle in the night as they move slowly along.

Coming down to this camp today we crossed the main trail the boys will take from base camp to join us for the trip back to Champagne. We found horse tracks on the trail going toward Champagne which can mean only one thing, and that is that some of the horses from base camp have played hookey and are on their way home.

It doesn't make much difference since our load is lighter than when we started, and we certainly have no meat to pack back out. There are twenty-six ewes and lambs on the mountain behind us, and a small ram is on the mountain across the lake. We expect George and Joe in tonight. I hope they come and I hope they have a sheep. I'm hungry.

Unless we have a break in the weather or Alex comes up with something definite, we will probably head on out tomorrow.

Thursday, September 27—Cold early this morning until the sun came out. Freddie and Pal tried to get out on the trail at eleven o'clock last night. Alex ran them down and tied them up. Also had to tie up Indian and Skeezix. Joe came in afoot at 7 A.M. from base camp looking for horses. Alex went back with him to move the camp to this place.

Ole stepped on my fly rod last night. Patched it this morning with wood splints and spruce gum. Then I wrapped it with cord and Don and I caught seven nice grayling. We took pictures of scaling and frying them, and then the sun left us and the heat wave was over.

After lunch we went fishing again but caught nothing. Our lines froze in the guides. Shot two ducks with two shots at about thirty yards, and then missed a blue grouse at fifty feet.

Back in camp we cut wood and then the gang came in with the outfit from base camp. George had gotten a sheep! Now we have meat.

6:30 P.M.—I'm sitting in the cook tent sniffing frying sheep. George and Joe had a rough time getting it. They hunted high up on snow in a snowstorm.

I saw a woodpecker today unlike any I've seen before. I have seen pileated woodpeckers and know it was not that. It was a bit smaller than a crow, had black wings, a light gray breast, and a spot of white near the shoulder. It flies like a woodpecker and chirps like a downy but louder.

This is the halfway Jo Jo Camp. It is called "Dinner Camp" because it is halfway between Mountain Camp and the Jo Jo Camp. If we get a break in the weather, we will hunt moose and grizzly there for a few days.

Snow started about 8 A.M. *and is still coming down.*

Friday, September 28, 6 A.M.—It snowed again this morning. About two inches on the ground even down here. The ceiling is very low. It doesn't look as though we will get any break at all. Five days of sunshine since August 18.

Ed is cooking sheep steaks and the wranglers are after the horses. Four more are missing now which leaves us twelve out of the original twenty-one. They will have to load them heavily.

7 A.M.—Breakfast of sheep steak, bacon, and eggs. Sheep is tops in my estimation.

6:30 P.M.—In the cook tent waiting for dinner. It started snowing about 8 A.M. today and is still coming down. About ten inches on the ground now. A semiwet snow that clings to the spruce. It will make a wonderful picture background if we get light in the morning.

This is the first time I have ever set up camp in this much snow. Don and I are snug in our tent with a stove. We have a big job drying out gear. My sleeping bag is a real comfort however. I have never gotten cold in it.

There were not enough horses left to move all of camp today, so the boys will go back tomorrow for the rest. If the storm clears Don and I will try for a moose on foot. We are now one day from Champagne. Will probably get out day after

A catch of Grayling.

tomorrow. Alex suggests a short hunt just off the Alaskan Highway. I don't know.

Saturday, September 29, 7 P.M.—The boys got back from the upper camp with the rest of our gear today. Alex, Don, and I went after a bull moose we saw near the top of the mountain across from camp, but he heard us and made off. Had lunch in camp, took a nap, and then Don and I hiked down to the north end of Jo Jo Lake. We saw wolf tracks and nothing else.

Leaving for Champagne in the morning.

Jo Jo Lake Camp.   *Jo Jo Lake.*

Sunday, September 30, 9 A.M.—In the coffee shop of the TAKU Hotel in Whitehorse, Yukon Territory, catching up on my field notes.

We rode straight through yesterday and got to Champagne at 4:30 P.M. It was then that I learned it was Saturday instead of Sunday. Ed had his car there and we got into Whitehorse at ten o'clock.

Yesterday, before we left Champagne, we talked with an Indian who had just come down from salmon trapping north of here. Said the grizzlies had been giving them trouble and that they were snaring them.

"Must take a strong snare to hold a grizzly," I ventured.

"Quarter-inch steel cable holds them okay," he replied.

It is raining today for a change. We need boots to walk on the sidewalk. Everything closed today. Much to do, general cleanup and packing.

Monday, October 1, 7 A.M.—Down in the coffee shop again. I'm in the habit of waking up early and can't sleep. Yesterday we went on a tour of the town with Ed. Saw Sam McGee's Cabin and the stern-wheel steamers that, until last year, traveled the Yukon and Klondike rivers.

We rode straight through to Champagne.

In the afternoon we had company. Jack O'Connor and Bill Ray, editors of *Outdoor Life* magazine, also Fred Huntington of California. They are up here hunting and came out the same time we did. They reported poor hunting too, but good weather. They were within 100 miles of us!

We could see good weather around us many times but always managed to be directly under the bad stuff.

We visited with these people for several hours. Then a reporter from the Whitehorse paper came up.

Sometime later Alex and Ron come in. Ron said the salmon run was on at Klukshu and wants to take us up there.

They stayed for half an hour. Don and I went to the O'Connor-Ray room for a few drinks, and then to Sonny's Steak House for dinner. Alex and Ron will meet us at nine this morning to pack gear for shipment and to clear customs.

It rained last night. If it clears we may make a try at shooting salmon. We need pictures. The ones we took in Alaska are dark, taken in the rain.

We have a date with the *Outdoor Life* group for dinner again tonight. I need a haircut badly. First day of deer season at home. . . .

Tuesday, October 2, 7 P.M.—Had dinner and said good-by to O'Connor and Ray last night. We got up at 6 A.M. and went to Klukshu this morning. Not an Indian or a fish there. It was cloudy, also. Stopped at Kathleen River and caught some grayling and rainbows on the way back. Made the trip in Ron's car.

We are waiting for dinner now at the Whitehorse Inn. Will do a final packing job and ship our stuff tomorrow. Have a date to show movies at a meeting of the Whitehorse Archery Club tomorrow evening.

Wednesday, October 3—We packed and got air freight shipment off. Toured the town and took more pictures. I showed movies at the air base to about fifty people. Martin Hanson, another archer hunting here, looked us up at the hotel at noon. He was with his outfitter and an Indian guide. Went out to their place (Marsh Lake) with them and visited and had a moose steak dinner before the movies.

We flew to Edmonton with Hanson. A modest and interesting fellow from Chicago. He beat me to the first grizzly with a bow up here last spring. Says he has good movies of three hunts he has had up here. Have invited him to hunt with us at Trout Lake in Michigan.

NOTE: The fly rod mentioned in these notes was given to me by Ernie Von Reis who manufactured them under the name of Orchard Industries. Upon my return I sent the rod back to him in jest, with the statement that there was something wrong with it, that a horse had stepped on it, but it was a small horse. . . . The rod was replaced without comment.

Chapter 3

BRITISH COLUMBIA - 1957

It was Glenn St. Charles who named this the Presidents' Hunt.

Another new experience in another new area. It is great and beautiful country, the Cassair district which lies in north central British Columbia.

PRESIDENTS' HUNT
COLDFISH LAKE—BRITISH COLUMBIA—
SEPTEMBER 7 TO OCTOBER 7, 1957

FRED BEAR–President, Bear Archery Co.–Grayling, Michigan
BUD GRAY–President, Whirlpool, RCA–St. Joseph, Michigan
ED HENKEL–President, Lamina Tool Co.–Royal Oak, Michigan
K. K. KNICKERBOCKER–President, Acme Visible Records, Crozet, Virginia

Saturday, September 7—Four hours and 400 miles north of Prince George, our Pacific Western pilot, Merv Hesse, eased the *Norseman* down to a gentle meeting with the mirror surface of Coldfish Lake. The floating dock was barely able to sustain the weight of the group assembled to greet us. Tommy Walker, our outfitter, and his wife, Marian. Tommy's partner, Rusty Russell, and his wife. Guides, both Indian and white, wranglers, and general help. On the brink of the hill by the corral fence were the wives and children of the Indian men. Behind them, the Indian village, and from farther back, the defiant bark of the sled dogs could be heard.

Big job unpacking and sorting gear for the pack trip tomorrow. Poring over a map we find that we are about 200 miles south of the Yukon border and equidistant from the Pacific Ocean and the Alberta line. A beautiful country of towering peaks as far as the eye could see. Glaciers fill their irregularities and start cascading streams that snake through the spruce and jack-pine valleys. To the east the Spatsizi River comes up from the south to empty into the Stikine. This river flows west and then southwesterly to empty into the Pacific Ocean at Wrangell, Alaska. Nearest outpost is the Indian village of Telegraph Creek on the Stikine 160 miles west. Thirty-five hundred square miles in which to hunt stone sheep, goats, grizzly bear, moose, and caribou.

We eased down on the mirror surface of Coldfish Lake.

Sunday, September 8—Ed, Knick, and I went with Tommy to the east end of Coldfish Lake to fish for rainbows while our outfit goes by horse on their way to Gladys Lake camp. They left saddle horses at our fishing site for our trip to camp later. We caught a great many beautiful, lively trout on small dry flies. These fish are hard of flesh, brilliantly red inside, and delicious. They averaged between one and two pounds. We took some with us and the remainder went back to base camp to be smoked.

Monday, September 9, After Dinner—7 P.M.—Rainbow trout, red and firm. Rode with Charles Quock today looking for sheep. Saw none. Saw four moose, six caribou, many goats, and a small flock of ptarmigan.

Ed, starting for the river to fish, saw some moose and did a stalk. No luck. Never did get to fish.

Knick went with Dale. Saw much sign, but no game. Tommy went back to base camp.

Tuesday, September 10—Charles Quock, my Indian guide, and I rode a long way up Connor Creek to the west branch. Lost some time trying for a moose on the way. Got there at noon and stopped by a creek to eat lunch. Located a lone ram bedded down high on the shale. Put the scope on him. "A full curl," said Charles.

We made a stalk. The ram had been facing away from us, but as our heads showed over the ridge he was looking at us at fifty yards. He got up and started away over the shale.

I shot an arrow at about sixty yards, but it didn't reach him. He disappeared around the mountain with us hot on his trail. The ram climbed a rocky peak and stood looking at us from the top. We continued along the side, planning to circle over and find him again on the other side.

After crossing the shale we were on a grassy, rolling, steep sidehill. Charles ahead and I panting along in back of him. Looking back I was surprised to see three rams in a depression we had passed. One was lying down and two were feeding. We kept on going because the lone ram we had seen first was the biggest.

Just before reaching the top, I, behind as usual, saw the big fellow crossing the next draw beyond. I signaled to Charles. He came back and we watched him go over the next ridge. We continued after him and routed a flock of seven rams on the other side. No time for them, however.

Circling back we peeked over a ridge beside a glacier. Our ram was about 150 yards below and just going over the next knoll. When he was out of sight we ran and slid down the fine shale just in time to see him disappear over the next ridge. We ran again and there he was about thirty-five to forty yards away. Just his head showing looking at us. He knew we were after him.

I do not like a head-on shot. Just a few inches off the mark will only wound and the hole through the rib cage into the chest cavity is no larger than a baseball. In addition, to shoot an arrow at full draw to clear the ridge would hit him in the head.

The only way was a short draw to lob it over the ridge and drop it into the brisket. If I had been alone, I would not have taken the shot. But Charles barked, "Shoot Quick!" I felt that I was on the spot and to hesitate would have been to lose face with the Indian.

The arrow went in a perfect line but I had a sick feeling that after it cleared the ridge it had dropped too low. The head disappeared and Charles ran over while I tried to regain my breath. When he got there he turned to me with a wide grin.

We found him jammed against a rock halfway down the shale slide. He had run about sixty yards and died on his feet. Then rolled down the mountain until he hit the rock.

He was a beautiful animal. Horns not broomed. A 41½-inch curl and 27-inch spread. He would dress out at well over 250 pounds. There was a big hole right in the middle of his brisket. I was very lucky to get such a large ram on the second day of hunting and would have been quite happy with a smaller one. A 42-inch ram is the biggest head that has been taken out of this area.

We had left our hats on the other side of the mountain weighted down with rocks to keep the wind from blowing them away. Charles said he would get them and told me to roll the ram the rest of the way down. I did so reluctantly and he came to rest on a bench far below.

It was four-thirty and raining. We were four hours from camp. We propped the ram up for pictures and then went down to the horses and back to camp. I was bushed.

The ram had rolled down the loose shale and came to rest against a rock outcropping.

Wednesday, September 11—The weather has been bad since we got here. But this morning the sun was shining. We went back with a big pack horse, took pictures, and packed the ram out whole. Another eight hours in the saddle.

Thursday, September 12—Charles dressed out the ram last evening by flashlight. We never found the arrow. The ram was facing me at an angle. The arrow entered the brisket center, cut the big jugular vein, skidded along the rib cage and shoulder blade, and passed out behind the front leg. I never saw a more devastating arrow wound. I would like to see the arrow, but am not going to climb back up there to look for it!

Coming back with the ram we saw a beautiful grizzly high up on a mountain. Saw another one on the mountain across from camp this evening.

Today was a rest day. We took pictures around camp in the morning. Went fishing this evening. Caught many rainbows. Tommy Walker came in this evening. Delighted with my kill.

*Tommy Walker and
Charles Quock flesh
the skin of the ram.*

Friday, September 13—Saw the grizzly (a beauty) on the mountain across from camp this morning. Being Friday the thirteenth, I was not sure I should stretch my luck and go after him. He was such a beautiful animal. Black with silver up his back, neck, and head with black rings around his eyes. Tommy, Charles, and I had planned a high trip for sheep pictures but I could not resist a try at that bear.

It was 10 A.M. when we left camp. Rode part way up and then climbed above the bear. But he was not there. Stayed up until three-thirty and then gave up and came back to camp. Had a bite to eat and just now (6 P.M.) spotted him on the next mountain. Spent the last half hour watching through the thirty-power scope. He is eating mossberries, blueberries, huckleberries, and cranberries—all of which are plentiful. Have one scope on the bear and another on a billy goat.

Knick went up to a salt lick in the area where I shot my sheep. Got back a few minutes ago. Built a blind and shot two blue grouse on the way.

Morris, our wrangler and woodcutter, is a young Indian. Robert, the cook, is Charles Quock's brother. Both he and Charles are around thirty years old. The Indians are a happy lot. They sing in harmony, very well. They pitched horseshoes at odd times.

8 P.M.—Dinner is over. Ed got in. Saw two caribou.

Charles has good eyes, is a good hunter, and is not afraid of grizzly bears. Emphasis is always on the word *grizzly*. It is never a bear—always a GRIZZLY bear. He is the first Indian I have ever seen who was not afraid of grizzlies. He also has a sense of humor. The night we left my ram on the mountain some suggested that a grizzly might get it and Charles said: "Where he get oxygen." The ram was up high. . . .

Had sheep ribs last night. Roast hindquarter this evening. Yum.

Several days ago, watching a bull moose through the scope, Charles said: "Make me hungry looking at him."

The Indians are singing at the dishwashing now. We have a campfire every night. I am sitting by it writing while the others sit on blocks of wood discussing horses. Tommy has top equipment in every department. His fifty-two horses are fat and gentle.

Knick and I share a tent. Ed has a smaller one. Tommy has a short-wave radio here. Talked to his wife at base camp this evening. I had him send a wire home about my good luck with the sheep.

Saturday, September 14, 7 P.M.—Sitting by the campfire. Got in at five o'clock and pitched horseshoes for a while. Ed came in a few minutes ago. He had seven ptarmigan. Got almost close enough to a big bull caribou.

Charles and I rode up the valley today where the bear went last night. Did not see him. Rode to within sixty yards of a big bull moose and cow but cover was too thick for a shot. Saw a beaver and four ducks on a small lake. I asked Charles if he shot ducks. "In the spring," he said. "Shotgun?" I asked. "No, .22. Miss a lot. Come back in spring full of lead." "Lead?" I asked. "Yes, shots from shots gun."

I asked Charles about his family. "Four sisters in Telegraph Creek." "Married?" "Yes, lots of kids." Of all things, he is having his dog sled shod with fiberglass.

This is a beautiful country. Not so desolate as the Yukon and more game. Weather has been fine since I shot my sheep. Last two nights have been cold. Freezes water at night. Very cold mornings until the sun comes up.

Sunday, September 15—Another freeze last night. Poplar leaves are beginning to fall. We all rode up Connor Creek this a.m. Ed and Laman went up into a low, wide valley. Tommy, Charles, Dale, Knick, and I looked over three valleys. Saw two sheep and some moose on the way. We were high and could see Ed down

Ed saw a wolverine and shot three more ptarmigan.

below us. Also saw wolves. Ed told us later that the wolves played in front of them for half an hour. Never more than 500 yards away. We could hear the wolves howling. They chased a band of sheep over the mountain later. Ed saw a wolverine and shot three more ptarmigan. Birds for dinner tonight. Very good.

Plan to go up to where I got my sheep tomorrow. Need sheep pictures.

Monday, September 16—Got in too late.

Tuesday, September 17—Got in too late.

Wednesday, September 18, 10:30 A.M.—Sitting by the fire. Camp is being torn down. We're moving to Rainbow Camp at south end of Coldfish Lake. Tommy and Knick hunting on the way. Ed and I going with pack train to get pictures and fish.

Monday we all rode together up Connor Creek. Charles, Dale, Knick, and I took the west branch. Tommy and Ed went up to the head of the creek. We saw eight sheep but they were too far away for pictures. Went up a different valley, then crossed a mountain and came back. Saw a bull and two cow moose just before dark. Met Ed and Tommy on the trail.

Twelve Noon—Just had lunch. Cook tent coming down now. The sun is warm but it froze a half inch of ice last night.

Tommy Walker came here from Bella Coola in 1949. Came to this country from England in 1929 to start a fur farm. It didn't work out and he has been an outfitter ever since.

Charles goes to Telegraph Creek by dog team before Christmas each year. It takes him nine days. He brings back presents for the family and also the Roman Catholic priest who stays for a few weeks. The priest tells them that if they have big families, they might have a mission here later.

Three families winter the horses at Hyland, thirty miles east of here, where there is good grazing. They live in log cabins and subsist on moose meat. Staple groceries for these people come in from Prince George by plane when they come in empty to pick up hunters.

Two goats have been on the mountain across from us all morning. Spotting scope is always set up. Looking in, we either see a goat, moose, sheep, or bear.

Rainbow Camp is where we hunt goats. Tommy says there are lots of them there. We need meat. We have eaten all the sheep. Expect to be at next camp for two or three days. Then to Coldfish Lake Saturday when Bud Gray comes in. Will hunt caribou from there for a week. After Knick and Ed leave we will pack in for a week. That will end the hunt. Frosts of the last few nights have hit the poplars hard. Leaves are off in most places.

Thursday, September 19—Knick and Tommy came in last evening after I had finished writing. Am writing at breakfast now. It is raining and blowing. We have a cabin for the cook and dining headquarters. Big and well made of logs. All lumber for the roof, floor, and window frames is whipsawed.

Knick came in last night, built a roaring fire in our tent, poured himself a drink and finally blurted out that he had shot a bull moose. Shot him in the back leg

Knick and moose.

cutting the big femoral artery and that was that. I'm going out with him this morning to get pictures. I hope the weather will clear up.

2:15 P.M.—Sitting on a hillside where Tommy and Dale are butchering Knick's moose. Black flies are pesky. It has cleared up somewhat. Warm and cloudy. Can see the two horses but not Laman, Charles, or Ed across the mountain. There are eight goats in sight.

Lots of meat in this moose. Antlers are about forty inches with sixteen points.

Ed and I did some fishing yesterday afternoon. Rainbow Camp is only about twenty minutes from our fishing spot. Waited for trout to rise in shallow water and waded out ten feet. Ed threw his fly, I focused on it and got the trout coming up and taking it. I want to get back there again to fish from my horse and take pictures.

Friday, September 20, 5 P.M.—Sitting by our fire in front of the tent. Knick shot a nice goat today.

Knick, Dale, Charles, and I rode up high on Goat Mountain this a.m. and saw a pair of goats bedded down in a draw. Charles and I moved down and set up the camera with a six-inch lens. Could cover the goats well. Knick made the stalk down. It was a perfect setup. The goats were directly below a big rock. Knick shot at about 35 yards hitting one of them straight through the middle. He ran about 200 yards, fell, got up, and fell in some buckbrush. A beautiful goat with ten-inch horns.

It is about time I started hunting again. Have not done any for a week. Too busy taking pictures.

This is the end of the first stage of the hunt. Tomorrow we will go up Coldfish Lake to base camp. Bud is due in tomorrow and we will reorganize and start off again.

We spend too much time riding. I hope to take my pup tent and ride off with Charles for the last week. Would like to camp wherever we are at the end of the day and start from there the next morning.

Wednesday, September 25, 6:30 P.M.—First notes I have written since last Friday at Rainbow Camp. We are now in base camp. Bud came in Saturday. He and Tommy and I went south to get sheep pictures. Ed and Knick went caribou hunting. They saw a great many, but no shots. We saw some sheep and got good pictures.

Monday we all went up to the caribou plateaus. Split up and Tommy and I saw two bulls in a valley flat. Spent two hours on a stalk and could not get a shot. Got into camp just after dark.

Yesterday Ed, Charles, and I went to caribou country again. Saw a band with large bulls on top of a mountain. We made a stalk and were pinned down from 3:30 to 7 P.M. when I finally got a running shot. A tremendous bull.

The shot was too high I thought, up near the shoulder. He ran to the top of a hill with the group and they stood there. His antlers were much bigger than my elk. He was gray in front and halfway back. With glasses I could see a blood streak down his white side. He kept his mouth open and seemed to be panting. I wondered if the arrow had gone lower than I'd thought—perhaps into the lung cavity and he was gasping his last. I handed the glasses to Charles and asked what he thought. "Him barking at cow," he replied, handing back the glasses. The rutting season was on.

We found the arrow later. Little penetration. A slight wound that didn't even interfere with his love-making.

There were three big bulls in this herd. Also some smaller ones and many cows. We watched them at close range through two siestas and a feeding period. Much pseudofighting, clashing of horns, and barking all the time. The long hour ride down the mountain back to camp was most spectacular after dark.

Three hunters from Tucson and L.A. got in from a hunt. Yesterday a.m. we visited while we waited for our pack train to be made up. They had three sheep, six goats, a moose, and a grizzly. One sheep was forty-two inches.

We said good-by to Ed and Knick who rode off for the day's hunt. They will hunt from Base Camp for two days and then go out Friday.

Bud and I, Charles, Dale, Robert, and Morris are on our way to Marion Camp, two days from Base Camp. It is now 9:15 A.M. Thursday the twenty-sixth. We are at Cache Camp halfway to Marion. The sun is warm as we sit in front of our tent. Have been waiting since daylight for Morris to bring the horses. Hear bells now. They must have gone a long way.

Charles and Dale are sitting with us. Charles is telling us his problems. He met his wife at a "gamble." Has worked for Tommy for eight years. His oldest child is seven now and he is worried about schooling. Does not want to send his children "out to school." "Come back no good." "Take things without asking." May go to Telegraph Creek for the winter. Can get a job for him and his dogs at survey on road work. Might trap "if they pay good for fur."

I have not talked much about our good horses. First I rode Whitey. Easy to ride and not a bad trotter. She wandered off one night and was not recovered until Dale went on a search several days ago and found her. She is now with our group of fourteen. Next mount was Snip. A gentle bay and the best climber of the group. He was affectionate and would steal the camouflage twigs from my hat or reach around and nip my saddle quiver gently, thinking it was my leg. Short, choppy steps and a hard rider. Since yesterday I've been riding Snookie. She is an easy rider and responds quickly to the reins. Not hard to urge into a gallop when I want to ride ahead for pictures.

I have more gear hanging from my saddle than a pack horse. The camera saddlebags weigh thirty pounds. Attached to the right one is my bow. Between them I have my rain suit and the big lens. From the pommel hangs my saddle quiver, handgun, spotting scope, and binoculars. My pockets are loaded with film, light meter, and camera accessories. Also lunch and a pint thermos of tea. On the hunt we sometimes tow a pack horse with the big camera and tripod and extra magazine.

10 A.M.—Four horses are in. They are being saddled to search for more.

11:30 A.M.—Still waiting. Bud and Charles took a stroll up the hill. I took some pictures of Dale making "fire sticks." Have camera set now on some pancakes as whisky-jack bait. Have them pegged down. They carried the first two away whole.

Bud and Charles back. Said they heard a shot. Think the horses are found. Very warm, sitting in shade.

The Charles Quock family by their home.

12:30 P.M.—Horses in. Cook tent coming down—packing begins. I took 100 feet of whisky-jack pictures. We will be late getting into Marion Creek Camp.

Friday, September 27—Just had dinner. T-bone steaks from a caribou I shot yesterday.

We had come over a pass with the pack train. Down in a flat valley ahead, in an area broken up by small ridges and mounds, was a big bull caribou. Bud and I dismounted and stripped for action. Bud elected to cut in ahead of him. I went straight toward him but he eluded both of us. The boys from the pack train whistled and pointed to another bull, a smaller one. I made a sneak on him, got behind a big rock, and waited. He came within twenty-five yards and stopped.

It seemed obvious that he would pass me on one side or the other. I was crouched to shoot either way keeping my head just high enough to see the top of

We had T-bone steaks from a caribou I shot yesterday.

his antlers. He stood for about a minute looking at Bud and then at the pack train. I wanted him to pass by for an easy shot at eight or ten yards but was afraid he would wheel and run back, so I decided to move out beside the rock and try a shot. Looking through the brush beside me I could see that he stood facing me at an angle of forty-five degrees, offering a good rib shot. I eased my feet to the side, checked my arrow, and started out. He had heard me and was looking my way. Before I completed my draw he wheeled and I loosed the arrow after him. As he ran down through the willows and brush, I could see about eight inches of it protruding from his flank. I saw the arrow come out about 100 yards away. Twenty yards farther on he stopped for a moment and stood with his head down. Then he walked into a hollow and did not come out. We found him there, dead.

Dressing him out it was evident that he died in less than two minutes. The arrow had punched through the far side and the insert blade had been shed inside. The hit was straight through, just nicking a bone in the rear quarters. Must have hit a large artery.

He was not a monster, although these Osborn caribou are large animals. Antlers are about three feet high and three feet wide, with a shovel. A beautiful, large gray-and-black body. Should weigh dressed out about five or six hundred pounds. It was too dark for movies, so we came back to camp.

This is a beautiful place, and for the first time, no rocks just under the turf to break arrows.

Before going in after the bull we counted twenty-two goats on the mountain across from camp. Bud and Dale went after them while we went to get the cari-

The Indians watch Bud sharpen arrows.

*Bud offered to take a
stand at one end
with his bow.*

bou. Took pictures in the rain. Got back about 3:30 P.M. Bud was in camp with a fine goat. What a start for a hunt. A caribou on the way in and a goat the first day.

Have been busy getting our tent in shape. Needed drying racks by the stove for our wet clothes and gear. Bud has been working on an elevated bunk for the past three hours. Stopped for a minute while I got a picture of his "beauty rest." Says he will make one for me but not tonight. This is the best camp I have ever been in. There have been only three shots fired in this part of the country in two years. We have great hopes for the six days of hunting that are left.

Knick and Ed were to go out today. No planes could come in at this low ceiling. Rain stopped about 3 P.M. but it is damp and the clouds are thick. Charles is steamed up to hunt GRIZZLY bear. Says we will find one, watch him until he starts digging for marmot, and when he has a trench dug and only his rear is showing, we will slip in and shoot him.

Tomorrow we will start. Charles has abandoned his .38 revolver in favor of a rusty 30-30 rifle. We should see other game on this trip. There are many caribou and goats, some sheep and moose. Bud's sleeping masterpiece is about finished. Time to go to bed. Have changed from daylight saving to standard time.

Saturday, September 28, 9:45 A.M.—Rained last night and off and on this morning. Thick overhead. Decided to spend the day in camp and get things dried out and everything shipshape. While the time is short, we have a good start on trophies and do not begrudge the lost time.

Camp was invaded last night. A pack rat cut almost all of the tent ropes off the guides' tent and toted them to his home in a big, hollow, leaning spruce tree. The tree was about three feet in diameter with a thin shell as hard as bone.

The problem was discussed from all angles at the breakfast table. Robert suggested a propped-up piece of wood to be triggered with "spikes to come down on him." Bud was for a set-gun type of installation with his bow but the problem of a release could not be solved. My suggestion was a set-gun with the .44. Snares

Drain streams are slowed down and muskegs are tightening up.

of various types were considered also. With no conclusions reached, Charles went out and started chopping at the trees that supported the dead one.

A twelve-inch tree did not release it. Nor did another eighteen inches, so Charles shinnied up the hollow tree and hitched a rope to the top and we pulled it off. The cavity produced an amazing assortment of supplies for the pack rat's winter. Short pieces of tent ropes. A half bushel of dried mushrooms, pieces of caribou hide, ptarmigan wings, and feathers. Bones, large bunches of grass, and various plant fibers. Willow leaves, pieces of bread, and other odds and ends. Both ends of the trunk were packed like this.

Charles poked a long tent pole up from the butt end and the rat could be seen from the top. Bud magnanimously offered to take a stand at one end with his bow and some blunts. Two well-placed shots dispatched the marauder and order was restored in camp once more.

Putting an end to the pack rat was considered of prime importance. Dale said that the rat would find the saddles and cut all the lacings which would cause quite a stir in the progress of the hunt.

Bud is doing some needlework while I write. His elevated bed needs only a canopy to make it complete. Inquiries among the Indians produced no one talented in beadwork and he may have to settle for burlap bags sewn together with scalloped edges.

Bud's total bag to date is the goat, a Yukon gopher, and the pack rat. It takes a lot of meat to keep an outfit like this going. Each of the crew eats what is equivalent to a good-sized steak with lots of pancakes and cereal for breakfast. Our meat pole is hanging full. We could live out a fairly long storm with it.

Same Day, 3 P.M.—Had lunch of caribou steaks, potatoes, and beans. Am beginning to understand how the boys can eat so much meat. I ate about a pound and half for lunch myself.

Bud and Dale went hunting right after lunch. The only two saddle horses available up to now. Charles is out looking for more. A timely suggestion was offered to hobble them tonight if they were found, in order to get a good start in the morning, rain or shine.

Aside from a short brush with caribou in British Columbia two years ago, this is my first experience with them. These Osborn caribou are the largest and carry the greatest antlers of them all. The Barren Ground caribou is the smaller—not much bigger than our deer. The species is something like the antelope of Africa

Sheep and goat country.

as far as intelligence is concerned. They become confused and are likely to run in two directions at almost the same time. From a distance of a few hundred yards, they are not alarmed by an intruder but at closer range, it is a different matter.

In my two close contacts with caribou on this trip, I have found them to be as alert as white-tailed deer. They can wheel and be gone in an instant like elk or deer; their senses are keen and they like a certain space between them and unknown sounds. I feel certain that they are quick enough to avoid a well-directed arrow at thirty yards if the shooter has been seen. They seem, like many other animals, to find security in numbers and this condition, with more noses, eyes, and ears to contend with, piles up more odds against the bowman.

Goats are somewhat down the scale from the caribou in IQ. If one does not mind climbing and can locate them from below, it is just a question of time even

The pack train plods on.

for the bowman to make a successful stalk from above. Moose would not be difficult in this country. There are enough for good hunting but it takes time to find them where bow shooting conditions are favorable.

Sheep are more difficult and to hunt a trophy ram with the bow is not exactly a relaxing pastime. It could take a long time to be successful. The grizzly bear is the most thrilling of all game to me. I have had several occasions to observe them through the scope. Most of them are mixed silver and black. They move with an easy, sure-footedness and carry themselves as if they had a gentle and inquisitive nature. While one senses dignity about them, there is power and fury hidden there that is unexcelled by any animal on this continent. The gun has taught him that man is his superior. I hope he will not recognize the limitations of the bow!

4:30 P.M.—Raining again. I have water heating to wash some socks. Bud and I shot off the Marion Creek Championship before lunch. He won, hands down. He is a good shot.

Sunday, September 29—In too late to write.

Monday, September 30, 8 A.M.—Waiting for the horses. Can hear the bells. Yesterday was another day without sun. Wind and rain squalls. We were in the saddle from eight to eight. It is good to get an early start and anticipate the luck for the day. Also good to come back to the campfire and comfort of our camp.

Last night, coming in, we broke out of the spruce to see the glow of the warm lighted tent. Bud had our usual outdoor fire going and everything shipshape.

Charles and I rode up Marion Creek yesterday past its source and came out on top overlooking the Stikine Valley. A beautiful sight with a low ceiling pierced by mountain peaks. While we admired the scene Charles pointed out his marten trapping grounds where he and a cousin had caught forty in forty days.

Sitting there on our horses we heard an almost inaudible sound. I thought it was ptarmigan chuckling, but Charles said "Moose." We made a stalk. It was a small bull with a cow. Charles took his chaps off. "Can't run fast if he comes after us. . . . Tongue going out and in; him mad."

I took pictures of the moose from several angles at about forty yards, then the horses got loose and the moose ran off.

During lunch a lone bull caribou saw us from the next hill. He started toward us to see what we were and I shot pictures of him at about 150 yards. I doubt if they will be good because rain was spitting on my lens. He was slightly larger than my bull but not what we were after.

We went around the mountain and saw about a hundred caribou in four or five groups and looked them over. One bull was very nice and we rode straight for his group. At 200 yards we left the horses and crept over a knoll to within 125 yards. We were deciding what to do when the horses strolled in sight and the caribou ran off.

I ran under cover of the ridge and got a running shot at the big fellow at about sixty yards. They continued on up the slope and began feeding about a third of a mile away.

We got the horses and started toward them again but they tried to cut in front of us. Charles spurred his horse and I switched mine for the race. The caribou were running at an angle to us while we tried to cut them off. It was like an antelope wanting to cross in front of a car, both at high speed.

I passed Charles. With my bow with arrow on the string in one hand and switching Whitey with the other, I had no way of steering. If I stopped switching, Whitey would slow down.

I finally got up to within forty yards of the bull and rode beside him, imagining myself getting close enough to sock an arrow into him at close range like the Indians did on buffalo. I found myself wishing for a roping pony. . . . The bull ran with that peculiar caribou pace—legs spraddled and apparently doing his best. My horse played out at last and the chase was over. I wish I had had a picture of it.

Some time later the same caribou were grazing peacefully a half mile away. We saw a large bull moose and a cow on the way home. The cow was quite gray. Charles called in his best moose voice. The bull was interested but came only a short way toward us.

It was five-thirty then and two hours from camp, so we did not go after him. Ptarmigan chuckled at us from the safety of spruce thickets as we rode past. They are not so tame on rainy days.

Tuesday, October 1, 11 A.M.—Sitting in the tent. We have a fire in our stove and one outside. Charles and I went out this morning at 9 A.M. It was raining. By the time we got to the top of the knoll above camp the rain had turned to heavy snow. Snowflakes hit hard against our faces. We rode on for about ten minutes and I noticed Charles was not urging his horse as usual. I asked him what he thought. "Real bad," he said, so we turned back.

Bud was glad to see this show of common sense. I took pictures around camp in the storm and again dried out my gear. Will try to catch up on my notes.

This Marion Creek area is an easy one to hunt and it seems to be the Osborn caribou capital of the world. They are here in great numbers and some have enormous heads. Charles told me that before Tommy Walker located here hunters sometimes rode all the way from Telegraph Creek (160 miles) to get big caribou. If we get nothing else, I hope for one day of sunshine to get pictures of those big bulls.

We have had no sun at this camp. Have not taken the big camera out since the long lens calls for good light.

Just took off a half hour to see who was archery champion of the day. Bud won again. Our arrows melted into the snowstorm.

Bud had a good day yesterday. Got two long shots at sheep. Saw goats and four caribou.

Charles and I rode up to where I killed the caribou to see if a grizzly had been around. We rode to the top and all sides looking continually, searching over miles and miles but no sign of bears. We saw at least a hundred caribou, twenty sheep and goats. We always see goats.

The trouble in hunting caribou with the bow is that while one can place himself in front of the herd, the cows come first and the big bulls last. This is the mating season and the bulls are busy chasing the young bulls away from the cows. They never seem to be looking around, depending on the cows for sentinels. A bull alone would not be hard to handle with a bow.

This is not a caribou migration. It is a gathering of the herd for the purpose of propagating the species. The wind was blowing a gale topside. We hunched in a little draw to eat our lunch. Later on we came upon another herd of about thirty.

They were bedded down beside a half-acre alpine lake. We watched and photographed them for about an hour. Some got up and stood in the water. Two fought standing in the lake and two more fought on shore. Much snorting and clashing of horns. The cows have horns, but smaller than the bulls.

When they moved off we tried a stalk. I shot two arrows at seventy or eighty yards but they hit the gale and went down sideways. If they had hit, it would only have been a slap because of the wind.

Back at camp just at dark. Bud not in yet. Raining hard. Bud came in half an hour later, soaked. It was a good day.

1 P.M. now. Still snowing. It is melting in the valleys but clinging to the hills. We unsaddled the horses and forgot about hunting today. Sleeping bag looks good. Bud is repairing arrows. Stove and outdoor fires going.

Wednesday, October 2—Too late to write.

Thursday, October 3, 6:30 P.M.—No time to write this morning. Am now waiting for Bud and Dale to come in. Yesterday we all went together. Took a pack horse and the big camera. Snow on the ground and cold and windy. Ran into about forty caribou. I set the camera up while Bud went to work on them. Got about 200 feet of film, although the camera was sluggish from the cold. It took both hands to turn the focusing ring on the lens. Bud got several seventy- to eighty-yard running shots.

Coming back we crossed a big grizzly track, over our tracks. If we had been a little sharper on the way out this morning, I might have gotten a shot at him. We had seen a bull caribou walking along the side of a mountain about a third of a mile from us and had seen him shy at something behind a knoll but had paid no more attention to it.

Charles and I left Bud and Dale and took the trail. It led us down into a steep spruce ravine where we left the horses and went afoot.

It proved to be a bad chase. Too late to go farther. Backtracking to where the caribou had shied, we found it had been the bear that he had seen. Got in about an hour after dark. Bud had the place warm and a drink waiting.

Bud got wet down from violent exercise chasing goats and is taking a bath as I write. Had a good day, he says.

Charles and I took off after the grizzly again this morning. Cold as hell last night and today. A small lake we passed in the a.m. was frozen over when we came back tonight. Trailed the grizzly several miles but had to give up. We think he winded us yesterday as we found running tracks today.

The cold yesterday brought snow about two inches deep and two-foot drifts at times. I had hoped it was just a forerunner of Indian summer but doubt it now. I believe it is the priming coat for winter. The alpine lakes are frozen and glaciers are stilled. Drain streams are slowed down and the muskegs are tightening up. It is the long winter settling in and this is the snow that will melt next year.

As always the first snow tells all about animals we have not seen. I have not seen a red squirrel. Have heard them, have seen many tracks, and have found their mushrooms drying on the spruce, however. Two wolverines made tracks last night not far from camp. Fox tracks mingle with those of ptarmigan and snowshoe rabbits. Weasels are around too, as well as the fisher.

We saw about six or seven bull caribou today. That is all.

Have had dinner. Goat ribs and delicious trimmings. Very cold outside. We're snug here in our tent.

The horses are getting tired. We should have a change in saddle horses. This ends our grizzly quest. Too scarce. We will concentrate on caribou. Have only tomorrow left, although we can hunt on the two-day trip back to Coldfish Lake. Looked down on the Spatsizi River today. What a big country this is. I wish I could capture all of its moods on film.

Friday, October 4, 6:30 P.M.—Got in at five-thirty. Had a bath. Washed socks and underwear. Shaved and am now waiting for Bud.

Charles and I started out this a.m. bent on caribou or moose. Ran into another grizzly track and spent the day on that. Found where he had watched two bull moose fighting. They had torn up the ground over half an acre. One had been down but we saw no blood. We assumed that the grizzly was waiting for an easy meal.

From here the grizzly wandered aimlessly until he got up out of the timber and he then headed for a pass. We went around by an easier pass hoping to pick up his track on the other side. Not so. We had to circle the mountain and come back over the one he had headed for. We found his tracks on top. He had turned back, possibly because of the cold wind cutting through the pass. He had taken a nap in a spruce thicket and then headed down for timber. There are blueberries down there even after this snow and cold weather.

The only living thing we saw today was a spruce hen. The last hunting day is over. We will hunt on the two days to Coldfish Lake. May get something. If we don't, it will still have been a good trip. To see and to photograph those big caribou was almost enough in itself.

Saturday, October 5, 7 A.M.—My wife's birthday and as always I am hundreds of miles away on this day. . . .

Up and dressed. Horses just came in. Waiting for breakfast call. Bud is dressing and telling about his goat. Bud and Dale got in at 8 P.M. last night, packing the head and skin of a big goat. Bud had climbed up for him with Dale giving signals from below. Bud made a good shot at fifty yards.

Sunday, October 6, 9 A.M.—Sitting at Cache Creek Camp. In the sun this time. Two inches of water froze solid in the tent beside the stove last night. The day is clear, and the sun feels good. Had a big campfire last night. Got away from Marion Camp at noon yesterday. Bud, Dale, and I rode ahead to hunt. Never strayed from the trail. Saw a band of caribou in the distance, but too far.

Little wind. Cold, but a beautiful day. Saw my first red squirrels. Two of them, big and fat. Bud shot a spruce hen. We saw wolverine and wolf tracks. Got here about 5 P.M. A good dinner of caribou steaks. Charles and Bud and I are about ready to take off ahead to hunt on the way to Coldfish Lake. We will take the long way in and hunt caribou. May be late getting in and it is not likely that I will have time to finish my notes until on the plane going home.

Monday, October 7, 12:30 P.M.—On the bush plane a half hour out of Coldfish Lake. Will go back to yesterday.

Bud and Charles and I hunted to Coldfish. Took the long, high route. Saw caribou antlers on the skyline. It turned out to be a lone bull lying on a knoll taking a drowsy rest. We split and made a stalk from opposite directions, out of sight of each other. The bull lay prone, one antler resting on the ground. I thought Bud had gotten in closer and had shot him. Later he said that he was about the same distance away and thought that I had shot him.

It would have been a good time to hustle right up to him in the open but much time had gone by and I thought Bud was close by and I was afraid of ruining his chances.

After fifteen minutes the bull woke up and at the same time I saw Bud still some distance away. He seemed to have run out of cover. I was pinned down also.

It wasn't long before the bull became drowsy again and when I could see only his ears above the buckbrush, I made a bold dash across thirty yards of open to take cover below the hill he was on. A careful stalk put me within sixty yards, as far as I could go.

I had been careless of the wind—and knew it—but hoped that if he winded me he would go on toward Bud who was downwind. There was a chance that he would get up and stroll my way, too.

Fifteen minutes went by. I could see Bud. I felt the wind change to blow on the back of my neck. I got ready to shoot.

The bull sprang to his feet, facing me, and snorted a few times. I had hoped he would turn slowly and offer a shot at his ribs. But he whirled quickly and made off; my arrow was too late.

He half circled Bud who got four arrows off but no damage done. We had spent an hour and a half on this job. . . .

Came down the mountain to Coldfish at dusk just as Merv Hesse was coming in for us in a Beaver plane. Got our first news from the outside world via Tommy's short-wave set. Learned about the launching of the Russian satellite and about a new granddaughter for Bud. Also learned that the temperature was plus three and plus six the last two nights.

Just stopped at Takla Lake for gas. Airborne again. Should be in Prince George by three-thirty. A bath, a change to street clothes, check trophies, and hope to catch a plane at seven-thirty to Vancouver.

Breakfast at eight this morning. Left some bows and arrows for Charles and Robert before we left. Bud gave an outfit to the pilot also and some lessons on the art of shooting. Well qualified for the job since he was champion of the Marion Creek contests.

I met and photographed the family of Charles Quock. Six children and a seventh expected. They live in a log cabin that looks small for a family of eight plus a mother-in-law. Got the slippers and gloves I had ordered from them. Left candy and gum for the children.

A busy time packing up. Many things to talk about and not much time left. Lots of film exposed. We finally got the ship in the air at 11 A.M.

It is always interesting at the end of a hunt in remote places to speculate about the number of game animals there. It would seem that where hunters are not at all numerous game would be most plentiful. Also, that the farther north one goes, the more game he will find. But this is not so.

Last evening in base camp we talked to Tommy about the amount of game in his hunting territory of thirty-five hundred square miles. He has been hunting this area for eight years and should be in a position to estimate a fairly close count. He figures there are about thirty-five hundred game animals of the five species found here—grizzly, caribou, moose, sheep, and goats. That means about one animal to every square mile.

In our northern deer states a population like that would indicate that the herd was practically extinct and the area would not attract hunters except possibly on fresh tracking snow and in an "any deer" season.

This so-called scarcity of game came to my attention not only in the Coldfish Lake area, but farther south in British Columbia two years ago as well, and again last year in the Yukon. Nature has established a balance and the small amount of hunting does not take the surplus. It is doubtful if game would increase, even without the infrequent hunting pressure, unless wolves were hunted.

But if there were no wolves, game would increase more rapidly and might soon destroy their winter food supply and die of starvation. This is a condition we have now in many states with our deer herd. While game is not plentiful in terms of animals per square mile, hunting is good for these reasons: the terrain and cover of these northern areas allow animals to be seen at great distances, either with the naked eye or with glasses. In Michigan, with its heavy cover and flat ground, it would be almost useless to hunt with such a low game count. But here, where one's view is unobstructed for miles, certain areas are known to contain sheep, others are the home of goats. Moose and grizzly bears might be seen anywhere. During the latter part of September the caribou gather on certain high plateaus for mating and can be found there.

With a condition like this, in open mountainous country, good hunting can be had even with a scattered assortment of game. The very remoteness kindles the imagination of the adventurous hunter. He likes to think that he is perhaps the first white man to have climbed a certain ridge or looked down into a deep, glacier-carved canyon. There is always a chance that he might collect a world record head. For the confirmed climber always anticipating the view from the next ridge, this country is Utopia. From the top of any mountain the challenge extends, far and wide, until the mountains meet the sky.

A short stop—welcome respite from the saddle.

Charles Quock learns about a modern hunting arrow.

Above the lake is the corral.

Chapter 4

LITTLE DELTA, ALASKA - 1958

In the fall of 1957, Glenn St. Charles of Seattle and Dick Bolding of Olympia, Washington, made their first hunting trip to Alaska. Bowhunter Keith Clemmons joined the two at Fairbanks and proceeded to the Brooks Range where they fished and hunted for ten days.

Back at Fairbanks, Dick McIntyre, outfitter and owner of Frontier Sporting Goods and Flying Service, suggested they look over an area due south in the Alaska Range. Marc Stella was the pilot when he and Glenn left in a Super Cub for the suggested country. En route, they became temporarily lost in the area of Mount Deborah, but soon found themselves flying over a beautiful valley harboring an abundance of game. Upon studying the map, it was determined they were over the west fork of the Little Delta River, and just below them was an abandoned trapper's cabin that would serve adequately as a hunting camp.

Flying on down this glacial stream, they came upon the Portage Creek Airstrip, approximately ten miles below the cabin. This lonely landing strip had been built atop a ridge by a survey crew and would accommodate planes of fairly good size.

Thinking ahead, Marc and Glenn flew back up the river and found a short gravel beach near the cabin that would lend itself, with no small amount of work, to a landing field.

Back to Fairbanks and a huddle with Dick and Keith resulted in another flight the next day. Marc, in a larger plane, flew the group along with limited supplies to the Portage strip from which they made their way on foot to the cabin. Within an hour of their arrival, Marc flew over and, using small parachutes, dropped additional supplies, including axes, shovels, and saws for the construction of the landing strip.

The trio spent a happy week in this area and had a good supply of moose and caribou meat along with some fine antlers stacked on the landing field when Marc came back at the appointed time and found the strip to his liking.

The valley would be the location of our party along with Glenn and other friends for this hunt in 1958.

GRUBSTAKE BOWHUNT 1958

Saturday, August 16, 8 A.M.—Am situated in a trapper's cabin about a hundred miles from Fairbanks in the Grubstake Area of Alaska. No other person is within a week's hiking distance since Dick McIntyre of Frontier Airways brought me in last Thursday in his Super Cub—the only type plane that could land and take off from the gravel bar left by the spring freshets along the nearby river.

Standing on the strip, surrounded by nearly two hundred pounds of gear, I watched the plane fade into the sky. I had the problem of packing a mile and a half to this cabin site, with two rivers to ford in the two hours of daylight left.

A good-sized bull caribou was at close range on the river flats and three more fed on the mountainside as I trudged off with the first load. It was soon apparent that darkness and a threatening rain would forestall plans to reach the cabin that night and I made camp about halfway there under the watchful eyes of a band of sheep lying near the top of the mountain. The next morning was bright and sunny and the move was completed before noon.

Hunting season is still four days off as I write this. When a trip is planned about this time of year my legs are suddenly too long for my desk and I usually find myself on my way several days ahead of schedule. Some business commitments in Anchorage took up some of the slack before the plane flew me into the hunting territory a short time ahead of the others.

They are due in some time today. Bud Gray of Benton Harbor, Michigan, his son Mike of Chicago, Glenn St. Charles, Dick Bolding, Bob Arvine, and Jack Albright, all of Seattle, and Keith Clemmons of Fairbanks. Keith is the holder of the first-place Alaska Moose in the Archery Boone and Crockett and Dick Bolding has the first-place caribou. Dick is on this trip to record events on 16mm color film. Keith is an expert on army survival technique with considerable Alaskan experience and has promised to keep us out of trouble and away from the squaws along the Yukon. Bud and I are especially interested in white Dall rams. The rest of the party would take great delight in topping Dick's caribou or Keith's moose as would we all.

This cabin was built in 1927. It is tight and weatherproof with a roof of half-round timbers leveled off with moss and covered with sheets of birchbark. The bark is weighed down by several inches of earth and gravel out of which willow brush grows to an alarming height.

The ridge pole is a peeled spruce log, eighteen inches on the butt end tapering to twelve inches at the small end that supports an eight-foot overhang. The cabin logs vary from eight to ten inches in diameter and are chinked tightly with moss and dressed off neatly inside with an adz to give the walls a clean flat surface. The wood floor shows circular saw marks and was quite likely brought in by dog sled along with lumber for the window frames, the two glass windows, and the pieces of birchbark for the roof. The half-round roof timbers have the irregular scratches of the whipsaw. While the furnishings also show these signs they are smoothed off nicely by a hand plane that hangs on a wall along with other tools of the resourceful backwoodsman.

A dog sled twenty-four inches wide and ten feet long, lashed together with rope

The cabin was built in 1927.

and rawhide and shod with steel, is preserved from the elements inside the cabin. A heavy sheet-iron stove with a cast-iron top serves for both heat and cooking and a trap door in the floor gives access to a storage space below.

There is no door. The shattered remains lie outside, the work of grizzly bears. Supplies left here by the last inhabitant are in shambles. Cans of food are punctured by teeth and smashed out of shape. There are brown hairs high on the doorjamb and on several trees nearby where the bears have scratched themselves. Still higher, considerably higher than my head, chunks of wood are torn out leaving the horizontal teeth marks of the foraging bears. The trail leading to the creek also shows telltale tracks of bears. Feet set down in the same place each time.

Outside, near the door and protected by the overhang, hang the tools of the trade, saws, axes, wolf and beaver traps.

Nearby are the remains of a smaller cabin and numerous dog kennels, all in a state of collapse, with decayed roofs and timbers crumbling to the ground. A food cache perched on two peeled trees too high for the grizzlies remains intact. Claw marks on the supporting trees bear witness to unsuccessful attempts to reach the food and destroy things in general.

This cabin was built for trapping in the winter and prospecting in summer. It has not been used by the owner since 1936 as the low price of furs no longer encourages trapping. It is about 500 feet above the valley floor along a rushing, icy, glacial stream. The weather is beautiful, with the landscape not yet colored by frost. A large bull caribou stands dozing in the sun on a hillside.

8 P.M.—Took the spotting scope and went for a hike this morning climbing the mountain back of camp. Four small caribou bulls were feeding on the hillside. Higher up I saw a ram bedded down in a lofty place. I doubt if I could get a shot at him there.

From the top of the mountain I saw the plane ferrying Glenn, Keith, and Bob into camp. The climb gave me a wonderful view of the country and helped to get my legs and lungs in shape. Saw more caribou, two big bulls and two smaller ones.

Back at camp at 5 P.M. The men were packing supplies from the river and had seen several caribou bulls en route. This evening we saw ten sheep on the mountain plus a bull and cow moose.

Sunday, August 17, 8 P.M.—I left this morning at 7 A.M. to try to locate the big ram I saw yesterday. It was raining so I wore hip boots and rain jacket. Went farther than intended. Finally located a band of sheep about five miles from camp. In the rain and fog, I could not tell if they were rams, but believe they were since there were no small ones in the lot. Saw a cow caribou with two calves and later a nice bull.

The weather cleared somewhat as I worked my way back toward the main creek and saw about thirty sheep on an opposite mountain but not close enough to tell if there were rams. After coming off the mountains and back through the spruce, two fine bull caribou passed me at sixty yards. Back in camp at 4:30 P.M. and bushed. Hip boots are not for mountain climbing.

Bud, Mike, and Dick got in. Everybody busy erecting tents and sorting gear. Glenn and Keith are establishing a second camp about three miles downriver where a big flock of sheep live. Glenn, Dick, and I will hunt from this camp for the first few days. My wife would love to pick blueberries in this country. Very big and very thick in places. Not so sweet as the ones at home, however.

My quarters is a pop tent. Bud and Mike bunk in a larger tent. Glenn, Dick, Keith, and Bob sleep in the cabin where we eat and relax.

Monday, August 18, 5 P.M.—It rained all night, sounding nice on my tightly stretched tent. No frosts yet. It is like late September in Michigan. Rained off and on this morning. Keith and I packed some gear down to the lower camp and Glenn came later with a pack. Put up another tent. Glenn, Dick, and I will go down there after dinner tonight and stay for a few days to hunt. Bud, Mike, and Bob will stay and hunt from here.

Four rams are on the mountain across from us. Two of them are either full or almost full curl.

Twilight here is between 8 to 9 P.M. Daylight about 3:30 A.M.

Got back from lower camp and had lunch. Bob went to the river for water and came back reporting a bull caribou on the opposite side. With the opening date a full day away it was decided to make a stalk and shoot a blunt at him for pictures. Dick and I both went in over our hip boots crossing the river. He got the camera set up on a knoll and the bull lay down. I made a stalk to within twenty-five yards and grazed his side with a blunt arrow. Should make a fine picture. A red fox ran up the creek bed as we sat on the hill to rest.

Tuesday, August 19, 8:30 P.M.—Dick, Glenn, and I came down to lower camp last evening. Went south in the mountains this morning. A fair-sized bull caribou came close and we got pictures. We saw many cow and calf caribou and four sheep. Also a cow moose and some ptarmigan. Had a feast of blueberries and got back to camp about 4 P.M.

Glenn got in from our hunt earlier than I did. Bud and Mike had paid us a visit reporting many caribou and a moose. All hunting starts tomorrow. Dick and I will scale the mountain nearby and see if we can find the rams we saw yesterday.

Friday, August 22 (Missed two days)—Wednesday morning Glenn woke us up (Dick and me) at three-thirty. Left camp at 5 A.M., headed for the top of the mountain. Got there at nine and located a large flock of sheep, probably sixty or so with one small ram in the lot. We spent three hours photographing and observing them. It was a warm day. At one-thirty we stretched out in the sun for a nap. Woke up at two-fifteen and sighted a ram a short distance down from the top about a third of a mile away.

We mapped a plan for pictures and the stalk. The ram was feeding on a grassy ledge and could be approached from above. We moved in to 200 yards and Dick took pictures. He moved to 100 yards and set up for more pictures of whatever action would follow. I went in behind a ledge about fifty yards from the ram to wait until Dick flashed a signal that he was ready. In the meantime the ram lay down looking out over his domain. He was somewhat concerned about a gopher that had been whistling at us.

Dick took some pictures, wound the camera, and signaled that he was ready. I stalked to a small ridge above the ram. Crouching low, with my hat off, I could see the ram through a crack in a rock. He had either heard or winded me and got up, turned my way, snorting softly. Then he pranced a bit, turned again, and came a few steps closer facing me at a slight angle. I raised up into full view and shot at about twenty-five yards. The Razorhead from the sixty-five-pound Kodiak bow went in near the back ribs and out through the opposite hindquarter.

The ram dived off the ledge, walked across some shale, and lay down in the buckbrush. He got up immediately, however, and walked out of sight around a ledge. I went in above and saw him lying below. I tossed a small rock down and he tried to get up but toppled off the ledge and rolled down the shale slide for about 200 yards which finished him. Not a big ram, nor heavy horns, but a full curl showing eleven annual-growth rings.

As in the Yukon two years ago, we have to cross a glacial river to reach the sheep country. In the morning the water is low and hip boots do the job. We leave these by the river for the return crossing in the evening when the water is higher and the boots not quite high enough. Between the current and the boulders it is difficult to keep one's footing. Coming back on opening day, Dick lost his balance and went down. Being an agile young fellow, however, he was able to keep the camera pack and precious film topside until he regained his footing.

Jack and Bob packed the sheep meat into camp, Dick and I following down the mountain behind them. When we came in sight of the river, Jack and Bob were swimming in the ice-cold water.

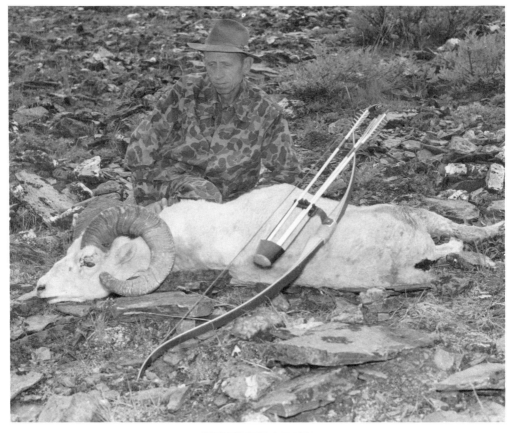

Not a big ram, nor heavy horns, but a full curl showing eleven annual-growth rings.

We leave our hip boots by the river.

Got back to base camp last evening in time for a banquet and reunion. Some of the party have had shooting at caribou, but no hits. Plenty of big bulls around. Glenn watched a grizzly eat blueberries all yesterday afternoon. The bear was a beautiful creature still in sight on the mountainside as we came upriver last evening.

Up at four-thirty this A.M., 7 A.M. now. Bud and Glenn have gone to the lower camp to try for a ram Glenn has been watching. Bob went to the airstrip to take mail and a grocery list to the plane expected in today. Dick and Jack picked blueberries for pancakes. A wonderful day. Bright and clear. Temperature just right for a much-needed bath, washing of clothes, and a general reorganization program plus a little rest. Have been climbing mountains for four days now and need this lazy day. May go down to Camp 2 and join Bud this evening.

9:30 P.M.—Just got back to base camp. Dick and I hunted downriver this afternoon. Ran into a big bull caribou but he outwitted us. Got to Camp 2 at 6 P.M. and went up on the plateau and saw the same bull but he won this time also. Back in Camp 2 at eight. Bud was in. He and Glenn told of an interesting experience with a grizzly. Came on him while climbing for a sheep. He was eating berries and paying no attention to them. They took pictures of him at fifteen yards. Had sheep for dinner, the best of all meat, and then came back to main camp after dark. Short of sleeping equipment and tonight is the coldest yet.

Sunday, August 24—Hunted yesterday morning along the trail to Camp 2. Before I left, Jack reported a hit on a caribou bull. Bob brought news to camp that they found it dead 300 yards away an hour later. A very nice animal with a fine set of antlers. Roasted sheep ribs last evening and had a feast. Wind blew hard last night. Just finished breakfast. Blueberry pancakes, bacon, and eggs, plus quarts of coffee. Will hunt upriver this morning and stop at base camp.

Monday, August 25, 4:30 P.M.—In base camp. We started up here from Camp 2 yesterday morning. About halfway Dick and I jumped a medium-sized bull caribou. He ran out on the dry river bottom but made the mistake of stopping to look at us at about forty-five yards. My Razorhead took him through both lungs. He staggered for a minute then crossed part of the river and expired on a small rocky island.

About this time our plane came in on its biweekly trip. The pilot saw our kill and took the news into camp. Keith and Glenn came down with packs and the meat is all sacked now and hanging at the cabin. Part of Jack's caribou was sent into Fairbanks when the plane went out.

After the packing job, Glenn, Bud, and Keith established a high camp on a spur of the mountain by base camp. I stayed here at base camp last night. Had a lazy morning and then took a hike with Keith up the valley where he saw the big grizzly several days ago. Shot at some ptarmigan and saw bear tracks along the way. Sighted a grizzly high on the mountain ahead of us, but did not try for pictures because of a wind blowing up the valley. The grizzly hunting season does not open until September first.

Back to camp and roasted sheep ribs for lunch. Spent the afternoon doing pictures, camp chores, and watching game.

Five big bull caribou have been feeding on a mountaintop north of camp all afternoon. At the moment there are five bands of sheep within sight, totaling

Keith and Glenn came down with packs.

seventy-five animals. As near as we can tell, all are ewes and lambs. We wonder where the rams are and hope they will show up later.

This is lush country. The caribou are sleek and fat. Small islands of willow are beginning to turn yellow and the buckbrush is blushing orange.

Keith is cooking more sheep tonight. Mike and Jack have gone down to Camp 2. We expect them back soon.

Dick and I plan to get up early tomorrow and go up Grizzly Valley. We'll take a lunch and perhaps top over and come back one watershed west where a band of sheep are feeding now.

Weather has been wonderful. Never below thirty degrees at night. Days around sixty and seventy degrees, about half cloudy and half sunshine. A little rain occasionally, like Florida. A quick shower and then sunshine.

Bud and Glenn came in at 8 P.M. Bud was packing a beautiful sheep head he had shot yesterday morning after a most difficult stalk up between the mountains opposite Camp 2. A great head with full curl and wide heavy horns. The plane had brought some refreshments and there was a celebration broken only by details of the stalk. Glenn also scored on a caribou bull that he classified as eating size.

Tuesday, August 26, 8 P.M.—Slept late this morning. After a blueberry-pancake breakfast Dick and I went up Grizzly Valley and ran into the black grizzly we saw yesterday. Ran about a hundred feet of film on him in poor light. We were about to move closer by circling a ridge when the wind changed and he left the valley. We saw a herd of caribou, eight or ten bulls, four of them with massive antlers. Hunted them the remainder of the afternoon without success. It started to rain and we got wet before reaching camp.

Keith got in at the same time with a big smile on his face and a spent arrow in his hand. Said he had shot a monster caribou just a short way from camp. More celebrating and rehash of Bud's ram stalk which was worthy of note. He shot the sheep from four yards!

Bob Arvine acted as signalman from a high point, directing Bud during the two-hour stalk. Much of the time Bud was in plain sight of the sheep but was able to remain undetected by careful movements and with the aid of his camouflage suit complete with hood. After the breathtaking circuit within view of the ram, cover became available to make the close approach.

The plane is coming in tomorrow at noon to start hauling meat to Fairbanks. Plan to get pictures of packing Keith's caribou out to the airstrip. My caribou, Jack's, and Bud's sheep are already hanging on poles at the strip.

Bob Arvine admires Bud's ram.

Thursday, August 28, 6 P.M.—We spent most of yesterday taking pictures and packing Keith's caribou in. A monster bull. The picture will tell the story. Packed meat and things to the airstrip. The plane did not get in as planned, so Dick and I hunted down to Camp 2. Back here at seven-thirty for a full meal of caribou tenderloin, onion rings, french-fried potatoes, and trimmings.

Got up at five-thirty this morning. Dick and I went about three miles up Grizzly Valley hoping to see the bear and caribou. We saw neither. We climbed the mountain at the head of the valley, hoping to drop down below, but ran into bad weather, snow and zero visibility, and, rather than take a chance, turned back. Tomorrow is our last day. The plane will be in on Saturday morning.

Packing meat and trophies to the plane.

Keith bagged a fine bull caribou.

Keith packs meat to the airstrip.

Friday, August 29, 6:30 P.M.—The hunt is over. Bud, Mike, and I got up at five and went hunting. Located two good bull caribou upriver about two miles. Back for breakfast and Bud and Mike elected to go after them. Right after breakfast Jack went for water, came back in a rush reporting three caribou bulls coming down the riverbed. A big dash for equipment and we headed for various places on the river. I stayed up on the bank to direct activities. Bud, Dick, and Mike melted into the willows in a bend on the river.

The three bulls came lumbering along and ran into a downwind from Bud and Dick. Bud shot two arrows about sixty yards. One struck the horns of one and they all made off. Never saw them again.

*Our only link to the
outside world.*

I dismantled my pop tent and packed gear, washed socks, and then went hunting with Dick. Saw one lone bull caribou and that was all. Bud and Mike are still hunting as Keith prepares dinner.

This was an unusual hunt in many ways. The best of it was that we had no guides. This makes for much greater freedom and provides opportunities to exercise one's own initiative. All decisions are your own. You plan the day, find your own game, and make the approach. If the stalk is successful there is greater pride in accomplishment. If it is a failure there is only yourself to blame.

Saturday, August 30, 8:30 A.M.—A rather drowsy gang this a.m. A great celebration took place last night to mark the end of the hunt. There was a shooting match in the rain, by gas lantern, at 11 P.M. Keith was the winner, being the first to extinguish the flame of a candle. The bush about camp bloomed with arrows this morning.

Up at 5 A.M. Bud and Mike went hunting. Back now eating another breakfast and hoping the plane will get in. Very wet and dull early today. Sun is shining now and the scope is on a half-curl ram on the mountain across from us. To date I have seen just two legal rams, the ones Bud and I shot.

I am slowly beginning to reach some conclusions about hunting sheep. I realize that it is dangerous to form opinions based on limited experience and may later wish that I had not said that sheep are 'stupid, but I think they are, and feel the same about mountain goats. Both make great trophies and while there is considerable physical exertion and much excitement connected with hunting them, when rams are located in rough country, it is not difficult to get quite close to them.

Of course I may not be giving these majestic creatures their due. It just might be that if a white-tailed buck were on a ledge on the side of a rough mountain, and the hunter had big rocks for cover and quiet footing, the buck could be approached closely, also.

Most likely, however, the smart whitetail *would bed down on top* where he could see his enemies. The weakness of sheep and goats lies in the fact that they do not expect danger from above and the hunter who knows this can bag fine trophies with bow and arrow.

Keith, Fred, Mike, Dick, Bud, Bob, Glenn, Jack

Chapter 5

LITTLE DELTA AND BROWN BEAR - 1959

During our hunt last year, in this magnificent hunting area, we had talked of returning. To share with other friends the beauty of late August and early September in a fantastic country, not yet spoiled by too many people.

Some of us arranged to leave earlier than the rest for another hunt of a different nature. We were to meet the Alaskan brown bear on the beaches and mountains along the coast of Prince William Sound. This was another first and we had no idea of the interesting experiences in store for us.

August 20, 1959, 6 A.M.—Seattle, Juneau, Cordova, Anchorage, Fairbanks, and to camp here in the Grubstake Area on the eighteenth.

Found camp in fine shape; the only disappointment is a new tarpaper roof on the trapper's cabin we use. We had repaired the door last year. Left it closed with crosscut saws nailed across with teeth exposed in an effort to discourage the bear who had demolished things last year.

Being thwarted, and his anger aroused, the grizzly went through our picturesque roof of logs, moss, birchbark, and sod. Not content to leave by the same hole, he smashed the door down from the inside after punching holes in all of the canned food with his teeth and destroying any other items that drew his attention.

McIntyre had the new roof installed two weeks ago. One-inch boards with tarpaper. This one will not hold bears either. When we close camp we plan to make a high cache outside and leave the door open.

Aside from this everything is the same as last year except that the season is not so far advanced. Blueberries are not plentiful nor are they entirely ripe yet. There has been no frost and the heavy summer rainfall has made the country lush and green.

Glenn St. Charles, who organized the Archery Division of the Boone and Crockett Club, flew in on Saturday the fifteenth along with Bob Arvine and Jack Albright who were with us last year. Newcomers are Bob Kelly and Ross McLaughlin also from Seattle plus Russ Wright from Grayling. These men and the rest of the group, in addition to nearly three thousand pounds of equipment and supplies, were flown in by Dick McIntyre.

Our old airstrip was one and a half miles from our base camp. Mac made a new one to ferry in the lumber and roof materials. It is short, limiting its use to a

The advance crew established Camp 2.

Super Cub, with large, low-pressure tires. This airstrip is only one half mile from camp which is a big improvement.

The advance crew set to work preparing the base camp and establishing Camp 2, located three miles downriver. This is a four-tent complex complete in every detail and eliminates the three-mile daily hike for those who wish to hunt this downriver area and the salt lick nearby.

Last year the packing-in job was quite a backbreaker. Ross McLaughlin brought in a rig called the "Merry Packer" which is a sort of wheelbarrow with handles at both ends and a wheel with a low-pressure tire in the middle. The wheel is driven by a gas engine and V-belt to a gear-reduction unit to the wheel. Two speeds are available by changing the belt to different pulleys. A lever on the handle operates the clutch. It will carry seven hundred pounds and comes apart to carry in the Super Cub.

First impression was that the Merry Packer would be useful only on fairly level terrain. Actually it will go almost anywhere, through muskeg, over rocks, and up and down the mountains.

I met Judd Grindell from Siren, Wisconsin, on the eighteenth and Mac flew us into camp that evening. Yesterday we looked the country over and tried our office legs on the mountains. Some charley horses interrupted sleep last night.

Hunting season opens today. Judd plans to hunt down toward Camp 2 along the mountainside. I think I will go up Grizzly Canyon where Dick and I saw so many caribou and two grizzlies last year.

August 20, Evening—Went about a mile up Grizzly Canyon this morning and saw a good caribou bull a short way up the mountainside. He was near a creek lined with willow brush that provided a fine approach. A good wind was blowing with some rain and sleet mixed in.

He expired on the hillside.

The bull was feeding in the open about thirty yards from the creek. Because of wind direction, I was forced to take to the open and stalk through the low buckbrush on hands and knees. At forty yards I released an arrow with an experimental head on it. An exact replica of the Razorhead but larger, having a blade and insert width of one and one half inches. With the feathers wet down the arrow went in right and low, going through a rear leg just above the knee. He ran about 400 yards down the creek, crossed it, and expired on the hillside. The femoral artery had been severed.

Judd came in sight saying he had watched the whole episode from across the creek through his binoculars.

In the afternoon I hunted toward Camp 2 along the hillside to look down into the spruce bottoms by the river. Two full-curl rams and a smaller one were half-way up the mountain across from me. I watched them with the glasses for some time until they went out of sight. Got one more glimpse of them about a mile and a half from me. They seemed to be feeding along the river. I rushed down there only to see them take off over the mountain on the other side.

Also saw about twenty-five caribou, mostly bulls.

Judd came in just at dark lugging the heart and liver of a fine big bull he had shot up near the head of the canyon. A great start for our meat supply on the first day in a bowhunters' camp.

While we were hunting the rest of the gang put the final touches on Camp 2 and brought the balance of supplies from the airstrip in on the Merry Packer.

Friday, August 21, Evening—Mac brought in Dick Bolding early this morning. We went down to the natural mineral or "salt" lick near Camp 2 and built a photographer's platform in the edge of the spruce and a shooting blind near the lick.

I took a hike across the mountain. Made a stalk on two caribou bulls but was

The Merry Packer brings supplies from our airstrip.

thwarted by Yukon gophers (parka squirrels) that are here by the thousands this year. During the warmer part of the day, it is almost impossible to make a stalk with those rascals whistling their alarm signals.

Knick Knickerbocker of Charlottesville, Virginia, came in this afternoon. More charley horses last night but getting into shape even quicker than last year.

August 22, Saturday Evening—Dick set up his camera on the platform this morning and Knick went into the blind. Three caribou came in but did not come close enough for a good shot. They also saw a cow moose and a porcupine.

Russ Wright went to pick blueberries and took his bow along. Shot a fine young bull caribou close to Camp 2. Should be good and tender. Mac flew most of our meat in to the freezer at Fairbanks.

I went on an exploring hike back into country where Dick and I had hunted last year. Whistlers again prevented a successful stalk on a caribou bull of good size. Had some fun with four sheep. I slid most of the way down a shale slope to land at the bottom within fifteen yards of them. There was one small ram in the lot, not of legal size. We looked at each other for a few seconds and then they made off up the mountain. Later I saw several more sheep but they were all ewes and lambs.

It cooled off toward the end of the afternoon—too cold for the whistlers—and I ran into three caribou, two cows and a calf, while making a stalk on a medium-sized bull. I got within fifteen yards while the cows fed on the grass and the little fellow nuzzled his mother.

Camp 2 is operating full time now. Five of us here. Glenn and Ross have established Camp 3 about two miles upstream from the main cabin. This is for sheep hunting later.

August 23, Sunday Evening—Did some work around camp this a.m. Knick went up to the plateau but reported no game in sight. Judd came in at noon with the news of two caribou bedded down. Said he was going to go back and try for a

Glenn and Jesse Rust pack up near the Yanert Glacier to establish a sheep-hunting camp. They named it the "Yanert Hilton."

Camp 2 is operating full time now.

Camp "Yanert Hilton."

shot when they got up to feed. He glassed the mountainside where I had seen the caribou and found a small bull moose on the spot. Jack decided to try for him and left at once. Bob Arvine, Dick, and I loaded Russ's caribou and camera on the Merry Packer and came back to Camp 1 where we had some pictures to do and some things to take back to Camp 2.

Judd came in about 6 P.M. saying he had been progressing well with the two bulls when Jack came along stalking the bull moose and spooked them away. He was foiled again when Dick and I barged out into the clearing nearby and scared six caribou bulls he had been stalking.

Jack and Bob Kelly came in a little later, Jack brandishing a bedraggled arrow with which he had killed the moose Russ had failed to reach. Glenn and Russ came in from Camp 3. Glenn had killed a small bull caribou.

Monday, August 24—Still raining and has rained all night. We have had only one clear day up to now. Temperatures steady between forty and fifty. No frosts. Moose and caribou antlers are all in the velvet—last year at this time about half of them were rubbed off.

Dick and I had planned to hunt on the way down to Camp 2 this morning but the rain changed that. Stayed here in Camp 1 instead and just finished masterminding the film we will make on this hunt.

Bob Kelly and Jack are warming up the Merry Packer to bring Jack's moose in. Judd went to Grizzly Canyon about 9 A.M. and Dick and I are going back to Camp 2 when the rain lets up.

Judd came in at 9 P.M., soaked. Had made a good stalk on a very large bull caribou but he was too cold to shoot accurately.

Tuesday Evening, August 25—Since it rained all day yesterday we didn't get here to Camp 2 until this morning. Knick and I went up through the pass by Eagle Nest Rock. We fooled around with some sheep and then Knick made a stalk on a caribou and missed three long shots. Back to camp early. Russ had gotten two long shots at a ram. No hits.

Wednesday Evening, August 26—Temperature went down to twenty-two last night. Just what we need to freeze the velvet on the antlers and start the animals down to timber to polish them off. Caribou are not in here like they were last year. The salt lick is hardly used. Moose are in the timber but hard to see with velvet still on their horns.

Knick and Bob hunted up to Camp 1 and will stay there tonight. Dick and I went to "Gray Creek" (where Bud shot his sheep last year) this morning and climbed Black Mountain from the back. Made a climb to get above a ram but he either winded us or just wandered off. Ran into several ewes and rams. Coming down, about 6 P.M., we looked back and there, 200 yards away on a cliff, were two rams looking at us. One was a big one but there was nothing we could do about it and they finally ran over the mountain.

Back in camp at 8 P.M. Russ had spent the day washing and cleaning things up. Said that Ross McLaughlin had dropped in for a visit from Camp 3 and that Glenn had had a long shot at a good ram. No news from Camp 1 for two days.

Thursday, August 27—Weather is cloudy. We went up to the flat above Camp 2 this morning intending to hunt back past Eagle Rock, coming in over the mountain to Camp 1. Ran into a bull caribou and did a stalk. He saw us when we were maneuvering to get the camera in line. He stared at us head on for a minute at about forty yards and then started circling downwind to get our scent. I shot under him at fifty yards, under again at sixty, and low again about seventy. Dick had the camera going and we should have a fine strip of film—maybe even better than if I had made a hit. The caribou never did seem to get our scent and stayed around about 200 yards from us finally ambling off over the mountain.

I am beginning to have more respect for caribou. It is important to wear camouflage, to make use of all available cover, and to make no moves unless the animal is facing away or quartering away from you. Their eyes cover a wide radius and their ears are quick to pick up strange noises.

By the time this caribou incident was over, the rain started again and we decided to hunt through the spruce, along the river bottom toward Camp 1, to learn about activities there during the past four days. As it turned out we didn't hunt since the light was too poor for pictures. We found Bob Arvine shivering beside the stove in the cabin. He had waded the river to try for a moose. . . . Knick is hunting downriver toward Camp 2.

Just as we finished lunch Judd came in, soaked to the skin, and wearing a very wide grin. He had dropped two fine bull caribou within fifteen yards of each other. The first one with a long shot and the second at closer range where the Razorhead did its job quickly. The details of the hunt took almost an hour to tell and all the time Judd still had his pack on his wet back!

Jack Albright shot a big bull caribou with a fine, wider-than-usual rack. Judd saw a wolverine yesterday. Bob Kelly came in followed by Jack. They were also wet down from the rain.

After coffee and tea, we went to photograph Judd's trophies. This was on the way to Camp 2, so I filched some tenderloin to replenish the larder at our camp. Judd's caribou are two mighty fine animals and looked great in the viewer. He has now filled his license on caribou. There are moose in the alder thickets along the lower slopes and in the spruce in the valley.

Before we left Camp 1, six rams were bedded down high on the mountain across from us. Twenty-five ewes and lambs were in sight also. We think the rams are moving into this territory. And the freeze of two nights ago seems to have driven the caribou down lower. We have not seen a grizzly nor any sign. With the shortage of blueberries they have doubtless gone elsewhere.

Camp 2 suffered another blow in prestige when our team of Knick and Bob Arvine were trounced soundly at cribbage by Judd and Bob Kelly.

The plane was expected in today but clouds hung low and prevented it. The hard freeze has changed the scenery from green to all the fall colors. Buckbrush is now red and orange. Cottonwoods along the creeks are lemon yellow while the poplars show a burnished gold. Some of the willows are turning but the hardy alder are still hanging on to their dark green.

I wonder if I've talked about the bridge across the river near Camp 2. Last year the water was not too high for wading and we could cross it in our hip boots. But this year was a different story—the frequent rains turned the stream into a raging torrent too high for any kind of boots.

Bob Kelly, Judd Grindell, Fred Bear, Jack Albright, and the two caribou Judd downed.

A bridge was built across the river.

Arvine, Kelly, and Albright made a survey of the problem and found a spot where two spruce trees leaned far over the water in strategic positions. They tied them together in such a way as to form ladderlike rounds. Then they dropped two heavy spruce poles into the center of the river and anchored them at the base with piles of rocks. The poles were further supported by guy wires anchored to a tree across the river. These poles were also fashioned with ladder rounds. In conclusion, two more poles were used to make a sort of suspension section which reached the opposite bank. Handrails completed this fine piece of backwoods engineering and served us well for the entire hunt.

Sunday, September 6—Dick and I came here to Camp 2 last night after a fine dinner of caribou tenderloin smothered in mushrooms, hot biscuits, and other delicacies.

Got up at 4 A.M. for a 5 A.M. start up the mountain. Sky clouded over. Looked worse at 6 A.M. Snowing at seven and still at it now at eight. We are waiting in the tent by the stove.

There was trouble with the pressure fuel lantern last evening. It was hanging from the drying pole overhead in the tent when flames began spurting from underneath. I backed out of the tent with it and tossed it as far as I could where it lay on the ground burning. We thought it would burn out but about ten seconds later it exploded. Could not find any pieces with a flashlight and deducted it all went into orbit.

Don Loesche, our bush pilot, had lunch with us yesterday. He told us of an experience he had last spring flying charter for a prospector in the mountains. The prospector had seven hundred pounds of supplies, mostly food, done up in small bundles for a free drop in an area where it was impossible to land. Don had never been in there and instructed the prospector to mark the drop area well, preferably by pegging a tarp flat on the ground.

At the appointed time, after the man had hiked in, Don took off from Fairbanks with the load and found the place without difficulty. It was marked by two arrows made of brush pointing to the tarp.

The plane made many passes dropping several bundles each time and Don was delighted with the accuracy of his drop—mostly direct hits and the rest close misses. He was encouraged, he thought, by the prospector jumping around, waving his arms, and yelling, on the fringe of the area.

After the drop was completed he went in low in a tight circle to appraise his work and found that his target had been the prospector's tent which he had flattened to a shambles!

7 P.M.—At 9 A.M. we decided this would not be a day for pictures so we started off by ourselves to hunt. I went downriver intending to go to where we saw the moose. Got into a wet blizzard about three miles down and returned to camp and then on to Camp 1 to get dried out and pick up my hip boots.

Just did a washing and plan to return to Camp 2 after another of Bob Kelly's dinners. Tomorrow Dick and I will pack downriver and set up a spike camp regardless of the weather.

Don had said that there were many caribou on the flats below and he had located a short ridge that he could land on when the wind was just right if anyone wanted to set up a spike camp there. Bill Wright and Jack Albright quickly packed limited supplies and Don set them down on the ridge.

Just about the time Dick and I were ready to start on our downriver project the fog began to lift. When we could see part way up Black Mountain there were four rams halfway to the top. Plans were changed and we took off.

We did not find them. Russ told us that they were alarmed by the plane that made three trips up the valley to ferry Jack and Bill out to the ridge.

We found a spot where a grizzly had dug out a marmot on the mountaintop and saw his tracks in the snow. Saw wolverine and fox tracks also.

Coming down the mountain we saw a fine bull moose in a spruce grove surrounded by high, thick willows. Could not do anything with him as we spooked him off.

The plane made an air drop of a corrugated box containing among other things an airmail letter from my wife. Really airmail, all the way. . . .

Kelly came down to Camp 2 to keep Russ company as Camp 1 is deserted. Glenn and Jesse and Russ are siwashing up to the glacier to look for rams.

Good weather today. Cloudy but some sun. Temperature twenty-eight now. Will freeze tight tonight. A cow and calf moose were on the salt lick as we came by on our way in.

Tuesday, September 8, 8 P.M.—An unusually long hike today. Abandoned, at least temporarily, our siwash expedition downriver and took to Black Mountain again expecting to find the rams on the back side. The sun was out when we left so we dressed light. Got about a mile from camp and that was the last we saw of it. We did not find sheep and went to the very top where there was a foot of snow. Continued east along the top and had to move along to keep warm. A grizzly had been wandering about. Also a wolverine, fox, and porcupine had crossed over. Shot a hoary marmot for his skin and then started down through the basin where I shot the ram last year. Halfway down we saw a ram near the top and went back up again. He was traveling. We followed for about an hour but finally had to give up to get off the mountain while there was still daylight. Wet snow started to fall, making us glad to see the glow of camp lights across the river.

Since cold weather has stilled the glaciers, the river can again be waded with hip boots. This saves a half mile to the bridge and back. The sleeping bag felt good.

Wednesday, September 9, 7 P.M.—A blizzard, with an inch of snow already down, greeted us when we got up this morning. Visibility zero and temperature thirty. Spent most of the morning taking a series of camp pictures with the snow coming down steadily. It was finally decided that the comforts of the cabin at Camp 1 were too overwhelming, so we loaded packs and started upriver. Got some fine pictures of the swinging bridge along with some good footage going through snow-laden spruce.

Shot a spruce hen. Kelly says that if we all keep shooting at these and the ptarmigan, we might have enough for a dinner near the end of the season. It is hard on arrows in these rocks and tundra.

As we neared Camp 1, the blizzard still raging and visibility nil, we were surprised to hear the drone of a plane. It was Don flying low up the river. He left mail and supplies but took off before we could get to the airstrip.

He was back in half an hour and before landing dropped a note listing supplies needed by Bill Wright and Jack Albright at their spike camp on a ridge in the

*A blizzard greeted us
this morning.*

foothills. Also a note from Jack saying they had shooting at caribou and a big
grizzly and that they planned to stay until Friday.

Glenn and Jesse Rust must be having a rough time on their sheep hunt upriver
near the glaciers. This snow, still coming down, will end their activity. It is dangerous, and very hard work, to hike snow-covered mountains. Also, the sheep
season closes tomorrow.

Alaskan residents have never seen such weather at this time of the year. We
are still hoping for a break and a fairly long look at the sun.

I forgot to say in yesterday's notes that Russ climbed the mountain across from
camp and routed a grizzly in a willow thicket.

We see quite a number of cow moose. Occasionally we see a bull but the latter
are staying in thick cover. We hope the rut will start soon and we can have some
fun with our moose calls.

There are no birch in this part of the country; however, the birchbark from the
roof of this cabin can be made into moose-calling horns.

Except for the men hunting caribou in the foothills, whatever hunting luck we
might have from here on rests with the moose and the rare chance of a shot at a
grizzly. Have not seen a caribou since Judd left. We have a new theory. While
these are non-migratory caribou such as the large herds in the north, they do
move from an area west of us to the lowlands along the Delta river.

All of the rain we have had has been snow up higher, leading us to think that

*Birchbark from the
cabin roof is made
into moose calls.*

some normally used passes are closed now. This reasoning is substantiated by reports from the Dry Creek area where hunters are having good luck with caribou. This is across a mountain to the north of us.

Thursday, September 10, 6 A.M.—Up at 6 A.M. Two inches of snow here in the valley. Temperature twenty-two and snow crunchy. Spent the morning making two moose calls—one for this camp and one for Camp 2.

This afternoon, Dick and I went up Grizzly Valley to see what game had moved and to check on the wolverines. Saw no tracks of any big game. Twenty-nine sheep fed just above the willows, but they were all ewes and rams. We find there are rabbits here. Saw their tracks.

The wolverines have eaten all the remains of both Judd's and Jack's caribou.

Had expected Glenn and Jesse back tonight but so far they have not shown up. The men from the ridge camp are due tomorrow. They will probably need a day to dry out and reorganize, although the weather has been better down that way. Dick, Russ, and I will go down to Camp 2 tomorrow to spend a few days trying for moose.

Friday, September 11—A confusing day. Bill Burke is due in. The "Ridge Runners" are due back. Glenn and Jesse are scheduled to get back from their siwash up the valley by the glacier. Everybody's anxious for mail.

Camp cleanup and an outdoor shower for all kept us busy during the morning. Plane came in with Bill and some mail. Don could not land at the Ridge camp because of a bad cross wind. He dropped a note on the way back to Fairbanks saying that he would come in at 6 A.M. tomorrow.

Dick Bolding and Bill Burke traveled along the mountainside toward Camp 2 this afternoon. They intercepted a bull moose coming over the snow-covered mountain. They got within 100 yards but were defeated by tricky winds.

Packing up to spend the remainder of the hunt at Camp 2.

Glenn and Jesse got back from their outing up near Yanert Glacier. Called

Camp cleanup and outdoor shower for all.

their quarters the Yanert Hilton. No luck with the sheep. There were rams there, thirty-six in one group, but because of the snow and their high location they could not get to them.

Camp 3 was evacuated and moved to the strip with the Merry Packer.

Saturday, September 12—Plane brought Jack Albright back from the ridge early this morning. They have made no kills but have had interesting brushes with caribou, moose, grizzly, and black bears. He picked up more provisions and went back asking for a pickup Wednesday.

Dick and I packed to Camp 2 and then went on a hunt along Sheep Creek and

Black Mountain. Tried my moose horn but only succeeded to put a cow and calf to flight. Bagged another blue grouse.

Bill Burke and Russ Wright hunted the south side of the river. Bill qualified for membership in the "Little Delta Bowhunters" by crossing the bridge without a mishap. He still has to do an hour on one end of the Merry Packer to become eligible for membership in the Great White Packer's Association. Glenn came down to join us this evening.

Sunday, September 13—A beautiful morning. Sun came up over the white peaks to start the thermometer up from twenty-six degrees. We threw our tent flaps back and ate breakfast with the warm rays on our backs.

Bill Burke hunted en route to Camp 1. Dick and I put our hip boots on and went six or eight miles downriver. We kept high on the right side and kept watching the left mountain which was covered with thick, high willows, tag alder, spruce, and buckbrush in a setting of knee-deep tundra.

Started back about 2 P.M. Sat down to scan the hillside at three-thirty and saw a fine bull moose and cow with calf, about halfway up. We marked him down well as he stood in a small clearing while the cow and calf wandered off downwind and disappeared.

We checked the bull again and went up; the wind was just right. With more luck than good planning, we came upon the bull lying down slightly below us about seventy yards away. I stripped my boots off for a close stalk. Dick was to photograph the event from my starting point as there were dry leaves on the ground in that raspy buckbrush.

At this point, the variable mountain wind changed and the bull got up and looked at us broadside. I started grunting to hold his attention while I picked up my bow and took a shot. The big, experimental broadhead made a beautiful arc as it streaked down the mountain, bending into what looked like a sure hit through the ribs. It did not drop enough, however, and went over his back.

The cow, apparently attracted by my grunting, came over to see what was going on but the bull had made off after the shot.

Farther up the river another fine bull was sighted along the mountainside but it was too dark for pictures and too late for another stalk.

The gas lanterns lighted up our white tents like jewels as we came in after dark. The aroma of broiled caribou steaks hastened our steps.

Got caught up on the news of the day through intercamp gossip as related by Glenn and Russ.

Kelly and Jesse, bringing supplies to Camp 1, saw a big bull coming downriver. He seemed to be heading for the salt lick where some cows have been hanging around. Russ and Glenn went to look for him but didn't locate him.

Don took Bill Burke out to the ridge camp. A black bear had gotten into their camp while they were out hunting and messed things up a bit.

Monday, September 14—I'm writing by the light of our campfire. This is a cold night but this morning was bright and sunny. A slow start for Dick and me after our long hike yesterday. We went up Sheep Creek to take some pictures. Came back down and climbed part way up the mountain across from camp and looked for moose. Saw none. Saw nothing today except sheep.

Glenn went up in the Eagle Rock basin. Saw a grizzly track and watched a black fox trying to catch a parka squirrel. Kelly and Jesse made a high cache today to store Camp 2 equipment.

Don, our pilot, told us yesterday that he made a mercy flight before he came in yesterday. A local outfitter had flown three hunters from Texas into a hunting area and had not returned. They found the party on their airstrip. Plane needed a new prop and some landing-gear parts. On the takeoff a hunter ran in front of the plane and was killed. The pilot wrecked the plane trying to avoid him.

The moose are not co-operative. The mating season has not yet begun and they seem reluctant to come out of the timber.

Tuesday, September 15—Another beautiful day. Am writing in our cabin at Camp 1. We spent the morning taking pictures of Camp 2 and putting the finishing touches on the high cache platform for Camp 2 tents and supplies. Four spruces, each about eight inches thick, standing about six feet apart, form the supports. Timbers wired and spiked to these make up the framework for the logs that comprise the floor which is about twelve feet from the ground. The trees are peeled to keep them from rotting and to discourage animals from climbing them.

Word reached us that a large bull moose was on a flat across the river from Camp 1. This information started Dick, Glenn, and me on our way. Kelly and Jesse were out hunting. Glenn offered to climb the mountain back of camp and try to direct us to the moose if he could locate it. We were to climb the opposite mountain and try to locate him from there. It is always difficult to see game on the same side of the mountain one is on. Mountains look clean from across but are a jungle once you get there.

We planned to be about two miles apart which made it necessary to arrange that each of us be in a designated spot on the mountains, so we could locate each other with binoculars.

There was another camp of hunters several miles upstream. Early in the season a wounded caribou expired on the hillside above camp. Glenn said he would signal us from there.

When we were halfway up the mountain, we looked across for directions. Glenn seemed to be sitting right on the carcass. This did not make sense since the remains of the animal had been there so long it was bound to discourage proximity.

Dick and I passed the binoculars back and forth and finally decided that we were looking at a grizzly. Not just one, but two.

It was 4 P.M. Not enough time to turn back and still have light for photography. Besides we knew that Glenn was quite likely photographing the bears from cover in the spruce at the bottom of the mountain. So we decided to stay with the moose, which incidentally didn't show up. We got to camp in good light and studied the bears through the scope at about 1,000 yards.

They had eaten their fill and were covering the remains with rocks and grass, taking time out to play and tumble now and then. Apparently it was a sow and yearling, although it was not possible for us to determine how big either one was from that distance.

The discussion tonight is whether the small one is this year's cub or a two-year-old. We think it is a cub. The game law reads that it is not legal to shoot sows with cubs. Aside from this it would take a hard heart to shoot either one of them after having observed the affection of the mother for her offspring.

All things considered, this is not a good situation for a bow. Almost all maulings occur from one of three reasons. A female with a cub. A bear that has assumed ownership of a carcass. Or a bear surprised and taken off guard. We have right here a combination of the first two. We hope they will come back tomorrow and that the light is good for photography. Some good footage of them playing will be more valuable than a hide on the wall.

Don Loesche, our pilot, was in today and brought the following messages from the Ridge camp:

Kelly—The boys love your cooking but will settle for Jocko's grub and the animals they have to shoot at here.

Bill Burke got a shot at a 70-inch moose. Also Wright got a shot at another big moose today. Kelly, can you send me six more of your broadheads; have you got any that shoot six inches lower? (Missed another Black again today.)

The two Bills are going up in back of camp for moose. We had the spotting scope on a beautiful silver-and-black grizzly. I'm going to give it a try tomorrow. Pray for me.

We can use the following as we plan to stay until at least Thursday—perhaps longer: Orange juice—Vel or Joy—candy bars—canned Ham or anything along those lines— butter, meat (one quarter will do, sheep, please).

Jack Albright

Jocko has been doing his best to keep me off my dead ass. Now, not only do we hike all day, I now walk all night trying to find where he relocates camps. So weak can only half draw the bow. Send us an extra hunting knife. I'm getting desperate.

Wire Whiskered Willie (Bill Wright)

Mess Sgt. Jocko (and I Do Mean *Mess*) is doing great. He's kept me on my diet. Am in great shape. Please send me two rolls of Tums. That's T-U-M-S, for the tummy.

Skinny Billy next to Willy (Bill Burke)

Bill Wright would like his lens adapter for his camera. It is in the metal box in my tent.

P.S. Why don't you guys grab a tent and come down for a bit of shooting. Why pay air freight on arrows back to Seattle?

Dear Fred: In case I don't see you before you leave, thanks for a wonderful trip.

The boys are having a good time and are getting shots every day.

Bill Wright is having a ball on the trip. He should get a moose, at least, before the trip is over.

If possible I would like to order a 70–72#, 60″ bow from your factory with camouflage job on it. You can send it to my home COD or just bill me.

The boys from Windy Ridge said to have the Merry Packer ready, "Tomorrow is the day." Bill, Willie, and Jack.

P.S. Have a good Bear trip.

Thanks again, Jack

Wednesday, September 16, 9 A.M.—At 6 A.M. the bears were playing on the frosty hillside by the carcass. Later mama kept busy raking more debris over it. As the sun warmed the air they settled into a sound sleep. The sow draped over the caribou with Junior curled up in a ball on the tundra above.

The female has a dark brown coat, silver tipped on the back and sides. The offspring is a handsome young fellow. Silvery, with black circles around his eyes like a panda.

The affection of the mother is beautiful to see. The young one wants to play and wrestle all the time but receives no harsh treatment even when she is busy covering the banquet and the young one is nipping at her heels.

She lies on her back with all four feet in the air while he crawls all over her. Sometimes she holds his head in her paws and licks his face while he struggles to avoid the washing, like a boy I know.

The sun is not yet shining on the hillside. Glenn and Dick are tuning cameras as the hour approaches for a stalk and pictures.

11 A.M.—Just returned from photographing the bears. Exposed eighty feet from the cover of spruce some 200 yards away, using a 300-mm lens.

Junior bear tried to climb a dead spruce about thirty yards above the carcass to which I had tied a white handkerchief to serve as a wind sock.

As the sun warmed things up there was a wind change and the old bear got a breeze laden with our scent. With dripping jowls she tested the air and was a very uneasy bear from then on. She finally chose a tasty morsel from the carcass, walked up the hill with the cub following, ate it, and then lay down overlooking the larder and our position as well.

Right now she is sleeping. The sky was clouded over. We hope they will wake up refreshed and that the sun will be out so we can get some more pictures of them playing.

9:30 P.M.—The plane came in at noon and frightened the bears into the alders. We decided to dismantle Camp 2 and started down the river. Met Russ at the bridge. He had just shot at a big bull that crossed the river at the bridge, almost ripping it out when he became tangled in the guy wires. We all went after him and saw a total of three bulls. Glenn and Kelly each got shots but no hits.

By this time it was late. Had dinner at Camp 2 and just got here to Camp 1. Jesse, who had the heaviest pack, forged ahead saying he wanted to get here before he got tired. I got here first and put a gas lantern in the cabin. Jesse got in last. The lantern had lured him from the hillside near the bears which was quite a bit off course.

This business fouled up a well-planned day. Russ had seen a good bull caribou but no shooting.

The bull moose that Kelly shot at was grunting which is a sign that the rut is about to start.

There seem to be a lot of moose around now. With antlers polished and no longer tender they are beginning to come out of the brush.

This is the last day of the hunt for Dick, Russ, Glenn, and me. Plane coming for us at noon tomorrow.

I have not heretofore had the pleasure of hunting with a finer group of men. All true sportsmen dedicated to the handicap of hunting with the bow. Thrilled by a kill but satisfied with a good stalk or a close miss. I hope we can do it again another time.

Perhaps we can photograph the bears in the morning. If not and no moose or caribou show up near camp, we can end the hunt with these lines. The Ridge Runners are due back in the morning. Long tales to tell but little time to listen.

» «

TRIPS TO FAR OFF PLACES MUST BE PLANNED WELL IN ADVANCE.
IF GUIDES ARE NOT ENGAGED, IT BECOMES A MONUMENTAL TASK TO PROVIDE
FOR A RATHER LARGE PARTY.
FOLLOWING IS A LIST SHOWING COMPLETE BOOKKEEPING FOR SUCH A HUNT.

December 1, 1959

To all members "Little Delta Merry Packers' Association"

Gentlemen:

Have finally completed the bookkeeping on our Alaskan hunt. I realize that just before Christmas is a bad time to hit you between the eyes with the bill, but here it is with a fairly complete report.

My accounting is not in detail but the totals are taken from invoices in my possession, which I will be glad to send to you upon request.

Things come high in Alaska, as you well know. Also, it has been our policy each year to write off all costs. This means that all gear except the merry packer was left either in the cache at Camp 2 or in the cabin. It is less expensive to leave it than to take it out.

The paying members are the six whose "man days" have been extended on the Man Day sheet attached. Bill Burke, who supplied air transportation between Seattle and Fairbanks and return for our workers, plus air freight on our gear and one half the air freight meat bill to Seattle, is being charged for only his flying trips in and out of camp.

Glenn, who found this spot at no little expense three years ago and did the brainwork on organizing the hunt both before and during, has been classified along with the remainder of the group who supplied the muscle for the many and various chores that needed attention.

To those who secured meat and took it home, I have tried to divide these costs as fairly as was possible. If I have made mistakes, I wish you would call them to my attention.

Enclosing some photos. If you want more, I can get them for you at a buck each. Also including photos of our bear hunt. My field notes will be sent to you later.

I think, to the last man, that we had a wonderful group of fine fellows, all fourteen of us. Word trickles down from the north that an Alaskan guide law will be in effect next year. Most likely it will call for a guide for sheep and grizzly only. Not final, but that looks like the way it will be. Anybody want to go back next year?

Merry Christmas,

Fred B. Bear.

FINANCIAL REPORT—LITTLE DELTA HUNT, 1959

Flying between Fairbanks–Little Delta (see flying sheet attached)	$2,892.25
Frontier Sporting Goods: Blazo, Merry Packer repairs, game bags, etc.	507.09
Ray's Super Market: Groceries	884.83
R. Wright: Excess baggage and license	70.00
Bob Arvine: Advance	500.00
McIntyre: Advance	700.00
Northern Commercial Co.: Dishes, silverware, etc.	139.97
Miscellaneous: Tents, cots, sleeping bags, air mattresses, Railway Express, phone calls, stoves, air freight (½), Keith Clemmons' possessions at cabin, plus Camp 2 tents	1,194.15
Quality Meat Co.: Freeze and meat storage (Albright)	36.18
TOTAL	$6,924.47

121 man days divided into total=$57.23 per hunter. Based on man days, as per IN and OUT Schedule, the costs are divided as follows:

Fred Bear:	30 days × $57.23	$1,716.90
	Plane—September 4, personal	70.00
		$1,786.90

Dick Bolding:	29 days × $57.23	$1,659.67
	Plane—In and Out	140.00
Bear's photographer—his expense		$1,799.67

Bill Burke:	Plane—In and Out	$ 140.00

J. Grindell:	13 days × $57.23	$ 743.99
	¼ of freezer and meat storage bill	36.18
	Meat flown to Fairbanks	70.00
	Air freight Fairbanks–Seattle	32.60
		$ 882.77

R. Kerr:	14 days × $57.23	$ 801.22
	¼ of freezer and meat storage	36.18
	Meat flown to Fairbanks	70.00
		$ 907.40

K. Knickerbocker:	13 days × $57.23	$ 743.99

W. Wright:	22 days × $57.23	$1,259.06
	¼ of freezer and meat storage	36.18
	Meat flown to Fairbanks	70.00
	Air freight Fairbanks–Seattle	32.60
		$1,397.84

HUNTER MAN DAYS—LITTLE DELTA, 1959

Name	In	Out	Days
Arvine	8–15	9–5	—
Albright	8–15	9–21	—
Kelly	8–15	9–21	—
McLaughlin	8–15	8–30	—
St. Charles	8–16	9–17	—
R. Wright	8–16	9–17	—
Bear	8–18	9–17	30
Bolding	8–20	9–18	29
Burke	9–11	9–20	—
Grindell	8–18	8–31	13
Kerr	8–30	9–13	14
Knickerbocker	8–21	9–3	13
W. Wright	8–30	9–21	22
Rust	9–5	9–19	—
TOTAL MAN DAYS			121

FLYING REPORT—FAIRBANKS TO LITTLE DELTA, 1959

Date	Detail	Amount
8–15	Arvine, Albright, Kelly, Ross—In and gear	$ 350.00
8–16	Freight—In	175.00
	Freight—In	70.00
	R. Wright, St. Charles—In and freight	110.00
8–17	Freight—In	70.00
8–18	Freight and recon with St. Charles	122.50
	Bear and Grindell—In	140.00
8–20	Bolding—In	70.00*
8–21	Knickerbocker—In and freight	140.00
8–25	Freight—In. Albright moose—Out	70.00
8–28	Grindell meat—Out	70.00*
8–30	W. Wright and D. Kerr—In. Meat and Ross out	140.00
8–31	Groceries—In. Grindell—Out	70.00
9–3	Groceries—In. Knickerbocker—Out	70.00
9–4	Supplies to camp and Recon (see bottom of sheet)	108.00*
9–5	Supplies to camp and Recon	97.00
	Jesse Rust—In. Arvine—Out	70.00
9–9	Supplies—In. Shuttle to ridge	111.00
9–11	Burke—In	70.00*
9–12	Supplies—In. Ridge Stops	87.50
9–13	Ridge shuttle. Kerr—Out. 2nd trip for Kerr meat—Out	187.50*
9–15	Trip to ridge. Ridge Runners decided to stay	70.00
9–16	Gear—Out	70.00
	R. Wright to Portage—Out	70.00
9–17	Bear, St. Charles to Portage—Out. Ridge Runners back	166.25
	St. Charles, R. Wright, and Bear and Gear	
	Portage to Fairbanks (Bonanza)—Out	67.50
9–18	Bolding—Out	70.00*
9–19	Jesse Rust—Out (bad weather)	87.50
9–20	Burke—Out. Merry Packer and gear—Out	140.00*
9–21	Kelly—Out and Portage shuttle. W. Wright and Albright	
	—Out and gear and moose meat	192.50*
9–21	Bonanza from Portage—Personnel and gear—Out	120.00

TOTAL STATEMENT FROM FRONTIER $3,452.25

Deduct:	One trip each for Grindell, Kerr, Wright meat (3 @ $70)	$210.00	
Deduct:	Burke In and Out	140.00	
Deduct:	Bolding In and Out	140.00	
Deduct:	F. Bear—personal September 4	70.00	560.00

$2,892.25

LITTLE DELTA EXPENSE STATEMENT

Per Glenn St. Charles, Northwest Archery Company

Check from Fred Bear	500.00
Misc. expenses from Seattle thru Fairbanks to Little Delta. Hotel, food, gas for Mac's car, etc., for St. Charles, McLaughlin & Russell Wright.	48.83
Alaska Airlines Invoice 8836 (Freight Bills)	12.92
″ ″ ″ 8837 ″ ″	19.95
Seattle Tent & Awning—Waterproofing	4.16
Seattle Tent & Awning—Tent Poles	2.31
7–13–59 Hunt & Mottet (Camping Gear)	16.74
8–2–59 ″ ″ ″ ″	10.09
8–5–59 ″ ″ ″ ″	85.80
8–5–59 ″ ″ ″ ″	104.68
Washington Hardware Invoice ⚡03526	17.94
Washington Hardware Invoice ⚡03135	17.94
Warshal's (B-4809)	28.04
Railway Express Collect for two tents	24.71
8–13–59 Phone call to McIntyre in Fairbanks	21.18
Expenses for Arvine & Albright thru Fairbanks to Little Delta, hotel & food.	50.06
First-Aid Kit bought on way in	13.80
Gas for Mac & Don's Car	11.18
Five fifths of Scotch	35.00
Export Meat Tag on way out	6.00

Other camping gear taken to Fairbanks from Seattle:

2 Air Mattresses @ 7.50 ea.	15.00
1 two-burner stove	10.47
1 Scout Sleeping Bag	8.17
1 4 lb. Dacron Bag	22.35
One airline ticket for Dick Bolding	202.24
One half of Alaska Airlines freight bill ⚡9211	65.16

Camping gear by Keith Clemmons at Little Delta sold to us
for $200.
Material furnished for the $200 by Bear Archery Company

@ 40% :	6 doz.	H-4 Razorheads	17.82	
	300	D5 Speednocks	5.40	
	1	C280 Bow Case	1.50	
	1	60″ Kodiak AA023	36.00	60.72

Remainder of material to cover the $200 furnished to Keith
Clemmons by the Northwest Archery Company $139.28
less an additional 20% so that we may realize cost only: 111.43

$966.15

STATEMENT CONTINUED

	560.72	
Less amount from column two	$405.43	BALANCE

Balance due Glenn St.
Charles and Northwest
Archery Company $405.43

INVENTORY

CAMP ☒1

STOWED IN TRAPPER'S CABIN

3   Single Burner Coleman Stoves
1   Single Burner Kool-Lite
2   Single Burner Army Lights
1   Small Single Burner Coleman Mountain Stove
1   Single Burner Coleman & Heater
1   3 Burner Coleman Stove
2   2 Burner Coleman Stoves
1   Large Oven
1   Dutch Oven & Lid
1   Large Griddle
1   Round Griddle (cast iron)
1   Cast Iron Skillet & Lid
2   Large Tin Skillets

2   Water Buckets
1   Canvas Bucket
2   Plastic Washbasins
1   Plastic Dishpan (rectangular)
3   Dishpans

Plates, Cups, Utensils, Pots (no bowls) enough for 12

1   Grub Hoe
1   Hudson Bay Ax
1   Scotch Ax
1   Hammer
1   Meat Saw
1   Hand Saw
1   Buck Saw
1   Old Double Bit Ax (broken handle)

1   Small Red Pack Board
1   Army Meat Board

4   Coleman Stools
1   Folding Table Set

1   5 Man Mountain Tent
1   Trail Tent
1   9×11 Wall Tent (up at strip)
2   Pack-a-Beds
1   Army Mummy Bag (outer warm)
2   Dacron Sleeping Bags, 4☒ (good)
1   Small Sleeping Bag (warm weather type)

1 Air Mattress
3 Air Mattresses (blue with pillows)
1 Tire Pump

2 pr Rubber Boots
3 pr Totes
1 pr Portable Waders
8 Dish Towels
6 Dish Rags

   S.O.S. Pads
60 Tea Bags

   Have some: Beans, Peas, Spinach, Applesauce, Peaches, Pears,
      2 lge. Quick, 4 lge. Powdered Milk, 5 Bisquick,
      3 Pancake Mix, Beets, Corn, Black Pepper, 2 ⚹ Crisco.

   Have lots of: Canned Tomatoes, Tomato Sauce.

   NEED
   Splitting Maul & Wedge
   Ax Handle
   Bowls

                        INVENTORY

                        CAMP ⚹2

                   STOWED ON HIGH CACHE

2 White 10×12 Tents
1 Trail Tent
2 White 6×10 Tarps

2 Mummy Sleeping Bags (inner—cold)
3 Air Mattresses
2 Pack-a-Beds

1 Hatchet
1 Cruiser Ax

1 Yukon Stove
1 3 Burner Coleman Stove
1 1 Burner Coleman Stove & Heater
2 1 Burner Coleman Lamps

1 Oven

   Dishes & Utensils for six

1 Griddle
1 Cast Iron Skillet
1 Small Tin Skillet

2 Plastic Washbasins
1 Plastic Bucket
2 Dishpans

2 cans OFF

Don came in and flew us to Fairbanks in four flights. The last trip brought news that Bill Wright had shot a world-record moose. It had come down the mountain opposite camp and Bill crossed the creek and downed the monster with one arrow.

We flew by commercial airlines to Anchorage and then on to Cordova to join Ed Bilderback for a brown bear hunt along the shore and on the islands of Prince William Sound.

We got news that Bill Wright had shot a record moose.

Knick examines the trapper's sled.

It was Bob Kelly's day to cook. Note the flat-sided cabin logs chinked with moss. Note also the bars on the outside of the window: They are birch, hard and dry. They held against the grizzly bears.

Saturday, September 19, 8 P.M.—**Aboard the "Valiant Maid" anchored in Sheep Bay**—Got into Cordova on Cordova Air Lines at noon today. Glenn St. Charles, Dick Bolding, Russ Wright, and I. Met Ed Bilderback at his home and decided to buy provisions at once, board his boat, and get on our way.

A two-and-a-half-hour run brought us here. Just returned from a trip up a creek at the head of the Bay. We traveled in Ed's skiff powered by a big outboard engine. Humpbacked salmon were going upstream in great numbers with many dead ones decaying on the banks. It was too late in the day but we had light enough to observe bear trails through the high grass on the delta flat.

Returned with the tide and are now heating a large vessel of water to cook Dungeness crabs. We saw a good-sized black bear as we entered the Bay.

The *Valiant Maid* is a sturdy boat built in Seattle thirteen years ago. She is sixteen-foot beam and fifty-eight feet long, powered by a six-cylinder diesel engine

Caribou ribs roasted by hot coals!

Leaving Cordova for a great adventure along the Alaskan coast.

of 115 horsepower. Gross weight thirty-five tons. With a sleeping capacity of nine, five of us are comfortable in the combination cabin-galley.

Ed's business is most interesting. During the summer he fishes commercially and in the winter he runs a mail route that takes five days twice a month. Mail is carried by plane during the summer when the weather is better.

Sunday, September 20, 6 P.M.—My quarters in the bow bunk, second deck, are very comfortable. I chose it because it is the largest, even though there is no port for ventilation. We were up at three-thirty for a daylight start at four. Got in the skiff and went up to the creek again. Sighted three brown bears. Something scared them and they ran into the thick alder and devil's-club. Later we saw a wolverine and believe that is what scared the bears.

Went up the creek afoot. Many salmon. Saw nothing else. Coming back the three bears were out on the grassy flat again near the brush. One fair-sized bear and two smaller ones. Made a stalk along a bear trail. Got up to thirty-five yards. The big one saw us and ran off. This alerted the other two who stood head on and looked at me. Both Dick and Glenn were running their cameras behind me.

This was my first sight of brown bears. These two did not look very big. At the time, I guess they would weigh perhaps three hundred pounds. One of them turned slightly and presented an opening for a shot at his rib section. I had hoped they would stand up for a better view and give me a chance to estimate their size. The larger one I would have shot without hesitation.

We looked into another creek, went back to the skiff, and were running some film on the salmon when a black bear came into sight on the grassy flat. Glenn made a stalk on him, got a shot, and he and Ed went into the brush following the bear into the bear tunnels. I followed them later but became confused by the many trails. Hearing a twig snap a short distance ahead and thinking it was Ed and Glenn I said, "How are you doing?" There was no answer and with brownies in there I decided to get out.

It was a great first-morning start for our hunt. Beautiful weather and bears sighted. I have turned down early-season shots at game before and later regretted it. It could be that events will prove that I should have shot one of these as Ed thought they were fair-sized bears. We shall see. They were beautiful animals. Well fed, with silvery coats.

We made another run of two and a half hours to Gravin Bay and checked some creeks there this afternoon. The fish run was about over and there were few fresh signs of bear. We are now on our way to another bay where we will hunt in the morning.

During this trip, our enjoyment was heightened by the sight of a black whale, quite a few seals, many ducks of assorted kinds, some Canadian geese, and a land otter. We also saw two dozen goats on a mountain and shot two silver salmon for food.

Forgot to mention that we had a feast on the crabs last evening. Ed says we can catch red snappers where we anchor tonight. Temperatures down to freezing last night. Took a nap on the aft deck at noon.

My first brush with brownies was not different from what I expected it to be. The stalk was not difficult as the grassy flats with head-high grass and spots of brush made ideal conditions. The bears were not suspicious. All four of us were in sight. I was forward, Dick and Glenn behind me, with Ed backing us up with

Dungeness crabs were a welcome addition to our larder.

his .375. With two cameras running and four people in sight, we were not surprised that the bears saw us. A hunter alone could have gotten close enough to throw a spear.

The business of an archer hunting big bears with rifle backing brings up the question whether this might be beyond the realm of bowhunting sportsmanship. An analysis of the situation, however, brings out the fact that hunters with guns are backed by guides, too. The bow requires a much closer approach to the animal. This is our handicap which does make the odds more even.

In big bear hunting I carry a 44-magnum revolver. This is not the entire solution to a bear that takes exception to being shot with an arrow but it is some comfort, and the .375 in Ed's hands tips the scale considerably in our favor.

Monday, September 21—In Fort Fidelgo Sound. Got in at eleven last night. I was asleep but the anchor winch woke me up. Got up at four-thirty. In the skiff at six going to a big flat where several creeks spill into the ocean.

We saw two black bears along shore as we approached the bay. Thousands of gulls, hundreds of crows, and dozens of bald eagles swarming along the creeks where the spawning humpbacks and dog salmon make their run. Canadian geese by the hundreds took flight from the grassy flats and overhead the familiar V formations honked their farewells as they winged south.

We found many bear trails in the tall grass at the edge of the mountains but no fresh signs except those of blacks. Perhaps the brownies have had all the fish they want at one time and have turned to other food. Looking over two more creeks without any luck we returned to the *Valiant Maid* at ten o'clock. Three killer whales surfaced frequently as we got under way while breakfast cooked on the galley stove.

What beautiful country. Mountains ending abruptly in the sea. Sometimes with sheer walls. Coastlines etched with fjords. Creeks grow out of smaller streams cascading from pockets of snow in the mountains above.

Ed made a two-hour run to show us the Columbia Glacier today. It is three miles across the base and rises to a sheer height of 200 to 300 feet. Large chunks of blue ice drop off at frequent intervals hitting the water with a roar like thunder and sending out swells like tidal waves. In an area of five miles the ocean was dotted with icebergs varying in size from footballs to perhaps hundreds of tons. We gathered some of the small ones for our icebox.

After checking several creeks with no results, we are running now at 7 P.M. for a safe anchorage. At midnight we will make another run to reach some creeks or an island at daylight.

We rammed a small iceberg with the skiff while photographing the glacier and punched a hole in the side. Winched it aboard to do a patching job and it does not leak any worse now than it did before. We carry a good bailing scoop aboard.

Ed made a run to show us the Columbia Glacier.

One could get out of shape easily on a hunt like this. Most of our time is spent either on this boat or in the skiff. Ed is trying hard to produce bears. We have done a lot of traveling. On a direct course the distance to Cordova is about fifty miles. Rained today while we were at the glacier. Have had very little wind. May get into some on the morning run through open sea.

Tuesday, September 22, 3 P.M.—Went to bed at nine last night. Ed started the run at midnight. Ran into bad weather. Winds 35 mph with gusts up to 50. My bunk forward was not the best place to be and I soon began feeling uncomfortable. Staggered up to the galley and found Glenn there in the same condition. Russ and Dick showed up later.

No one talked much. Water was pouring over the cabin and coming off the back on the rear deck. This closed the passage to the head and we had to improvise. Lots of traffic in and out of the galley through the early morning. Reached shelter here shortly after daylight and now have 600 feet of ⅝" cable tied to a big spruce on shore. With the anchor out at right angle we have a two-way tie.

Everybody still groggy except Ed who was up most of the night also. Things were pretty well shuffled around and the floor is littered with all kinds of gear. We are at Hinchinbrook Island now. The rain is still coming down in sheets with wind beating it horizontally. Can't hunt tonight unless things change.

7 P.M.—Weather getting better. An hour ago we launched the skiff and went into a flat nearby to look for Canada geese. Found them and got three with a

We shot some geese on a flat nearby and Glenn found a bear trap.

shotgun. Dinner is being prepared now as we sit around the table discussing events of the last twelve hours and making plans for tomorrow.

This is quite an operation. The skiff, which is fifteen feet long and weighs about a thousand pounds, is kept on the aft deck which is big enough to accommodate three automobiles. It is winched aboard by an overhead boom. The 35-hp motor is handled the same way. Hip boots are a must on board and when hunting. Saw several sea otters and seals this evening. The former are tame but the latter very wary. There is a $3.00 bounty on them and their skins are very much in demand.

Wednesday, September 23, 6 A.M.—We have an oil-fired cooking range in the galley. It operates like a blast furnace and quickly warms the place up. The wind has gone down but it is raining and we are rather well fogged in. There are so many things to photograph here but so little light to do it. Yesterday we saw some rock islands shaped like mushrooms—their bases corroded to small stems by the tides rushing by. The tides are sometimes seventeen feet high.

Someone is making coffee. We're going to look for bears and then come back for breakfast. The timber here is chiefly hemlock with a small percentage of Sitka spruce. Farther south, the timber is much bigger. Ed tells of Sitka spruce that he and his father harvested. It was thirty inches at the top and 189 feet long. The butt was seven feet and it yielded 16,900 board feet of lumber.

The underbrush along the creeks is alder mixed with devil's-club and berry bushes. Higher up the mountains this growth gives way to rocky cliffs and basins with snow pockets scattered here and there. This is where the goats live.

7 P.M.—We hunted all day. Went from one creek to another but saw no bears. The salmon run is over and the bears seem to have left. Shot a spruce hen and this evening we raided Goose Bay again. Russ got the only one. Two bears had crossed our tracks of the night before.

Not sure what to do from here on. Thinking about going back to Sheep Bay where we saw the brownies the first morning. What we do depends on the weather in the morning. Have four geese. Two have been skinned and boned to be parboiled and then fried. The other two will be roasted.

We did a lot of walking today through the forest on bear trails along the creeks. Rain-soaked, moss-covered rocks and logs lay under trees adorned with lichen. The limbs of these trees are covered with a green moss that swells a two-inch branch to eight or ten inches in diameter. We saw trees six feet at the butt and in some areas ate red raspberries and currants from growth along the way.

It rained off and on all day. We are always in boots and slickers and pay very little attention to rain anymore. From the skiff we saw many sea otters. They are cunning animals, coasting along on their backs. We ran the boat to within seventy-five yards of them sometimes. They are protected the year around and have no reason to fear man.

Everything is well wet down. Water came in a ventilator during the storm last night and soaked some gear we had stored in an empty bunk. Hardest job is to keep feathers dry. Even plastic bags get wet inside. Binoculars fog up, too, and have to be handled carefully.

Thursday, September 24, 7:30 P.M.—Up at 5 A.M. In the skiff at six. Rained all day. Hunted many creeks but no bears. Back on the boat at ten and pulled the cable from the tree, lifted anchor, and ran here to a snug harbor, Port Chalmons. Sounds like a town but there is nothing here except safety in a storm.

Checked a number of creeks but no bears here either. Found some high bush blueberries as big as the cultivated ones we get at home. Back to the boat again at 3:30 P.M. for a snack of stewed goose. Very good.

Went seal hunting at 5 P.M. Ed shot four with his 22 Hornet in a few minutes. From there we hunted a creek until dark. Plan to go back to Sheep Bay in the morning. Will use the seal carcasses for bear bait. This will be another night run. I hope it will be more pleasant than the last one. Ed says it will take about seven hours. That means we start about ten tonight to get there at daylight.

Friday, September 25, 7 A.M.—Fog last night. Could not start until daylight. We had rough seas for a time but are protected by islands now. Everybody is up sitting in the galley drinking coffee.

Ed Bilderback, our outfitter and guide, is thirty-three years old, 5'8" tall, and weighs 160 pounds. He has unbounded energy and bubbles with enthusiasm. He loves this country and does mostly what he likes to do which is hunting and fishing. He has twinkling brown eyes and a lively sense of humor and sharp wit. He is as alert and quick as a cat and very resourceful, stemming, I am sure, from his background of hazardous occupations.

Yesterday he shot at a seal with the .375 he carries for bear. The shot was wild and he decided to target the gun. He adjusted and zeroed in the sights with his one tool, his hunting knife. This morning at one point, the gun didn't fire. The cure for this was to squirt some oil on the firing pin inside the bolt.

We picked blueberries yesterday for some pancakes to serve with seal liver, which we are told, is a great delicacy.

» «

7 P.M.—This was the day. Dropped anchor at 11 A.M. and immediately set out in the skiff to place the seals for bear bait. As we approached the end of a bay where two creeks empty, we spotted a black bear on the beach. Motor was shut off and Ed sculled us to shore with an oar. Glenn was to try for the blackie and Dick and I handle the photography.

Just as we started out Ed saw a brown bear swaggering down the edge of the creek on our left. We watched as two more followed him. Blackie was forgotten. Ed and I took cover and started the stalk followed by Dick and Glenn with the movie and still cameras. Russ stayed with the boat since we couldn't take chances making noise by beaching it.

We rounded a point but the bears had left the narrow beach and gone into the woods. It was too thick and dark for photography so Dick and Glenn stayed behind as Ed and I took a bear trail walking quietly along the side of the mountain. A slight rain was falling and we had gone about 100 yards when I saw the last of the three brownies walking up a big moss-covered log looking down at us. He was clicking his jaws, not sure he had really seen anything. He was about sixty yards away, too far and too thick for a shot. The bears then went up about 100 yards and lay down on a knoll with their heads hanging over looking our way.

Using big trees for cover we cautiously bellied our way toward them. At twenty-five yards we ran out of cover and could proceed no farther. We watched them for an hour hoping they would expose themselves for a shot through one of several openings. They were very fat bears. The short climb to their perch had winded them and they lay there panting. Two of them went to sleep while a third stood guard, although his head would nod lower and lower until he'd jerk it up again for a good look around. The wind was blowing from right to left. Finally they apparently smelled the men at the boat. All of them got up and moved around restlessly. They came about five yards closer but still no opening for a shot and finally they moved out of sight around the knoll. We went after them but they were swallowed in a tangle of alder and berry bushes.

This ended the episode but that hour was worth the trip. We had made a good stalk and had practically lived with the bears as they lounged in their bedroom. I can still see those massive heads with their rounded ears, mouths open as they panted with lolling tongues.

We made our way back to the boat and sat there talking when I noticed another brownie coming down a different creek. Again we sprang into action. Followed by two cameramen we made our way to a grassy point where the bear would pass if he continued his course.

Another bear followed him. The first one slowly walked into view broadside at about forty yards. My arrow missed him, on the left. He whirled and stared back where he'd come from. The second arrow went left also, just missing his head. The third one at about sixty yards went over his back as he hurried away to join his mate who was eating fish up the creek. Apparently neither bear knew what was going on. They might have thought the swish of the arrows sounded like gulls flying close to them.

I was out of arrows with two brownies in sight. Usually I carry four broadheads but with so many smaller targets around I had substituted the fourth for a blunt. Watching carefully I crossed the small creek while the bears were not looking my way. My first arrow was retrieved from the mud and gravel bank. I removed the insert, sharpened both it and the blade, replaced the insert, washed the mud off in the creek, and started the stalk, using the brush along the bank for cover. Thirty-five yards from the bears I ran out of cover and stepped out on the gravel, kneeling low to clear some overhanging branches. One bear saw me and turned broadside to head for cover. Because of some branches I had to wait until he got just to the edge of the brush.

The arrow entered the rib section with a crash. I saw red blood as he rose on his hind feet and bellowed, turning to disappear in the brush. The other bear followed. We took up the course of my bear and found him dead on the trail about seventy yards from where he was shot.

The Razorhead had done a remarkable job. He was a two-year-old, fat, well furred, and weighed, we estimated, about 450 pounds.

Those first two bad shots worried me. They were made in the open at a good range with no excuse for shooting to the left. As I remember they did not get away clean and crisp. The sing of the string was muffled. I think I know what happened. The .44 I carry in a shoulder holster under my shirt is not easy to get at. When stalking bears I take it out of the holster and tuck the barrel in my pants under my belt. To get at it quickly I must leave my jacket open. I think the bowstring was striking this open jacket. At least this is the best excuse I can think of for two poor shots. It is fortunate that the bears were so co-operative.

We're having seal liver for dinner tonight. Ed has improvised a crab trap which now rests on the bottom of the bay beside the boat.

Saturday, September 26, 8 P.M.—Checked the creeks this morning. Saw a blackie but he was sharp and we could do no business. Bait seals were not touched. Back to the boat at ten o'clock and skinned the bear. The arrow we thought had gone through the ribs broadside had actually gone in at an angle shearing ribs, nicked the heart and plowed through the brisket. The lungs were not touched and the slit in the side of the heart had done the job.

Sunday, September 27, 4:30 A.M.—Waiting for breakfast. Moon and stars are shining bright. Looks like we might end the hunt in a blaze of sunshine as we began it.

This has been an entirely different kind of hunt from any I've ever been on. Living on a boat with eyes glued to binoculars, watching shorelines, sneaking up creeks, sidestepping dead salmon as well as live ones, stalking bears on shores that at low tide are slippery with eel grass and slimy rocks.

After a few days one gets used to the rain. Hip boots are standard equipment with a slicker on and off as the skies open and close.

7 A.M.—Had just toast and coffee early and went hunting. Air frosty. Saw nothing. Back on the boat. Anchor up and running for another creek. Picked the

Ed, Fred, Glenn, and Russ

crab trap up. Had crabs in it but the harness had become fouled and the Dungeness beauties were spilled back into the sea. Breakfast is ready. Blueberry pancakes with butter and honey, fried ham, fresh peaches, and pots of coffee.

Passed some sea lions on a rock. Checked more creeks. No bears. Everybody gathering personal gear as we head for Cordova. Things tucked away everyplace and some of it considerably scrambled by the blow last week.

I have mementoes of the trip as has everyone else—a bear trap, driftwood, glass floats from Japanese fish nets, and bear teeth pulled from a skull found near an old cabin.

Hunting from a boat is an interesting variation. Except for the climbing required to hunt those coastal goats, it is an easy hunt and one could turn tenderfoot fast.

For the Midwesterner, living away from salt water, the sea food is a delicious change of fare and life on a boat quickly becomes routine except when running through a blow in the night.

This is the stronghold of the fisherman. Hands calloused by salt spray. Faces weathered by wind. Ed takes life seriously when hunched over a book on a stool in the wheelhouse. He reads by a small light—one eye on the book and the other on his navigation charts. He steers, when reading, with his foot.

We will not forget Prince William Sound, the *Valiant Maid,* the white-collared, white-tailed eagles, sea lions, seals, goats, the dainty-footed black bears and the strutting, pigeon-toed brownies. Nor the screaming gulls as they crowded the mouths of creeks to prey on the salmon. Or the fog and the rain which really did not seem to matter too much.

We have plans to come back for a spring hunt next May.

Chapter 6

BROWN BEAR - 1960

Our brown bear hunt in the fall of 1959 in the Prince William Sound area was a new, exciting, and interesting experience. Before saying good-by to guide Ed Bilderback, we made plans to return the following spring to observe the mood of his country at that time of the year.

We would journey farther this time. Do some hunting on Kodiak Island, and then across the treacherous Shelikof Straits to the Alaska Peninsula.

There would be no spawning salmon in the creeks we trudged along last year. No gulls, eagles, and crows would be circling above, and waterfowl would just be returning from their winter in the south. Leaves would have dropped from the alders and there would be snow in the high places. Bears would be just out of their dens, grubbing around, slowly getting their digestive systems in operation again following their long winter sleep.

Our hunting would be done mainly with binoculars, sweeping the grassy hills in an effort to locate bears from the boat or mountainside. We needed, desperately, pictures of Kodiak bear country and the actual shooting of one of these largest bears in the world.

We met Bilderback and his crew at the city of Kodiak following an unsuccessful polar bear hunt at Point Barrow. Bob Munger was my photographer this time.

I will not recount the details of our hunt on and around Kodiak Island but will begin as we make preparations to cross Shelikof Straits to the Alaska Peninsula.

KODIAK ISLAND, ALASKA–ALASKA PENINSULA MAY 4–MAY 11, 1960

Wednesday, May 4, 10 P.M.—Sent mail home from here (Larsen Bay) at noon today. The *Valiant Maid* is tied up at the dock.

After lunch we took the skiff and ran up to the head of the bay. Hiked overland one and a half hours to the Karluck River and caught some rainbows and Dolly Varden trout. Back at 8 P.M. Ed now frying the fish.

Plan to start at midnight to cross the Straits to the Alaska Peninsula.

Thursday, May 5—No running last night. Straits were too rough. Started at 6 A.M. this morning. Not too bad. Got into a cove at one this afternoon and into the skiff to look for bears. Saw a fine big bear and sow high up the mountain. Watched them for an hour until they lay down. We started up. At about sixty to seventy yards the bear heard us and got up to look. We were screened by the alders and he did not know what made the noise. After about five minutes he walked on a trail around a knoll and Ed ran over to see where he had gone. Ran head on into him just over the knoll at twenty-five feet. Ed waved me over but before I could draw, he took off. A fine big bear.

Almost had a big bear. I like this country better than Kodiak Island.

Friday, May 6, 9 P.M.—Up at six. Took the skiff to where we had seen the bears yesterday. Saw a horse and a wolverine but no bears.

Went out to a sea lion island. Shot a good sea lion; one with long whiskers. Should have a good film. Caped and skinned him.

Back on the boat and running for another cove twenty miles away. No crabs in the pot today.

Saturday, May 7, 8 P.M.—Got into Alinchak Bay at ten last night. Lowered the crab pot at the entrance.

Up at six this morning. Located a big bear from the boat. Watched him for an hour until he lay down and then we put off in the skiff and went across the bay to look for him. As it turned out, he was a wise one. He saw us and kept watching as he slowly made his way up to the snow, through it and over the top. We are lucky in seeing big bears but not yet lucky enough to get a shot at one.

Checked another bay. Saw a fox but no bears. Dug some razor clams and checked still another bay with no results. Wanted to lift the crab pot but could not find it. Will try again in the morning when we change location to Puale Bay.

Found some Japanese glass floats on the beach. Also some floating rocks. This is the land of Mount Katmai the volcano that erupted in 1912, the source of these floating stones.

We are living off the land. Last evening our dinner was seal liver, a rabbit, and some oyster crackers. . . .

Sunday, May 8, 10 P.M.—Woke up at 4 A.M. with the boat pounding hard. A strong wind was blowing and the anchor was slipping in the sandy bottom.

Ed hauled the anchor up and headed toward shore. The skiff with outboard motor that was hitched to the boat, broke its ¾″ rope and went adrift heading for the shore of the bay. Another skiff, carried on the aft deck was winched overboard and Ed rowed after the runaway. The wind carried him to the shore about a half mile from where it was pounding on the beach.

While we held the *Valiant Maid* into the wind, Ed tried to launch the skiff and get the motor started. Finally did and got back to the boat. Too risky to go back for the other skiff and too rocky to get close with the big boat. We could see it for some time with glasses and then it disappeared from view. Either swept out to sea or destroyed. Will look for it if the wind ever stops blowing.

Confined to the cabin of the big boat all day. We are anchored in the lee of a mountain and riding out the storm in comfort. Lifted the crab pot and had four small king crabs.

Our Sunday dinner of razor clams and king crabs was appreciated. I wrote cards, cleaned cameras and gear, dried clothing, played cards, read and slept the day out. Very comfortable and warm with the stove going round the clock in the cabin, although the inactivity is despairing.

We were reminiscing about the bear we sneaked up on several days ago. If I had followed Ed after that bear instead of taking a higher course, I would have had a twenty-five-foot shot at the big fellow. Going to bed.

Monday, May 9, 9 P.M.—Anchored in Puale Bay. Up at 7 A.M. and wind still blowing. At 3 P.M. decided to make a run for it from Alinchak Bay here. Not too rough. Got here at 7 P.M. Anchored the boat and went ashore in the skiff. Found some glass balls and saw a bear on the beach about a half mile away. The wind was blowing harder than I have ever seen it. Not a chance to stalk the bear, so we decided to let him alone in hopes we could find him tomorrow.

Tuesday, May 10, 8 A.M.—Wind blowing still harder this morning. The anchor slipped. Yesterday we found the legs and shells of many king crabs on the beach. Some of them monsters. Have great hopes for a fine catch. Useless to go ashore in this gale. Wind must be 60 mph. Could not shoot an arrow. There are about thirty emperor geese on the beach at present.

Same Day, 11:30 A.M.—Breakfast of pancakes and eggs. Wind still blowing but we are getting ready to put ashore in the skiff. We plan to climb to a high point and glass the country. Still almost too windy to shoot an arrow but it is, at least, something to do. Want to check the tracks of the bear we saw to find out how big he was.

Bob feels that he should be starting home. Ed is trying to make contact with Kodiak by radio to get a plane to pick him up. Can't get in with a wind blowing like this.

» «

Same Day, 10:45 P.M.—Wow! This was the day. Got a beautiful brownie. As soon as we put ashore at eleven thirty this morning this beastly wind went down. Started across a lagoon to climb a hill to look the country over. Ed climbed the rise ahead of us. Came running back saying that a bear was on the beach near the skiff we had just left.

We hurried back and he was still there. I did a stalk but about this time the bear decided to head over the mountain. When he got over the top we got into the skiff and went around the mountain.

As we had hoped, he came over the top. Halfway down he started to run and disappeared in the valley.

We climbed higher for a better view but never did see him again. Climbed another mountain and saw nothing. Did a lot of hiking in hip boots but did not see any tracks. Very tired, after so much hiking.

We got back to the boat at 6 P.M., ate a snack, and went ashore again. I was interested only in walking the shore and looking for Japanese floats but Ed, walking ahead down the beach, suddenly flagged me over.

The bear we had been on the beach last night was there again about two miles away. It was too late for pictures, so Ed and I started after him alone. He was eating king crabs and other delicacies from the kelp piles that littered the beach. His home was in the tag alders that lined the shore and we made the stalk through them on his own trail.

The last hundred yards was thrilling. We had scant cover along a trail that left even the alders as we neared the bear. The only cover was logs and driftwood for the last fifty yards. Ed stopped there. I took the lead and got up to within twenty yards of the brownie. He was standing broadside eating something as I loosed an arrow into his midsection and the air was immediately full of action. The bear growled and spun around in circles. The hit was good and I felt sure of my bear.

I was on his trail and he came straight for me. I dropped the bow and whipped the .44 out of my belt. Had the hammer halfway back with the bear five steps from me when Ed yelled, "Don't shoot; he is a big one." In other words, don't spoil this trophy with a bullet hole.

At the sound of Ed's voice the bear saw me and veered off to the side disappearing in the alders.

We hurried up the side of the mountain and watched him drop in the alders 250 yards from where he had been hit a few minutes before.

A beautiful bear. Died with his feet in the air from a Razorhead through his liver.

Bob and Harley had been watching from two miles up the beach. They saw the action through glasses and came down in the skiff.

It was too late for pictures and we needed an ax to clear the alders, so we left him until morning. Got back to the boat at 10 P.M. Just about dark. Dined on king crab and to bed at twelve o'clock.

He died with his feet in the air.

Wednesday, May 11, 4 P.M.—Ed woke us up at 4 A.M. A very short night. Wind had changed to the southwest and he said we had two hours to get pictures and skin the bear—otherwise we might be there for a week as the Shelikof Straits really got rough in a wind from that direction.

We took flash equipment and an ax and set out without breakfast. Everyone working at top speed had the area brushed out, pictures taken, and the bear skinned in two and a half hours.

We're back to the *Valiant Maid* now and on our way toward Kodiak Island. Crossing is not too bad. We are headed for Spiridon Bay where we will probably tie up for the night and then on to Kodiak tomorrow.

Harley is working on the skin as we speed along through rough water.

Harley is working on the bear skin and skull as we speed along through the rough water. The skin squares ten feet, two inches. The very biggest ones are ten feet, six inches. Skull measures twenty-eight inches. Record is thirty inches.

I am very pleased with this bear and think I will have a standing mount. His skin is in fine shape. No rubbed spots. We did not have enough light for movies which was a disappointment, but the size of my trophy compensates.

Almost forgot to mention that last evening, as we got to the beach after the bear hunt just at twilight, a big bear was silhouetted on the skyline up on a cliff. That one made a total of eight brownies we have seen on this trip.

Hunting brown bears with a bow is exciting business. They are big and powerful but a Razorhead lays them low. They look very big at twenty yards and bigger still at five, head on.

This has been a thrilling trip. Action with both polars and brownies, with wolves and sea lions thrown in for spice. I have learned at least one thing. Those big heads are good for deer but are not needed on bigger game. The regular Razorhead does the job nicely and they fly better on the one shot a week one gets under difficult hunting conditions such as these.

Same Day, 9:30 P.M.—Running for Kodiak, five hours away. Will get there about 2 A.M. Plane leaves Kodiak at 11 A.M. If we can get on and the weather is right, we will take off in a stupor. I am beat. Will call home from Kodiak.

Looking forward to seeing my wife and getting home. Must stop at Juneau and talk with conservation people there, a day in Seattle and then home.

Chapter 7

KISPIOX RIVER, BRITISH COLUMBIA - 1960

This was a hunt for grizzly bears in the fall of 1960. We traveled to Hazelton which is on the highway that connects Prince George and Prince Rupert in British Columbia.

We were to hunt with Love and Lee Outfitters in the beautiful Kispiox River country.

The river is famous for its steelhead fishing. Salmon also swim up from the ocean to spawn in its tributaries. These spawning fish are the main diet of grizzly bears during the summer and fall.

There were four in our party. Knick Knickerbocker of Charlottesville, Virginia; George Griffith, Chuck Kroll, and myself from Grayling. Knick and George were interested in the steelheads and Chuck and I were after bears.

Monday, September 19, 6 P.M.—Got into Smithers yesterday at 11 A.M. A fine flight from Vancouver via Prince George. Jack Lee and Bill Love met us at the airport with two station wagons. Went into Hazelton for last-minute supplies and then to Bill's house for lunch and on to Jack's place where we changed from street clothes. Also changed from station wagon to jeep pickups for the twenty-mile drive to Jack's hunting camp at Corral Creek.

Mrs. Lee, who will do the cooking, and Bob Roy came with us. Bob is from Vancouver, here to do some hunting also.

It took about two and a half hours to get to camp. Chuck Kroll shot two ruffed grouse along the way. Chuck and George rode with Bill, Knick, and Bob in a pickup, and I rode with Mr. and Mrs. Lee. The road was rough as we followed the Kispiox, finally reaching camp just before dark. A beautiful spot on a high bank overlooking the river. Eleven saddle and pack horses munch grass in an enclosure that surrounds the camp. Our cabin, for the four hunters, is new. About eighteen by twenty, solidly built from huge spruce logs. A spruce floor and a roof covered with tarpaper.

Wilford Lee, son of the Lees, is here to help with the guiding. We got a late start this morning. Much gear to sort and assemble.

Knick, George, and Wilbur went fishing. Chuck and I did some practicing with our bows and then took the jeep upriver to check two places Jack had baited for grizzly. No fresh signs at either place. Went to the "Coho" hole, had lunch, and

Our cabin was new, solidly built from spruce logs.

Our view of the Kispiox from the cabin.

fished until an hour ago. Knick and George joined us here. They had four coho but no steelheads.

We are sitting on a log about 200 yards from a bear carcass—a bear killed by earlier hunters. Have just been in to see if there were any bears there. Going in again before the light gets too poor for pictures.

Friday, September 23, 5 P.M.—Have not written since Monday. Too much to do and too fresh from my office chair to be other than dead tired after the heavy dinners we eat following a day of vigorous outdoor exercise.

This country is forested with spruce, hemlock, balsam, poplar, willow, lodgepole pine, cottonwood, and some white birch. Ground growth is extremely heavy, varying from thimbleberry and wild rose to bracken higher than my head. Alder grows to an amazing size along the river and in draws. The spruce grows tall and slender, each one trying to outdo the other in an effort to reach sunlight. Beautiful timber for cabins such as ours.

Tuesday we packed waders, fishing tackle, cameras, lunch, and bows and hiked into a point of land made by a hairpin course of the river. It is about 2½ miles and will hereafter be referred to as "the point." Jack has a bait there which we checked and then to the end of the point for fishing. Caught quite a few Dolly Vardens, several coho, some cutthroat trout, and hooked a fine steelhead but did not land him.

Knick and George fished at various holes along the river and caught many fish but no steelheads. Fine weather, temperature just right, and the sun shining. Wednesday, Bill, Chuck, and I checked the two upper baits to find them unmolested. Did some fishing with assorted luck and came back to camp to learn that George had broken our luck and caught a steelhead thirty-two inches long. Had it for dinner. Excellent.

Wednesday night it rained and Thursday morning the river valley was filled with fog. A good sign for a clear day, said Wilford.

George has been suffering with a toothache and he and Jack went to town for some attention. Knick and Wilford hiked into a lake and had good sport catching cutthroat trout on flies. Bill, Chuck, and I planned a trip to the point to check the bait and to fish if there was no action at the bait.

When we got to the river it was high and not very clear. This ended our fishing plans, so we decided to still-hunt and visit the two other baits. I should have mentioned that Bob killed a moose on Tuesday and Bill put the entrails at our bait site #2.

We found that a bear, a blackie, we thought, had visited the bait and liked what he found. We went in to have a look this morning. He had been back during the night but was not around then.

Resting with my back to a spruce tree about 400 yards from the bait. It is now six forty-five and we have been in to look twice. Will go in again in a few minutes and stay until dark. It is already too dark for pictures.

Wednesday, October 5—It has been a long time since I last wrote up my notes. Except for fine food and good companionship there has been a decided lack of excitement. We take horses frequently and have pleasant rides through the woods and always an enjoyable campfire and tea boil at lunch places.

Chuck slipped off a log and wrenched his knee badly last week. He limped

Knick and Jack at our Sweetin River lunch stop.

around camp on a homemade crutch for a few days but is up on his own again now. In fact he is doing fine.

Early last week Jack and I hiked from the end of the trail at the Sweetin River up to Nangeese Creek. Jack packed a rubber boat and I packed camera, gear, and lunch. It was quite a hike and rough going for three hours. We saw two bull moose but could not get a shot. We floated down the Kispiox and checked the bait on the point. Had hoped to see a bear or moose but saw only eagles and ravens.

Bears, both black and grizzly, are scarce. The humpback salmon run did not occur this year and the bears seem to have gone to high country for berries and to dig out whistlers and other rodents instead. Of our three baits, only one has been visited and that, we think, by a black bear. Apparently he is feeding nights as we can never catch him there, although the tidbits we leave each time are always gone. He is a clever bear and does not seem to mind man scent. Sometimes does his dining right in our blind overlooking the bait spot.

Knick and George went home last week leaving Chuck and me to concentrate on our hunting. It was then that bears began coming to both the bait on the point and the one on the Sweetin. This was too much action all at once as they are too far apart to watch by one hunter, so on Monday we split up.

Chuck and Wilford went to the Sweetin bait and found a big black eating there with a grizzly standing up in the tall grass beyond watching him! The wind was not good and both scampered off before they could get a shot. Jack and I visited the point bait every hour making our last trip at seven-thirty but the bear did not show up. Yesterday we all went together to the Sweetin bait but found that it had not been touched. Decided to let it cool off for a day while we went to the point for our hourly visits. The bear had been there sometime since the evening before but he seems to be a wise one.

It is now 3 P.M. Jack and I have a fire at the point. Rode in at ten o'clock. Bruin had had another meal since last evening but we still have not seen him. Will have another look shortly and then again just before dark. Plan to stay until we cannot see. Chuck and Wilford went up to Sweetin this morning.

Friday, October 7—We checked the bait again at 7 P.M. and stayed there until long after dark. Wind was not good. We heard the bear or bears just at dusk. Heard them break dried parsnip stems and also heard them growl. Jack thinks there are several including a sow and cub. They made a half circle in front of us but would not come in sight. We had built our blind on high ground overlooking a river flat grown up with fireweed, bracken, and wild parsnip. Darkness comes here now at eight o'clock. We got back to camp at ten, to find Chuck and Wilford in high spirits.

Just before dark Chuck got a good hit on a beautiful grizzly. They found the bear about 200 yards away. A fine, mature animal, silvery-blond on top tapering to black legs and feet. The arrow had gone through a hindquarter into the abdominal cavity and into the lungs.

Late in the afternoon Jack and I rode up to the point again to have another try at the bears. Got there at seven-thirty and had excitement soon afterward. The bait was almost cleaned up but we heard something walking in the weeds. The bears were circling again. I could faintly see a place about 100 yards out on the flat where the weeds were tramped down and saw three bears come in at the far end of it. One little one, definitely a cub, came right toward us through the opening. He was whining and squealing like a little pig. The bigger bears moved off into the weeds to our left. We stayed until it was too late to see anything.

The day before we arrived at Jack's camp, a black bear had torn up his smokehouse and eaten the fish he had in it. Just back of our cabin the ground slopes sharply down into the river. The smokehouse was on the edge of this bank. It seemed like a good place to have a try at black bear. We hung some spawned-out salmon on a pole that bent over with their weight. To the end of the pole we fastened a fish line and ran it up the slope and in through a crack in the cabin wall to a cowbell we hung from a roof beam.

There was no action for over a week. Then two nights ago we were wakened by this alarm. The night was not dark and I had all I could do to keep from laughing out loud as Chuck tiptoed cautiously toward the drop-off in his shorts, bow in hand, through the frosty night.

I had unfolded some corrugated cartons and fastened them, light side out, on stakes just behind the bait to silhouette the bear so we could see him in the dark. At the top of the bank, we placed some balsam boughs as a sort of blind for the shooter. But no bear was to be seen. We waited for a few minutes and then crawled back into our sleeping bags.

Ten minutes later we had another alarm. I stayed in my snug bag and Chuck made another trip. The bear was there but saw him as he raised up and made off in haste. No more alarms that night. Bruin had taken the fish and a moose heart, however.

We have replenished the bait but have not had our sleep interrupted since. We sleep with the cabin door open. Bats, apparently looking for a place to spend the winter, fly in and out all night and last night I awoke to hear the clatter of small claws on the bare floor. By the time I found my flashlight there was nothing there. I suspected a marten as we have seen them several times around camp.

Last Friday, having no baits to attend in the morning, Jack suggested that we go down to "Nobody Much" to hunt a big mule deer buck that both Knick and Chuck had seen twice on this hunt. Might also see a moose, Jack said, and we could look for bear sign. "What is 'Nobody Much'?" I asked and he explained that it was a creek that got its name when the road was built through here. The creek required a fill and during the work, until the fill was completed, nobody much could get across it.

We had gone just a short way climbing to the top of the ridge, when Jack stopped, pointed, and whispered to me, "There's a bear as big as a house." Strolling through the spruce and hemlock forty yards away was a very big, dark-colored bear. He measured up to the qualifications of a big grizzly. His head was small compared to his long body. He was going in the opposite direction from us, just passing in the bush I thought. Jack was in the open and could see better than I could.

After he was out of sight I blew my varmint call. Jack, who could still see him, said he turned and made a few steps our way and then stopped. Not knowing this, I gave another blast and he moved off to fade into the trees. We made a circle to try to head him off. Reaching a high point, we waited and listened. Heard a stick crack down in a ravine. We went down there and found where he had taken off on a run. Backtracking, it was determined that he had been circling us inside of our circle. Apparently got our scent.

We proceeded then down the ridge that terminated at the outlet of the lake. Jack went down one side of Nobody Much Creek and I took the other. About halfway to the road, while stopping on a knoll to look and listen, a bull moose came out of the alders in the creek bottom about fifty yards behind me. Apparently he had seen or winded Jack as he would stop frequently to look back. I was standing in thimbleberry bushes up to my chest. The bull came around the knoll at the bottom with nothing visible but his back. As he slanted up the draw it was not until he started to enter thick bush that I could see his rib section. The distance was perhaps forty yards and the arrow hit well. The bull turned and ran about fifty yards down toward the creek. Then walked another fifty yards until he went down.

The kill was timely as we had been on a diet of fish for the last few days. It was well placed, too, being in the territory of the big grizzly who would find the entrails and make himself available, we hoped.

The dignity of bears always amazes me. The one we saw today knew we were there but walked by us without looking our way. I have seen it before in both black and grizzly. They are clever animals with an abundance of patience plus a good sense of humor and a surprising ability to think.

Jack Lee, who is fifty-four years old and has spent one third of his life hunting or trapping in the bush, says that this fellow was the largest bear he had ever seen. Jack is a modest person not given to exaggerate. Information that might seem a bit egotistical is hard to pry from him. Hunting and trapline tales flow rather freely though. Take the case of the white, black bear:

Jack was trapping on the Simonette River in Alberta a few years ago and a small black bear had been pestering him around camp. Although he had had several opportunities to shoot him, he had not felt inclined to do so as any company was welcome in his lonesome existence. To keep his grub supply intact he had hung edibles on a high pole under a tarp. Among the items was about twenty pounds of flour left over from a 100-pound sack.

Returning to camp one rainy evening, Jack was startled to see a white bear dart away from the area. It was not hard to guess what had happened. The bear, standing on his back legs, had ripped the flour sack open and flour poured down on him over his wet fur and clung there as he ran off.

Another story concerned a trapper named Frank Eklund who lived on the Findlay River. His trapline was made up of a string of cabins on the Ospida which was a tributary of the Findlay. Frank carried a 30-40 Kraig and had considerable respect for grizzly bears. Returning to his cabin one day he discovered that a grizzly had broken in. The bear had created wide and general disorder. What he didn't eat was broken or destroyed. His stove was torn apart and the pipe smashed flat.

Realizing that this was probably a gaunt, hungry bear or he would be in hibernation, Frank felt that extreme caution was necessary and made a high cache by building a platform on four spruce trees he sawed off about ten feet up where he stored his food, including a moose quarter.

This was no ordinary bear. He chewed two of the trees off, ate the supplies, and was asleep in Frank's bunk when he came back. . . .

» «

This is Tuesday the eleventh day of October. We have been watching the baits but never seem to have our visits timed with the bear's eating schedule. A big grizzly has taken over at the black bear bait. We packed my moose head in there and wired it to a log. Two nights ago he came in, tore it loose, and toted it off. An Indian killed a moose near the road here several days ago and we sewed the remains up in the hide and dragged and packed it in for bait yesterday. We went in at daylight this morning but the bear had not been there.

We do not sit and wait at a bait. Wind currents are too unpredictable. We go in, look, and come straight out. If the weather is bad as it was this morning, we hole up under a spruce, dig a nest in the pine-cone cuttings like a bear, and sometimes take a nap or write notes as I am doing now.

We had a hard rain last night and through part of the morning. The Kispiox is running higher than it has been since we came. A big boulder upriver from camp is totally submerged and driftwood is coming down.

The weather has not been cold. Only two frosts but the season has taken its toll of the leaves. Poplar and cottonwood are shedding first with the birch trying hard to retain theirs. Bracken is completely dead and brown and the fireweed and alder leaves are turning black. Everything was green when we came but now the hillsides of dark spruce and hemlock are gilded with aspen.

It is becoming monotonous to write that we are sitting under a spruce tree but we are, and it is raining. Jack is napping and Chuck is reading a paperback. Events of the last twenty-four hours have been interesting. Yesterday morning it was decided to remove the remains of my moose to the site where the black bear had been living high off our offerings. After this chore was finished and it was not a small one, we went by jeep to the fork of the Kispiox and the Sweetin. It is on the point of land formed by these two rivers that we have set the bait. It is here, also, that Chuck shot his grizzly. We got in there at six forty-five enheartened to learn that another grizzly had found our bait and covered it with grass. This is a sure sign of a grizzly. Blackies never do this.

Just a year ago, on the Delta River in Alaska, I watched a sow grizzly with a cub cover a caribou carcass. Walking away from the carcass about thirty feet, she dug up grass, sod, and moss with her powerful front feet and claws. Backing up and clawing at the same time she managed to roll up a ball of the mixture underneath her belly and roll it up to the kill. The cub, that weighed about fifty pounds, cunningly tried to imitate her at the same task. Surprisingly he did very well and got a fair-sized ball about halfway to the goal when it either tickled him or he decided it was more fun to play. He fell over on his back taking the ball with him on his belly and played with it until it disintegrated into tufts of sod and grass again.

Even older bears like to have fun. Once I watched two two-year-old brownies engaged in a playful tussling match that was as entertaining as a circus act. . . . Black bears are also known for their clowning. But the blacks are afraid of grizzlies and would not consider a dispute with one.

This morning Jack rounded up Scrappy, Spud, and Ranger and we rode out to the jeep that had stalled last night. In a few minutes, working in daylight now, we discovered that the feed wire to the coil had broken off. This was quickly repaired, so we threw the saddles in the jeep and the horses were happy to start back home with a slap on their backsides.

It was now time for another trip to the bait and then back to the river to fish a little. River is still high but fairly clear. Fishing produced no results. Hourly trips to the bait were fruitless also. Rain fell as we neared camp and it continued all night.

Friday morning we made our first visit at daylight and went in at regular intervals throughout the entire rainy, stormy day. The wind blew upriver and in under the spruce at our luncheon spot. Each trip took twenty minutes one way. Drying out beside a big fire took up the remaining twenty minutes when another visit was due.

Nothing came in all day. We saw martens, eagles, ravens, crows, grouse, blue

He had a grizzled face and a skin marred by many battles.

and stellar jays, magpies, and the usual assortment of red squirrels who pile up the spruce-cone chips at the base of the trees we sit under.

Rain continued all night and by the next morning the river had risen to near-flood stage. Patience is one of the virtues of a good hunter. We felt that we had almost exhausted our limit. The hunt had been booked for two weeks. The purpose, to bag a larger than average grizzly. Sunday would mark the fourth week and our departure from Smithers on the once-a-week Sunday plane was a must. There remained only Saturday morning to hunt. Surely the big fellow would find the moose bait or one would come to the spot at the Sweetin.

It was still pouring as we left camp at daylight in a rain that had continued for thirty-six hours. A stop at the moose remains was a blank. The light was too poor for pictures, so Chuck stopped to fish at the point while Jack and I continued on to look at the bait. As we got near we saw wolf tracks on the muddy trail, plunging our spirits to zero. Wolves are the kings of bait stealers and come in at night. (Grizzlies do not dispute their rights.) They had eaten the bait completely and seemed to have eliminated the last glimmer of hope for the remaining hours we had left.

This bait was one fourth of a mile from a horse trail Jack had cleared along the river to Nangeese Creek. Chuck's grizzly carcass was on a bench just a short way off this trail. There were wolf tracks going that way also and it seemed like a good idea to have a look at it.

I eased my way up the steep side of the bench and Jack continued along the trail to scout the area ahead. I had no way of knowing that the stage was set for a drama soon to unfold before my eyes.

It was difficult to gain the top of the bench quietly but as I reached the proper level I soon saw that the bear carcass was not there. Rising one more step I could see part of it off to the right and scanning the brush beyond, black blotches protruded from both sides of a large spruce tree. It was a black bear.

Back at the river I had shot two arrows at a grouse sitting high in a tree. The other two arrows in my bow quiver had a plastic bag over them to keep the feathers dry. By pulling slowly on the top, I was able to remove the bag without alerting the bear.

Arrow on string, I advanced two steps, cautiously looking for a hole in the brush. Putting my foot down at the second step I was in line with a shooting hole but I cracked a twig. The bear was standing behind the tree. As the twig snapped, the bear quickly swung his head out and looked my way. He was not certain where the sound had come from and turned his head to look the other way. I wasn't sure of the wind direction but if the bear moved I would not get another chance through that brush, so I shot at his head hoping to hit him in the base of the neck. The arrow missed and chucked into a log beyond. Having been harassed by wolves and grizzlies he instinctively sprang up the tree with woofs and growls.

It was not a difficult shot. Jack had heard the rumpus and hurried over. We examined the bear. He was an old animal with teeth well worn, a grizzled face, and a skin marred by many battles.

Chapter 8

BROWN BEAR - 1962

One of the advantages of making a hunting film is that another trip is usually called for to pick up footage of key shots that were not obtained on the previous trip. It is not hard to convince the office that the movie would be a disaster without additional film and a follow-up trip is indeed necessary.

Following the 1960 hunt, however, this underhand scheming to get away was not necessary since we had obtained no film of the big brownie . . . bad weather, too late in the day, no light.

So . . . the hunt began at Cordova, Alaska, where we spent two days scraping and painting the hull of the *Valiant Maid* and loading her with supplies. Bob Munger was my hunting companion again.

The trip resulted in the most spectacular hunting footage we have in our entire film library.

Friday, April 27—Aboard the *Valiant Maid* again. Ed Bilderback, Skipper; Harley King, Guide; Dan Korea, Cook. Left Cordova at 11 A.M. today. Went into Sheep Bay to check on bears. No sign anywhere. Will sleep here tonight.

Saturday, April 28—Came over past Montague Island and tied up at the cannery dock at Port Ashton. It rained this morning, but cleared into a fine day. Am concerned about the heavy snow still here. Most snow they have had in twenty years. The bears will sleep late this spring.

Sunday, April 29—Dropped anchor this evening in Nuka Bay after an eight-hour run from Port Ashton. Thought this might be a good place for black bear. We saw a coyote and some whales but no bear. Too much snow here too. We are early for bears. Heading for Afognak Island hoping it will be warmer there.

Monday, April 30—The weather was bad last evening. We dropped anchor for the night in Chugach Bay with its small coves and arms. Not so much snow here. Black bears in this area. We saw one in an open place on the side of the mountain. Went ashore and made a stalk, but the wind crossed us up. Took the skiff about five miles downshore and located another bear on a small beach, but he wandered off into the woods. When we saw a third bear on a beach nearby, we were almost within range when the wind changed and he made off.

We scraped her bottom and painted her sides.

Later, on another beach, we located more bears and circled through the woods until we were close. One of them came off the beach and bedded down about twenty yards from us. I shot some film of two on the beach. Later the one who had bedded down joined the others. They are digging kelp buried in the gravel. Bob shot an arrow at one and they scampered off into the woods. We scattered and sneaked after them through the spruce, trying to get within range. One had crossed a small frozen pond and I crossed after him. About halfway over I got an opening and shot the bear at about twenty-five yards. It was a lung shot and I kept after him. With my eyes on the bear, not looking where I was going, I walked into thin ice, and broke through to my hips. I found my bear a hundred yards away.

We saw a total of six bears today.

Tuesday, May 1—We're anchored near an abandoned cannery in Graham Bay —too rough to cross to Barren Islands. Got here about 10 P.M. and immediately saw two black bears on the side of the mountain. We decided that Ed should show us how to do it this time. He started off with his bow and arrow. Grass very dry and noisy. The bear heard him and he got only a running shot. We did not see it again.

Did some scrounging around the cannery and an abandoned sawmill. Getting back to the *Valiant Maid* we found her listing badly. There had been a minus tide and she was on bottom. Tide came back in and we are afloat again.

Wednesday, May 2—Made the first half of the run to Afognak. Threw anchor in a bay off an island this morning and got in the skiff to go seal hunting. We got a few nice skins. This country is covered with brant, yellow legs, honkers, sandhill cranes, swans, all kinds of ducks, cormorants and gulls and terns by the millions. The wind is blowing a gale. Hope it calms down so we can move on to brown bear country. Wonderful weather all the time except for the wind.

Thursday, May 3—The wind is even stronger today. We went ashore to hunt marmots. Ed shot one and I saw a parka squirrel. Back at the boat by twelve o'clock and departed for Shuyak Island. This is off the tip of Afognak, a short run of about three hours. It was not too rough. We plan to do our brown bear hunting here and on Afognak. It is doubtful if we will get to the Peninsula.

After dropping anchor we got in the skiff and went bear hunting, checking the beaches for tracks. Found some and later saw two bears, about a mile ahead, coming toward us. Perched on a high point overhanging the beach we watched for them to come nearer, but after about ten minutes they had not come in sight. Our time was short as Harley had the skiff with orders to come up the shore an hour after we left. It was time for him now and we were afraid he would flush the bears. We decided to move toward where we had last seen them. There was a small gully behind the beach and coming down off the point, I was suddenly faced with two bears, looking at me from about twenty yards away. I guess I felt relief when they ran off into the spruce and we saw no more of them.

Getting back to the boat we had a great dinner at 8:30 P.M. This is the nicest bay we have anchored in. Not a breeze is stirring. Ducks are quacking and geese are honking. The low island is almost covered with spruce. We think the bears will have to come out to the beach for food. They, both the blacks and brownies, like to dig among the logs for kelp buried by the storms.

Friday, May 4—Dropped anchor in Seal Bay on Afognak. Saw a bear near shore from the *Valiant Maid,* but he saw us and made off over the mountain. We hunted all the bays in the area and at 8 P.M. saw two bears on a grassy hillside, but they also saw us.

We went after them. Ed and Bob went one way and Harley and I another. We climbed up beside a big spruce thicket and stood there about ten minutes. A bear cracked some brush near us, but we did not see him. Had to leave then because of darkness. We saw two foxes and two otters and caught six king crabs in our trap. One crab measured forty-eight inches across.

One crab measured forty-eight inches across the tips of his legs.

Saturday, May 5—No bears today. There does not seem to be too many in this area. Perhaps they are not out of hibernation yet. Saw seven foxes though. All color variations from grays through reds to blue and silver. Some were very beautiful. We ate three king crabs tonight, keeping the others alive hung from a cord in the ocean. Weather still holding fine. Sunny and not too cold.

Sunday, May 6—Continuing our search today we went down along the east side of Afognak to Isut Bay and saw a lone bear about three miles away in the hills but did not try for him.

I stalked and photographed a fox today. He looked like a cross between a red and gray. These foxes are the largest I have ever seen. They live by beachcombing at low tide—starfish, mussels, sand fleas, and other oddities.

We had a three-hour run back this evening and got here at seven-thirty. Going ashore we found that a bear had been combing the beach while we were gone. We plan to stay here now and hunt the area tomorrow.

Weather is beautiful. The reason we stay on at Afognak is that this definitely is a late spring. Afognak, being low country, is warm and we reason that the bears should be out here earlier. Kodiak Island is higher and has more snow. Two years ago, with an earlier spring, many bears were out there at this time. Had planned this hunt for the Alaska Peninsula, but that is closed for hunting this year from Puale Bay, south. There is only a short strip of open hunting area north of the National Katmei Monument Park. Hardly worth the hazardous trip across. Plan to put a seal carcass out for bait today to see if we can create some action. Saw a herd of about forty Afognak elk and got pictures. Filmed whales and a sea lion eating a fish. Going into a cannery tomorrow for supplies.

Monday, May 7—Shot a sea lion this morning and a seal for bear bait. Placed them on different beaches and built a blind near each. A good way to photograph eagles and foxes also. We needed water and ran into Port Williams where we also stocked up on meat and groceries. We met a hunter from Flint, Michigan, and got some bear information from him. He said there was good bear hunting farther down the west side of Afognak. We decided to check it out and made a run into Big Bay. Took the skiff and ran over to a likely beach. As we rose to look

Brown bear country.

over the bank above the beach, there was a bear just beyond, among the logs on the high-tide mark. We tried a stalk but the wind was wrong and he made off into dense spruce. Checked several bays afoot and found many bear signs. This seems like the spot we have been looking for. As a matter of fact, it looks almost too good.

Tuesday, May 8—Went hunting afoot this morning. I got busy photographing some eagles and had to track Bob and Ed down. Finally found them and Bob had a big brownie dead on the beach. He shot him with a .375, but I did not hear the shot. Measurements will not be available until the head and feet are skinned. He has a monstrous head and should measure up well. There was another bear with the one Bob shot. Ed and I spent an hour looking for him, but no luck. Ed packed Bob's bear skin and headed back to the skiff. We weighed it when we got to the boat; 175 pounds. After a snack we went foot hunting again. Cut across land to some beaches. Back from the hunt at 8 P.M. I'm tired.

Wednesday, May 9—Went to look at the bear and seal carcasses to see if any bears were there. Cruised some beaches and came upon a medium-sized bear. Took some pictures of him and then decided to maneuver through the brush and try to get a shot at him with a blunt for pictures. The bear was about thirty yards out on the beach from us. As we were just about to come out of the spruce, somebody cracked a twig. The bear stood on his hind legs for a full thirty seconds. Bob had the camera and Ed was in front of me. I took the camera and started to run film as he made for the spruce to our right. He was huffing and puffing and I got some pictures of him before he was gone and I was out of film.

Another beautiful day. Ran four hundred feet of film. About two o'clock we left the area to scout the country north of us. Plan to give this place a rest and then come back if we don't get a bear before that. Dropped anchor at 4 P.M. and went scouting afoot and by skiff. Found some tracks that look promising.

Thursday, May 10—Took the skiff and went out cruising the oceanside this morning. Saw one bear, but he heard the motor and ran off when we were half a mile away. Got back in at 3 P.M. Found two rubber crab-pot floats. This makes seven we have found on the beaches as well as a good supply of half-inch nylon rope. We do a lot of beachcombing when looking for bears.

This country has a very comprehensive bird population and we spend a lot of time trying to identify them. The most unique, I believe, is the parrot duck. It has an orange, parrotlike beak, a black body, and black-and-white head. The harlequin duck is splendid, too, as are several variations of cormorant and the noisy, orange-billed oyster catchers. Land otters seem to be the only animals besides the bears.

Went out again at 6 P.M. Back at ten. Rained all day today, not hard, but steady. Located a bear at eight-thirty. He came toward us grubbing along the beach. We were hidden in the edge of the spruce. At seventeen yards he turned broadside and I started my draw. He saw me out of the corner of his eye and made off. I got a bouncing-away shot at forty yards. I was not too disappointed since he was rather small. We are well wet down tonight. Having the last two king crabs for dinner.

Friday, May 11, 6 A.M.—On our way back to the big bay we left a few days ago. Almost all tracks are headed south and that is a country that is easy to hunt on foot. We are leaving at this hour because we need high tide to get the big boat out of the bay. Rained all night and is still coming down. Fog settling in now.

I learned a lesson yesterday in my encounter with the brownie. I thought he would stare at me at least long enough for me to complete my draw, but the first slow movement and he was gone in a flash. He was forty yards away before I could get the shot off, bounding like a rubber ball over the sharp rocks.

Those smaller bears move like lightning. He ran into Bob and Harley who were waiting up the beach, turned and came straight back past the place we had first seen him.

The bears are not eating grass. Those we have seen are eating sand fleas. These fleas are one half to three quarters of an inch long and look like a small shrimp. They live in about a foot of beach gravel. The bears lick fleas up so greedily that they swallow gravel along with them. The stomach of Bob's bear had a handful of rocks in it.

Last night we tried to eat all of the two king crabs but could not do it. Dan plans to make a crab omelet for breakfast with the leftovers.

We are constantly amazed at the bird life. Almost every day there are new ones. Yesterday it was the beautiful eider duck. Among the logs on the beaches we saw a wren that Ed's Alaskan bird book says is the Aleutian wren. It is the only bird here with a melodious song the book says, but I have not heard it utter a note.

The rain has stopped and the fog clearing. 5 P.M. Hunted the beaches on foot in the area where Bob shot his bear. One fresh track and that was all. Back at the boat at 2 P.M. and finished up the crab. Went out again an hour ago and rain started coming down in earnest. Decided to abandon this area and go to the east side of Afognak.

On our way now. May stop at the cannery at Port Williams for fuel and supplies. I believe this is the first day we have not seen at least one bear. We feel that we have this area well polluted with man scent and should move on to fresh territory.

9:15 P.M.—Sitting in the galley. Dan and Ed are playing cribbage. It is getting dark and fog is settling in the bay. We are anchored near the mouth of a creek in Perenosa Bay. Bob and Harley went up the creek to see if they could catch some rainbow trout. Ed and I will go after them in a few minutes with the skiff. Saw a fox on the beach as we dropped anchor.

Saturday, May 12—Back at the bay where we placed seal bait. We had the seals wired to logs. Bears had broken the wire and carried them off. In late afternoon Ed and I were hunting beaches afoot and saw a bear. We hid in the edge of the spruce and waited as he slowly fed toward us. The wind was not exactly right, however, and he became suspicious and swerved off.

I photographed a silver, or cross, fox this evening and also a seal this afternoon. Start hunting at daylight in the morning.

Sunday, May 13—Went in to Tonki Bay with the big boat this morning. Located two bears on a beach. Got into the skiff, went ashore, and started the stalk. Almost overran them as they walked part way up the steep, grassy mountain that rose from the beach. Ed and I climbed to get above and ahead of them. Up to this point we had seen only a back or a patch of fur. We were carefully approaching the crest of a ridge when I saw a bear's head look over about twenty feet above us. At the same time I heard a snarl below me and there was a brownie prancing on his front feet and not liking the intrusion at all. I realized that it was a sow and the one above us a two-year-old. Fortunately the cub ran off and the sow was satisfied by his escape and also disappeared over the ridge.

Saw two more brownies on a hillside about two miles inland. Wind was wrong. May try for them in the morning. Caught some Dolly Varden trout for dinner. Clouding over and wind starting to blow.

Monday, May 14—A strong wind came up during the night, blowing directly into the bay where we were anchored. Pulled anchor in early morning and had a rough trip to the little harbor where we are anchored now. Ed pulled in alongside a small crab-fishing boat that was in here for the same reason—weather.

We planned to be on our way to Kodiak now to catch the early morning plane, but weather will dictate the time. It has been raining hard all night. Got four king crabs from the fishermen and had a fine meal.

Guess I will have to call this hunt a blank. I have been within thirty yards of four bears. One of them fifteen feet. Something always seemed to go wrong. None of them were monsters. Saw a great many Afognak elk yesterday. Some of them down close to the beach. Ed stalked some and shot blunts at them. Have picked up many shed horns.

10:30 P.M.—Still confined to our little harbor. Still raining hard, although the wind has let up somewhat. If it does not get worse we will make a run for Kodiak early in the morning. A lazy day. Have everything packed. Wrote cards, took a nap, and ate the day out.

Tuesday, May 15, 9 P.M.—Up at 3 A.M. this morning. Weather better so we pulled anchor and headed for Kodiak. Got here at 9 A.M. and tied up at the dock. We all had showers in a barbershop. Did some shopping.

I called home to see if I was needed and got orders to stay until I got a bear. Ed will give me a few days' bear hunting in between seal hunts and I have good hopes of getting a brownie. Bob left at five-thirty tonight for home.

We will be here tomorrow for some repairs on the boat. May leave in the afternoon—if not, on Thursday morning.

Thursday, May 17—Left the city of Kodiak at 4 P.M. heading northeast on the outside of Marmot Island. Ten thousand seals were reported here, but they turned out to be five thousand sea lions. Several beaches are covered solid with them.

Am sitting topside in a bright sun. Not a cloud in the sky. There is a slight breeze blowing and some rather heavy swells running. At eight-thirty we are rounding the north tip of Marmot to the mainland of Afognak to search the shores for bear. We will hunt north of where we were last Monday.

1 P.M.—Checked a whale that had washed up on the outside beach of Marmot Island. Apparently it went ashore last winter. Got some handsome ivory teeth from the jaw and pondered over the scrimshaw work done by becalmed sailors at sea in days gone by.

9 P.M.—Anchored in Seal Bay, really a part of Tonki Bay. The weather was closing in with an offshore wind and cloudy sky. Bow in hand, I walked the beach for a while. On the open beach ahead a dark object was identified as a bear. Our plan was to circle through the spruce and come out on the beach where the bear was.

He was about two hundred yards away, digging sand fleas and not greatly concerned about anything else since he rarely looked up. It was not possible to make the approach through the spruce as a cliff broke off between us. However, some large rocks furnished cover for the first hundred yards, and a few smaller ones from there on.

Ed had forgotten his .375 backing gun but had his .22 Hornet seal gun. Harley had nothing. I had my bow and a 44 Magnum. The question was, who was backing whom, and with what?

We took our hip boots off and made the stalk in stocking feet. There was a small rock near the bear that hid his head from us when it was down after the sand fleas. Almost no cover between us otherwise. Fortunately he was busy pawing among the kelp. Only once did he look up. We happened to be motionless at that time and he went right back to his meal.

We finally reached a point thirty yards from him that seemed to be the spot for action. Between us was noisy, loose gravel. The bear was broadside, but facing me slightly. His front leg was slightly back covering part of his chest. One more move and he would be in position for my favorite rib, lung shot.

The move turned out to be a look to scan the beach and there we were. Brownie ran off with much woofing and did not show up again.

Friday, May 18, 3 P.M.—Stopped at Port Williams and deposited some mail. Anchored in Big Bay now. Ed is changing oil and filters.

8 P.M.—Just came back from hunting the beaches that were so productive a week ago. Not any tracks since we left here. Disappointing and no need to spend any more time here. Plan to leave for the Alaska Peninsula at 3 A.M. tomorrow. Got some T-bone steaks and some Dungeness crabs at the cannery at Port Williams.

Saturday, May 19, 7 P.M.—Made a start for the Peninsula at two-thirty this morning. A southwestern wind made it impossible. Came back to Big Bay and are anchored peacefully here in the sun. Boating, like flying, is unpredictable. Plans can be made, but it is not always possible to follow them through.

9 P.M.—After the wind eased up we left Big Bay, came south, and went along the west side of Afognak to Paramanof Bay. Anchored in a small bay out of the wind about 200 yards off a small beach.

We were having coffee and cookies before leaving for a hunt in the skiff when I looked out the galley window to see a bear walking across the beach. He went into some alders that came down along one side of a creek. We rowed over, made a stalk, but the wind was wrong and he sneaked over the mountain through a draw. He was not a big bear.

We did some miles in the skiff. Examined beaches and found but few tracks. Went into a bay that drains an inland lake. Saw Dungeness crabs on the bottom in water five to eight feet deep. Speared a dozen with the long-handled spring gaff. Plan to go up this creek at daylight in the morning. There could be bears in the meadows surrounding this lake.

Sunday, May 20, 5 P.M.—Up at 6 A.M. Hunted with the skiff until two-thirty, but did not see a bear. Went around Ban Island and dug some littleneck clams. Saw and photographed two foxes. These are not good beaches for bear. No kelp. There seems to be no waterfowl either.

Left Paramanof Bay and just got in here to Malina Bay. Saw a single bear and a sow and cub high on the mountain as we came in. They made off as soon as they saw the boat. Planned to go ashore and hike in to Afognak Lake. Just got our gear on when the rain started. Decided to steam the clams instead.

Flowers are beginning to bloom and the brown hillsides are dappled with light green.

9:30 P.M.—Ate a mess of clams and then hiked over the rise toward Lake Afognak. Did not get to the lake, but looked over a little country. Very little bear sign, but quite a lot of elk activity, although we did not see any. Took the skiff and hunted down toward the end of the bay. Bad wind came up and we turned back. Finished up the littleneck clams. Very delicious. Cloudy all day and cold. Rain off and on. Tops of the hills have been in the clouds all day.

Monday, May 21, 8 A.M.—Rain and strong wind all night. Everybody slept in. Our generator quit working several days ago, delaying our move to the Peninsula. Voltage has dropped and we are now lifting anchor to run around the corner to a cannery in Raspberry Straits. Rain has let up but the wind is still blowing. Everything lashed down for the trip, although we will be on the lee side of the blow.

Ed climbed a cliff along a beach yesterday and was amusing himself rolling rocks down on the beach. Harley and I were on the beach appraising the results when the larger ones fell on logs. A big rock weighing five or six tons perched precariously near the edge was finally toppled over and came down thundering with earsplitting pandemonium as it crashed into the logs. Ed later told us of his efforts in dislodging this big rock. He put his feet on the rock and his shoulder against the bank and "gave it everything I had." He felt it move slightly and then "gave it a little bit more" and down it came. He didn't explain where "the little bit more" came from.

These rocks are hard on arrows. I have gone through two dozen blunts on this trip and have just six broadheads left. My bow is holding up well and so is the eight-arrow quiver. This has been a rugged test for it.

Yesterday we found a skiff pulled up on shore beside a Fish and Wildlife shack. Bear hunters had been there. We found a freshly killed bear skull, a fox carcass, and a skinned seal. This is the first evidence of humans we have seen on this hunt. Not even an old tin can or the remains of a camp site. Found a wrecked fishing boat on the beach in Malina Bay.

3 P.M.—Tied up at a cannery having their electrician repair the generator. A short in the brush holder. It was a good idea to take it out of the boat. It definitely needed a cleaning job if nothing else. Raining and still blowing. Very cooperative people at the cannery. I left my films there for them to run tonight. They will forward them to Kodiak for me. Left the cannery at 6 P.M. and dropped anchor here in a small bay. Hiked through a valley up a creek, but no bear signs. Plan to leave here at 3 A.M. in the morning.

Tuesday, May 22, 6 A.M.—Heard Ed start the engine at 4 A.M. Got up at five when the boat started to roll. We are headed for the Alaska Peninsula. We were wrong in believing it is closed to hunting. I did not know last night if we would go this way or to Kodiak. If to Kodiak, I would admit defeat and go back home. Dan has not been feeling well (the cook) and would like to get off the boat, but Ed is about as bullheaded as I am and he is the boss and we are heading for the Peninsula.

This surely stretches out this hunt and were it not for needing pictures I could have taken Dan's side and we probably would be heading for Kodiak. If I can get pictures of taking a bear, this will make the finest film in our library and I am pushing my luck to this end. Still overcast.

10 P.M.—Just got back from hunting with the skiff. Got here to Alinchak Bay at nine-thirty. Saw a sow and two cubs on the beach. Would have stopped for pictures, but it was raining. It has been raining almost all day. Chilly, too. There is snow on the hills. Saw no bears from the skiff.

Wednesday, May 23—On our way with the *Maid* southwest. Not enough bear sign here. Going back to where we saw the bears coming in. It is still heavily clouded over and some fog, but no rain.

9 P.M.—Ran into Puale Bay early this morning. This is where I killed the big brownie two years ago. Hunted by skiff and found the tracks of a medium-sized bear in a mud flat. It was fairly fresh as the tide had been out only a few hours. Failed to find him, however. Cooked up a mulligan and planned to hunt bears between four and dark.

Had an hour of sunshine this morning, but later we had rain and at four o'clock the wind started blowing the raindrops horizontally and we could not go out. Two crab boats came in here out of the storm and one anchored beside us. I took a nap, drank a lot of coffee, and dried my gear. Everything is wet down.

Keeping camera, gear, and feathers dry is a serious problem. Cameras are carried in my backpack which is not entirely waterproof. Have a heavy rubber pouch that I chuck the whole business in and tie it tight. Have to keep a plastic bag over the feathers of my arrows, even in fair weather, to protect them from spray.

Thursday, May 24—Did a skiff hunt for four hours, but saw nothing. Had a lunch about 2 P.M. and then went bear hunting again. Got back at 8 P.M. Saw quite a few tracks, but no bears.

Our eating habits are very irregular. Governed by the tide and weather and not so much by the hour. Low tide is about the middle of the day now. Had a few hours of sunshine this morning and then rain again.

» «

Friday, May 25—This was the big day. The sun was shining early and kept on shining all day. It was a good day for bears, seals, king crabs, and pictures. This was perhaps the most thrilling day of my hunting career, and not without some humor too.

Our hunting day did not start early. The crab pot was lifted first to yield three fine king crabs. One average size and two monsters. Next we took the skiff into Bear Bay, a rocky, shallow site with a short beach about three hundred yards long. As we rounded the point and the beach came into view, a fine bear chose this time to walk out of the alders into sight on the sand.

We were a good half mile away. The engine was quickly shut off while we studied the bear through glasses. He busied himself pawing and eating in the sand and kelp while Ed slowly and quietly rowed toward the rocky shore about two hundred yards beyond the edge of the beach. If we could make this without being seen, we would be hidden by a small point that came between us and the bear.

Harley watched the bear with glasses to alert Ed to stop rowing when the bear looked our way. It was touch and go. Brownie would paw and eat and lie down intermittently. The warm sunshine on his heavy winter fur doubtless brought out sleepy dreams of great summer days ahead gorging on spawning salmon.

Before we reached shore he waded out into the ocean, rolled over on his back, and, with his head and four feet sticking out, enjoyed the luxury of a salt-water bath. The tide was out. The narrow rocky shore met the thick alders at high-tide line. The mountain started up steeply from there.

While rowing across the bay I had shot some 16-mm film of the bear. On shore Harley was to pinch-hit as photographer. I reasoned that he could cover our stalk from a point some distance from us and would need the telephoto lens. As it turned out, the 25-mm would have been proper. Mounted underneath the movie camera lens, I have a 35-mm sequence camera operated by a push button on the fore part of the gunstock mount. This camera, a Robot Royal, will expose twenty-four pictures on one wind at the press of the button. In this way with one operator, both still pictures and movies can be taken. The 50-mm lens cover the same area as the 25-mm movie.

Leaving the skiff, we made our way toward a point that would afford a view of the beach and the bear. Ed and I ahead and Harley with his .270 and the cameras about twenty-five yards behind. When we were some fifty yards from the skiff we saw the bear's blond ears coming toward us. The wind was right. We motioned Harley to squat and be still. Ahead of us, there was a heaven-sent, big rock about four by four feet. Hunkering down we made our way to it. This was the only cover on this entire shore and we were very lucky that it was placed so conveniently.

We both knelt down in the shadow of the rock, Ed a bit to my left and I on one knee with the arrow on the string. We kept our heads down, sure that he would pass on the ocean side, and waited in great anticipation (not to say, apprehension) for the appearance of this alder king.

He was a good-sized bear. We had concluded that while watching him, through glasses, crossing the bay. Up to now, however, our only close look at him had been his ears and there seemed to be quite a space between them.

All kinds of thoughts go through one's mind in suspense-filled moments like this. Would he bolt like the one did two weeks ago when he saw me slowly start to draw the arrow or would I have only a frontal shot when he saw us and stared in amazement? We had to stop about ten feet from the rock because of some sticks that lay ahead. He would see us before he was even with the rock.

I was determined to place the Razorhead through the ribs close up to the shoulder. This would be a clean kill. There could be no excuses. I worried about the three strands of my bowstring that had chafed off on sharp barnacles as I got out of the skiff. Would it hold for this one shot?

We waited. Finally, he was in sight. Twenty-five feet away and coming closer. He turned toward us and looked us over, standing still. We remained as motionless and quiet as stumps and did not register in the bear's consciousness. We

*We are hidden behind
a boulder as the bear
approaches along the
water's edge.*

He continued along.

*The bear turns and
looks at us a few
seconds.*

He decides that we are something that came in with the tide. My bow is being drawn.

The arrow struck well and he is preparing to leave the area.

Weak hindquarters spell ebbing strength.

He expired on the open beach, not able to get into the thick alders.

He dwarfs my six foot height.

could almost see his mind working—"odd pieces of driftwood came in on the last tide. . . ." (Stationary objects are not considered harmful by the animal kingdom.) He turned broadside and walked to pass us. The sixty-five-pound Kodiak bow came back with the ease of a toy. He did not notice the movement. The Razorhead sank to the feathers near the front leg. The impact was considerable and as he roared and exploded down the shore straight toward Harley, we wondered what the outcome would be.

Harley, however, endowed with the tradition of good showmanship, stood his ground operating the camera until the bear began to fill the viewer and it seemed prudent to abandon the camera for the rifle. Cameras are delicate instruments and should be put down carefully. But life is precious. The open shore, between the steep alder-covered bank and the water, measured a scant twenty feet and Harley's position was squarely in the middle of it. The bear's direction of travel was also right down the middle.

In some alarm we saw Harley, legs and arms flailing the air, cameras in one hand, rifle in the other, trying to scurry up the slope to leave the open shore to the bear. Ed yelled in his booming voice, "Take pictures. I'm covering you."

At any rate, the bear passed him at full speed. A short way beyond it tried to climb into the alders, but could not make it and rolled back down the slope near the skiff. He was dead in less than a minute after he was hit. The arrow nicked a rib close to the front leg, passed through a lung, cut a heavy artery near the liver, went through the diaphragm, and just through the skin near the back ribs on the far side.

We took pictures and left him to go back to the *Valiant Maid* for a bite to eat. It was high tide when we got back and his feet were in the water. With ropes slung under him we were able to roll him into the skiff and winch him aboard for skinning on the aft deck.

With the carcass intact he tipped the scales at 810 pounds. The skin squared nine feet and the length and width of the skull measured twenty-seven inches. Ed paced the distance of the shot at twenty feet. The bear ran ninety yards from where he was hit.

It has been a very busy day, a very exciting one, and gratifying. A bear at twenty feet looks big when one is down on his knees looking up. Again it was proved that an arrow in the right spot will do the job quickly and humanely, regardless of the size of the animal. This was a day when everything worked out just right. The sun was out all day and the bear did his part in coming to us. Actually, it would have been a difficult stalk if he had remained on the open beach.

It takes breaks like this to be successful with either the bow or gun, except that with a bow the circumstances have to be more refined and the timing exact. This makes the fifth bear that we have been within thirty yards of. The other four times something went wrong. The range handicap of the bow is great, but the thrills of getting close to your target make up for it. A good-sized, bow-legged brownie strutting toward one at twenty-five feet is a thrill well worth the time and effort. It's a great privilege to match wits with a noble animal such as this that nature has so ably equipped to take care of itself.

Saturday, May 26—This was an easy day. Fleshing the bear skin. Cleaning the skull. Cleaning up in general. There was time to make a summary of brown bear hunting:

> They have only two enemies. Man and larger brown bears. As a result, small bears are jittery and alert, always expecting a larger bear to pounce upon them. The big ones are easier to stalk, having more self-confidence and an admirable cockiness that commands respect.

Chapter 9

KISPIOX RIVER - 1963

Again, the Kispiox River country was chosen for an adventure. *Life* magazine was interested in doing a story on hunting grizzly bears with bow and arrow.

Don Moser was the writer and Robert Halmi, the photographer. Love and Lee were the outfitters. Bill Love the head man with Kolbjorn Eide as assistant.

KISPIOX RIVER BRITISH COLUMBIA, 1963

Wednesday, September 25, 7 P.M.—Huddled in front of our campfire on Swan Lake where a creek leaves to drain into Stevens Lake. We flew in last evening in two "Beaver" flights and had camp up before dark. Our party consists of Bill Love, outfitter of Love & Lee; his helper and guide, Kolbjorn Eide; Don Moser, a writer from the staff of *Life* magazine; Bob Halmi, photographer; and myself.

This morning we hunted the creek between here and Stevens Lake. No bears were sighted, but lots of sign and plenty of sockeye salmon. Had lunch on Stevens and rested an hour before hunting back up the creek.

At the lower end of the creek, where I shot a grizzly two years ago, we surprised two medium-sized bears. Perhaps I should say that they surprised us as they apparently winded us and ran into some alders nearby.

We were on high ground and watched them for about ten minutes. Finally one of them picked up a fish and started up the trail we were on, the second bear following him. They were about seventy yards away when I started after them and closed the distance to about thirty-five yards. Bob and the others stayed back on high ground. The bear with the fish lay down in a depression on the trail to eat his catch. The other bear kept walking away and I had about decided to come out from behind a tree to try to maneuver for a clear shot when the far one turned back in my direction, whoofing weakly, sensing something was wrong. He was about twenty-five yards from me when I took a peek from behind my tree. The bear stood up for a better view and I heard Bob's camera clicking. I tried to get into shooting position but the first bear saw me and they both made off up the creek and we did not see them again.

About halfway back, however, we were startled by a good-sized, very dark grizzly bellowing, crashing brush, and charging toward us from part way up the hill across the creek. She came down to the edge, made three jumps along the

We flew in last evening in two "Beaver" flights.

Camp was set up before dark.

bank, turned and went back up the hill. I saw her beat the trunk of a tree with her front paw. She then made off and we saw no more of her. I think she had cubs up the tree, or maybe was just giving vent to her anger.

Don was greatly impressed with her savage actions. I was, too. Don says he plans to carry a rope after this—to get down out of trees. It rained almost all day.

Thursday, September 26, 7:30 P.M.—Cloudy this morning and a spot of rain but turned into a fine sunny day. Shirt-sleeve weather. We thought it best to rest the Swan-Stevens creek area and explore the Swan Lake creeks. This we did with Bill as guide while Kolbjorn went over into the Brown Bear Lake area to explore the creeks there. He reported no fish in the creeks and no bear sign.

We hunted two creeks. First one had no fish and no bears. Second creek, a short one, had fish but apparently only a lone bear, a big one. Because of dense cover along the creek we did not spend much time there but came back to camp about three-thirty and caught some rainbow trout in the creek here. Ravens are screaming at us from trees close by. Geese are honking their way south and whisky-jacks talk to us here at camp. Saw a water ouzel today.

Friday, September 27, 7:30 P.M.—Decided not to start early today. In this third year of hunting here we have seen bears only in the middle of the day. Left camp at ten-thirty this morning. Saw the two bears again we'd seen on Wednes-

They were fishing in the creek and put on a fine show for us.

day. They were fishing in the creek and put on a fine show for us for an hour or so. I finally took a shot at one but missed him. Bob Halmi snapped about a hundred pictures.

The bears caught fish, ate them, walked logs, made splashing rushes at fish in the shallow water. They would sit in the water after an unsuccessful rush and look about in seeming embarrassment to see if any other bears had seen them. It was a great spectacle.

Saturday, September 28, 9 P.M.—We saw seven grizzlies today. Went down the creek to Stevens Lake, and saw nothing. En route, fished at the river mouth and caught several big Dolly Varden, a rainbow, and some coho.

While fishing Bill looked upriver and saw a bear. We went after him and it turned out to be the twins again. Bob took many pictures. They ran into the brush.

After lunch we went up the river again and saw a big grizzly fishing. He caught a fish and took it into the brush across the river. Got myself into position for a shot and waited for an hour but he did not show and we continued on our way.

We decided to move camp to the Stevens Lake area where Jack Lee will meet us with the horses. Little use to stay here as there is nothing on Swan and the lower end of the river is best for bear. We will portage boats and all over to Stevens so as not to stir up the river.

Making our way along the trail we saw two bears, one a big one, across a small lake. They were going in our direction and we hastened to head them off. Our timing was off one minute, however, as they crossed the river at the end of the lake and went up the hill about eighty yards from us. I had just started a stalk when a third one came from the river.

Unfortunately, he saw me and so did the others—all of them went over the ridge. They were all fine bears. One of them a really big, beautiful one.

We portaged one boat and some gear over to Stevens Lake this evening.

Sunday, September 29, 7 P.M.—Have camp established now on the Kispiox River across from the lower end of Stevens Lake. Got an early start this morning and took the big boat and all gear across the neck to Stevens. Kolbjorn Eide is an extremely husky, thirty-five-year-old Norwegian. Six feet, two inches and about 205 pounds. In dragging the boats overland, about one half mile, he practically ran with them. We got to the lake with all the gear at noon, had lunch, and then started to hunt up the river but the wind was wrong and we came back. It started to rain and we sat in a downpour going the length of the lake to the trail. The portage from Stevens to the Kispiox is three fourths of a mile through willow and high brush and grass. By the time we got here we were really wet.

The advantage of this spot is that we can hunt Stevens Creek and also the lower end of Club Creek which is the only part of that stream that has any fish in it. It is a better camp, too. We have our tents under a big spruce right beside the river on the edge of a grassy clearing. The remains of an Indian cabin are here and a grave with pole fences around it bears the following inscription: "Martha Johnson Gowing. Died April 15, 1877."

This is where Jack will meet us with the horses in about two days. Plans are to go by horse one day and then use rubber boats to float down the Kispiox to Jack's camp.

We dragged the boat overland.

Tuesday, October 1, 5 P.M.—Up in a machan at the mouth of Club Creek, I can look down on nine Dolly Varden trout ranging from five to nine pounds. They are strung on a stick with a fifteen-pound nylon line tied to it which runs up to my platform. The string will be tied to a finger when I crawl into my sleeping bag. It is cloudy but I hope for no rain. We have had plenty of it since moving from Swan Lake. This morning the rain stopped, the sun showed for a few hours, and then disappeared again. Everything we have is soggy and damp.

We came up here to Club Creek this morning and discovered that some fish we caught yesterday had been taken by the grizzlies. This prompted the building of the platform in the hope that they would come again this evening or in the morning.

I did not write yesterday. Too wet and cold. Hunting with Kolbjorn we saw a bear across the upper river. I went down to the water's edge to get a close shot if he came in to the river to fish. About this time I discovered I was facing a good-sized mama bear and two cubs. She must have winded me and was whoofing to keep the small fry in the brush. I got out of there.

These three make thirteen grizzlies we have seen, not counting the twins we have seen three times. This latest trio were not the same ones we had seen before.

Wednesday, October 2, 5 P.M.—Up in our platform again. Bob and Don are with me and the weather is wonderful. Last night was a wild one, however, from several points of view. Rain started at 6 P.M. and kept up all night.

While docking the boat in the brush here early last evening I leaned my bow against an alder. The boat came up easier than we thought it would, resulting in

Bill stepping on the upper recurve. I heard it crack and the glass beside the string groove lifted. . . . I wound some rubber bands tightly around it and shot it several times. It seemed O.K.

At six fifty-five a big sow led three cubs across the river on a log about fifty yards from me upstream. A family we had not seen before. She dropped into quite deep water and caught a fish and the whole family went into the bush to eat it.

At the same time a good bear came out on a log about 100 yards farther up-

A good bear came out on a log.

stream. He looked the situation over carefully and then came straight down and started eating one of the fish on our pole. He was only fifteen yards from me and down at a rather sharp angle. I loosed an arrow and there was an earsplitting racket as that upper limb let go.

The arrow slapped the bow making still more noise and landed in the rocks about three feet off. The bear had a fish in his mouth and squatted facing me in a semisitting position, front legs spread wide and looking up to see where the noise came from. He seemed reluctant to leave the fish but in a few seconds made off into the alders dragging the pole and four fish still tied to it.

Rain was now coming down harder than ever and we were tempted to jump in the boat and head for camp. The wind was blowing upstream and soon the big sow was out fishing again. She caught a fish and was going ashore on our side when she caught our scent. It was nearly dark as she came up behind us in the bush, whoofing and snorting. She kept this up all night, intermittently, and did not leave until eight-thirty this morning.

We had no choice but to remain all night in our perch, although we were completely soaked from the rain. My fish bear, a beautiful black, silvery specimen, kept fishing. We heard bears all night and saw several upriver after daybreak this morning. We hope to come back up here again this afternoon, in good light. Bob Halmi is ready with cameras and Don Moser has his pencil poised. I will have my spare bow.

Thursday, October 3, Noon—At six-thirty last evening the twins made their appearance on the log upstream. Shortly after, the big sow who stayed with us last night, came out also. She fished for a short time and then something seemed wrong with her cubs on our side of the river. She roared and bounced across like an express train, grunting and whoofing.

She came up near us and began to huff. In the meantime my fisheater came out after another fish from our pole. I released an arrow which went into the river. The upper-bow tip hit a limb and again there was noise as my arrow went astray.

This naturally made the bear jittery and he raced into the brush and then went fishing upstream. He had no luck, however, and in ten minutes was crawling out on our side again and I was sure he would make a sneak through the brush to get our fish.

This proved to be the case. He stood facing me at a slight angle. I shot through the upper part of the shoulder blade, down through the lungs, and punched through the hide on the far side low. He jumped into the water going only twelve yards before he collapsed. Not a monster; 250 to 300 pounds, but a fine coat of fur.

We got back to camp at 9 P.M. and were greeted by Jack and Frances who had just arrived with the horses from Corral Creek.

We took pictures and skinned out the bear this morning. Will leave here early in the morning by horse. Float the Kispiox from the canyon down and reach Corral Creek in late evening. Don and Bob want to catch the Sunday plane from Smithers.

Same Day, 5 P.M.—We are all sitting on a hillside about 100 yards above the upper creek. It rained all the way here and until a few minutes ago. Drops coming down from the trees now.

This is our last evening, and we plan to stay until dark, hoping to see the whole

We skinned the bear this morning.

show again and get more pictures. If we run into the mad sow that has been giving us trouble, I am sure we will have to shoot our way out of here. Last evening there was a mighty roar up this way. A grizzly dispute probably.

Same Day, 9:30 P.M.—We ran into a fair bear on the second creek, made a sneak for pictures but she had two cubs with her and we backed out of there undetected. We saw the mad sow at the mouth of the creek but she only huffed and puffed and did not come too near us.

I believe we have seen twenty-three different bears, many of them several times. We are leaving for Corral Creek tomorrow.

Saturday, October 5, 11 A.M.—At Corral Creek. Came all the way from Stevens Lake and got here at 10:30 P.M. The trip was uneventful. We did not float from the canyon. It got too late. Don and Bob are going to Hazelton to catch a plane at Smithers. I have asked them to get me reservations to fly out next Sunday. I want to spend a week here with Jack trying to get pictures of that big grizzly. Two baits have been out for some time. We have not checked them recently.

Sunday, October 6, 8:30 P.M.—Don and Bob left yesterday and the silence is noticeable. I spent the day drying gear and getting rested. The walk from the canyon to Sweetin, Friday after dark, stiffened up some rarely used muscles of my body.

I never knew that horses could walk so fast. I kept a firm grip on Keno's tail

We went from Stevens Lake to Jack's camp at Corral Creek by horse.

and he pulled me up the ridges. In turn, I braked for him going down. He is a friendly, husky pack horse. Once I stumbled over a log and pitched forward headlong to bury my head between his rear legs. The good old square-sterned horse plodded right ahead.

I got my boots dry for the first time since we left Terrace.

There is a man here from Los Angeles, a photographer wanting pictures of grizzlies. He and another guide have been watching baits Jack placed for me. Last Friday this fellow shot a fine bear at one of our baits and Jack is plenty mad and so am I. Today he and Bill left for Stevens Lake. I hope one of those mad bears eats him up.

Fine weather today. The first frost of the season last night. That took care of the black flies.

Jack and I went riding this morning. Rode up to Clifford Creek and checked a bait that has been there for four weeks but nothing has touched it.

Went down Clifford to the Kispiox and caught five big cohoes to replenish another bait that has been reduced to bones. We then checked the far bait where the photographer shot the bear. Not much left of the bait but the bear carcass was there.

Tuesday we have planned to go back to a burn and hunt moose. We will take a pack horse and chain saw and build a raft to fish a lake that has not been fished before. I look forward to this as it should make a fine movie. I look forward to this week also. The pressure is off with the *Life* job done. Am alone in this beautiful cabin and lonesome, too, but dry and snug.

I like hunting with Jack. We understand each other and I can learn a great deal by observing his woods lore, which he acquired the hard way during forty years in the bush.

My day was further brightened by three letters from my wife.

Monday, October 7, 8 P.M.—A lazy day. Jack and I built blinds at both lower baits and then checked the upper one. This bait has been out for four weeks. The photographer who shot the bear was supposed to take pictures only. I can now only hope that a bear will come to eat the carcass he shot.

Nothing to do from here on except check baits. If a bear starts feeding, sit by it and try to get some pictures.

Tomorrow we ride into moose country with a pack horse.

Tuesday, October 8, 8:30 P.M.—Rain this morning. I wanted to take pictures of the raft building and fishing, so we did not go. Instead Jack and I hunted moose east of Nobody Much Creek. We hunted from horseback but gave it up because every time we separated our horses kept in touch with each other by whinnying. This afternoon we hunted afoot up Clifford Creek. Saw good sign but no moose.

No bears have yet come to the bait and nothing can be done about it. There is an abundance of berries this year to lure them afield and no humpback salmon for them to pick up along the Kispiox.

Thursday, October 10, 8:30 P.M.—Did not write last evening. Three men from San Francisco whom I had met two years ago stopped in and stayed until midnight.

Yesterday we rode into the untried lake. We got the raft built O.K. but then couldn't get the motor started, so Jack carved a paddle with the chain saw and we fished for three hours without a single strike.

This morning we checked the baits (no bears) and then rode out to the hairpin to fish. Jack caught a steelhead, about eight pounds. I had a big one hooked but was using an improvised swivel and it broke. Caught a dozen Dolly Varden trout. The weather has been beautiful since I have been here at Corral Creek. How nice it would have been to have had it like this at Stevens Lake.

Friday, October 11, 8 P.M.—Checked baits this morning. Thought we had a winner on the last one as the bait was torn apart. But on close examination discovered it was wolves that had been at it. This ends my chances for bear pictures as we leave tomorrow.

We stopped at a place below Sweetin to fish for a little while. I caught a steelhead, thirty-nine inches long. No scale to weigh it. Will freeze it and ship it home for mounting. It is a beauty.

Will head for Hazelton in the morning to get checked out with my bear and fish and get cleaned up for the flight out Sunday.

Aboard Plane, Sunday, October 13—I saw Bill Love today and got a report on his five days at Stevens Lake. No rain at all but few bears on Swan Creek.

The big, black sow had moved over to Stevens and she charged them vigorously with much roaring. She was coming strong, Bill said, and he moved sideways to clear a tree in case he was forced to shoot. He said he thinks that his quick movement may have changed her mind as she stopped at thirty feet, thought things over, and turned back. At this time the cubs, who had been across the creek, joined her and they went off into the bush. She must have followed them to camp as she was bellowing in the bushes behind their tent that evening.

Plenty of Dolly Varden at the mouth of the creek. They baited bears with fish and got good pictures of two sizable specimens at the place where I shot mine from the machan. Bill says that bears prefer coho to Dolly Varden and that the sockeyes had gone—even the upper creek had coho in it. Bill found my light meter on the portage between Swan and Stevens where I pushed the boat.

» «

Letter from Fred Bear to His Wife   10-15-63

On my way to Calgary to join Glenn St. Charles for the bighorn sheep hunt. Will give you a report since leaving Hazelton.

I had a bear hide, a frozen steelhead, and some trinkets when I landed in Vancouver. . . . The bear hide I sent to Jonas Brothers and the fish I shipped to Chuck Kroll. Ask him to put it in the freezer and hold it for me for mounting.

Also a box will come with some trinkets I bought from the Indians in Hazelton. In it is a plastic bag containing a coho head and a steelhead tail. Chuck should open this bag, add salt and water to cover everything, leave the bag open, and place it in a cool place awaiting my return.

One of the birchbark wastebaskets is for you and one for Julia. The horn ladle is for Chuck from Wilford. It came from the Indian cabin in the meadow at Stevens Lake. He will remember.

Don Moser (*Life* writer) had asked me to call him when I got out of the bush. This I did. He says he has 3,500 words written that he likes very much and thinks that I will, too. Expects it will be published about mid-November. Says they have some fine pictures.

Don, the *Life* magazine writer, turned out to be quite a guy. I had misapprehensions about him before the hunt, but he took hardships like a man and helped with the work. We had lots of rain at both Stevens and Swan Lakes and only open-front, lean-to tents. While our campfire was magnum size it was useless to try to dry clothes with one side getting wetter while the other dried by the fire. In short, we were, at best, damp most of the time. Bob Halmi (photographer) suffered most as he had only blue jeans and no long underwear. He did not complain, however.

In the lush country where Jack and Bill live in the valley near Hazelton, the soil is rich and rainfall heavy. We had strawberries fresh from the garden at Jack's place Saturday evening following a dinner of wild goose shot by Jack's son-in-law.

The shelves in their basements bend with home-canned food. Frances (Jack's wife) said that last fall she had canned over 300, 1½ quart jars of moose. We had some at Corral Creek and it was good. Bins hold apples, potatoes, cabbage, and squash. I saw raspberry stalks 2 feet higher than my head; so top heavy that the branches had to be tied together at the tops to keep them upright.

Their homes are spotless. Almost before the door is open in welcome, out comes the coffee pot followed by the frying pan.

Old barrelhead eluded me again this year. He was shot at twice this spring and seen late this summer. Am not sure if I mentioned in my notes that Jack found his tracks on a creek above the canyon on his way up to get us at Stevens Lake. He did not have a chance to investigate in detail as old Duke was mired up to his belly in the mud with a heavy pack on his back.

We had planned to check it out on the way back but we got a late start from Stevens, had trouble with packs, were short two horses and ran into some hornets.

We did find his tracks, however. He seems to have put on some weight in the last two years since his tracks are more rounded than before. He is probably suffering from fallen arches because of overweight from the heavy fare of fish and wild berries that are so abundant this year.

I am glad he had sense enough to move upriver away from the hunters who will go into the Sweetin River by road. Only with horses can one go beyond there and he is about ten miles above this.

You have probably guessed that I have plans to take his trail again next year. Jack and Bill and I spent several evenings planning a foolproof campaign. The assault begins in the early summer, reaches a crescendo in early September and old flatfoot falls to my Razorhead about October first. His hide is undoubtedly covered with scars from bullet holes and fights and his gut loaded with tapeworms but if his head is as big as it looked to me two years ago, he is big enough.

The emphasis on another trip is to make the greatest of all grizzly films. This can be done from carefully located platforms in trees at prominent fishing spots along Swan and Stevens creeks. Liberties can be taken with those sows from a platform without danger of having to shoot one, and the cubs would make very cute pictures. There are many brown bear movies but I know of no grizzly films. I did not carry my movie equipment on this bear hunt at any time. Did not want to mess up the still pictures.

We also want to explore a good-sized creek that flows into the Kispiox about fifteen miles north of Stevens. Jack took a military party up there with horses some years ago to locate a wrecked plane and found many fish and good bear signs. Coming into Calgary—more later. . . .

Chapter 10

INDIA - 1963

India: Land of romance and colorful history. One of the oldest wellsprings of mankind. Two thirds the size of Europe. The land of Buddha, the Bengal Lancers, Gunga Din, Mowgli the Jungle Boy, and Sher Kan the great Asian tiger.

In the spring of 1963 a New York photographer and I went to India to hunt tigers and make a film of the event.

We were guests of the Maharaja of Bundi at Phoolsagar Palace, Rajasthan, India, for eleven days and during this time I had to adjust from a cool Michigan climate and typical American schedule of breakfast at eight, lunch at noon, and dinner at seven, to one hundred degrees heat, breakfast at ten, lunch at two-thirty, and dinner anywhere from 10 P.M. to 2:30 A.M.!

We stopped off at Istanbul, Turkey, en route to see the ruins of marble monuments still standing at OK Meydan (the place of the arrow) on a hill on the outskirts of Istanbul. These pillars mark the distance of arrows shot from Turkish flight bows by the sultans of the fourteenth century.

Saturday Eve, April 20, Istanbul, Turkey—We are sitting at the "Cumburiyet Pavyonu" waiting for the belly dancers to appear. Our host is the Minister of News, Broadcast, and Publicity. The light is poor and the table very small. A thousand people here in a place big enough for three hundred. The performance is scheduled for sometime between 1 and 3 A.M. and is supposed to be the best in Turkey.

I hope I will be awake when the girls come out. As nearly as I can calculate, jet lag has us eight hours from our accustomed schedule already and the prospect of seeing this show through half-closed eyelids is not what I would have planned on.

We may not go to Pakistan as planned. Will try to set up a boar hunt here instead. I have just asked the minister about the flight-distance monuments at OK Meydan. He says these ancient relics may be involved in a housing development in that area but hopes we can find some of them tomorrow.

People are still coming in. Both men and women dress as we do at home and also dance the same way except here we see no one doing the Twist. The minister talks as we wait for the show to begin, sipping potent Turkish liquor. He tells us his countrymen suspect that Kennedy made a deal with Khrushchev to take our missile sites out of Turkey. He hopes not. They would like to have them here.

A woman sits outside the door of the men's room and dispenses toilet paper for a price. . . .

Sunday—We have just returned from a boat ride, guest of Orhan Gunsiray, top cinema actor and producer in Turkey. Our cruise took us along the Bosporus, the strait separating Europe from Asia. There were five in the party, including the Minister of Tourism and the man in charge of the boat. The waterway is about eighteen miles long and it took us three or four hours to sail this distance. We stopped at one point and bought a loaf of bread, wine, and several kinds of fruits and nuts for our lunch. The weather was cool and once it started to rain, so the skipper rigged up a canvas shelter for us. Gunsiray was handsome and a genial host but conversation was limited because of the language barrier.

While I was writing we were interrupted by a news reporter and photographer. Both seemed very much interested in our visit and took pictures for the paper. We're having dinner tonight at the Hilton, guests of the public relations man there.

Between the newsmen and public relations men we are never alone. They work in shifts, one rests while the other drills us and snaps pictures. Halmi's *Life* magazine card is a powerful instrument. His assignment for *Life,* trying to gather information on the methods of film companies in different countries, brings more of these fellows than we would normally have down on our heads. I don't know how long I can stand it.

Both of the newsmen are fine, intelligent Turks, however. One of them is a graduate of the University of Nevada.

We sat at a reserved table for the excellent buffet at the Hilton last night, getting a background of Turkish history from our host. We have an invitation to attend a Moslem service. I forgot to say that the belly dancers last night had quite beautiful eyes.

Monday—We went out to OK Meydan (pronounced Ox-Mi'-dan) today. Found it with very little trouble. OK Meydan is a more or less open field with a scattering of houses set among the pillars. Most of the shafts are crumbling now and while some of the inscriptions are legible, modern Turkish scholars cannot read them.

Back during the time of the Ottoman Emperors, however, it must have been a splendid place. *Anecdotes of Turkish Archery* says, "The Ottoman Emperors, with their Courts, frequently indulged in public in the diversion of archery, and there was an extensive piece of ground set apart for the purpose, upon an eminence, in the suburbs of Constantinople, commanding an extensive view of the city and harbour, called OK Meydan, or 'the place of the arrow.' This place was full of marble pillars, erected by those archers who had excelled in shooting their arrows at any remarkable distance. These pillars were inscribed with the names of the archers, the extraordinary distance at which they had shot their arrows, and usually with some verses in praise of their dexterity. . . . Selim, the reigning Emperor in 1797, . . . gave on several occasions very splendid public entertainments at the OK Meydan, where tents were pitched for him and his court."

We saw only ramshackle houses on the site. If a pillar interferes with the building of a house, it is ruthlessly knocked down. We took pictures of some of the best preserved. It may not be long before all evidence of this ancient place is erased. We talked to several people about this but no one has any money for such projects. It seems incredible that this historical spot where Sultan Selim is said to have shot an arrow that "drove in the ground at the distance of fourteen hundred pikes (Turkish measure), or nine hundred and seventy-two yards, two inches and three quarters (English measure)," should return to dust.

We also visited the bazaar where my wife would have spent half our fortune. I bought a large brass pitcher for her and also a gyroscopic tray with little bangles around the handle. On Wednesday we go to Ankara, one hour by plane, to photograph the archery collection at the museum there.

Tuesday, 3 P.M.—We have a date with Orhan Gunsiray for a preview of his picture, *Genghis Khan.* I will return the favor by showing two films we brought along of hunting in North America. We are also scheduled to visit "Ayasofia," the oldest church in the world.

Two million people live in Istanbul. There are sixty thousand taxicabs—all blowing horns at the same time. New York has only twenty thousand cabs. We hire a cab and driver for twelve dollars a twenty-four-hour day. The streets are narrow. Pedestrians lead an exciting life.

The Turks are very friendly, although conversation is difficult. We talk mostly with our hands. Twice I have had glasses of water upset on me at the dinner table.

Thursday—What a whirl we are in. There is not a minute of peace. We had lunch today with the owner of a fine restaurant and are invited to have dinner with him also, tomorrow night. Dinner is never served until 9 or 10 P.M. but since this man is trying to arrange a boar hunt for us, we can't complain.

Yesterday we went back to the shooting field of OK Meydan. A fabulous place we found it hard to keep away from. I shot a flight arrow out of sight and am watching the papers today to see if it came down on anyone.

We met the president of the Turkish Archery Club, who claims to be somewhat of an historian. We could not communicate because of the language but he promised, through an interpreter, to write me the answers to my questions after he has time for some research.

The museum at Ankara was like a flight into *Grimm's Fairy Tales.* One throne was adorned with diamonds, pearls, rubies, and emeralds and was valued at five million dollars. For two cigars the Minister got permission from the museum director to take some of the jeweled quivers and golden bows out into the sunlight for pictures. The bows had been made by sultans, he said, in the days when sultans were expected to learn some art or profession, and many of them chose the art of making bows and arrows.

Halmi took pictures of me yesterday during a wrestling match with a tame bear owned by a band of gypsies. . . . The mosque we visited is reported to be ornamented with fourteen tons of gold. We will leave for New Delhi Saturday if no boar hunt develops. Otherwise we'll go on Sunday.

Friday, April 26, Istanbul—We're having a beer with our Turkish Archery friend. It is difficult to converse but he has a few English words, picked up, he says, from the cinema.

The museum picture is finished. It will be a great story. One quiver we photographed had jewels valued at $100,000.

Saturday, A.M.—The boar hunt was arranged but we couldn't change our plane reservations, so will leave for New Delhi this afternoon. We are going to the film studio to pay our respects this morning and then to the home of our archery friend to see and photograph him and his collection.

Sunday, 2 A.M.—Aboard plane. We are about to leave Tehran. Next stop will be New Delhi in about four hours.

We left Istanbul at 6:30 P.M. and I was glad to leave, only because I need some rest. Too many friends all wanting to take us somewhere—phone ringing all the time. Wonderful people in a country rich in history. But not rich in money by any means. They do not have enough money to preserve the relics found here. We saw signs of poverty and hard living in many areas; people carrying heavy loads on their backs or leading donkeys who had the loads on theirs.

The food was excellent. Fresh vegetables, citrus fruits, fish, fowl, and delicious lamb. We will miss the cheese made from goats' milk.

Sunday, April 28, Ashoka Hotel, New Delhi—We got in early this morning and went straight to bed for a nap. This afternoon we visited the zoo and the Old Red Fort. It is very hot here. We made arrangements for a mongoose and cobra fight for pictures tomorrow morning.

We made arrangements for a mongoose and cobra fight.

Tuesday—Time for just one more note before we leave here. We are in our air-conditioned room at the hotel, glad to be out of the heat for a while. It may be quite a few days before I can write again. Apparently the palace is quite a distance from the town of Bundi with only "messenger" service between them.

The trip to Kota by train takes eight hours. We will have an air-conditioned compartment with twin beds.

We have finished everything we can do here. Spent the morning at the zoo taking pictures and studying tigers and leopards. A five-week-old tiger cub I held on my lap became overly enthusiastic and I had to change trousers. The people at the zoo were most co-operative. I tried catnip on both leopards and tigers with negative results. I did not try predator calls. This in the line of research for my coming hunt.

Characteristics of the Indian people seem to include a degree of inertness. An "argument" between our driver and a bus driver this morning sounded almost affectionate.

Today I ordered two suits and two sports coats and two silk shirts (the shirts to wear at the palace) from Indian tailors. After selecting the suit materials at two-thirty this afternoon the suits were ready for the first fitting at 7 P.M. this evening. The suits will cost fifty-five dollars each and the sports coats thirty dollars each.

My assignment begins tomorrow. The Bengal Tiger. If I am lucky enough to get one, it should be an exciting experience. And with a little more luck we could have an opportunity for leopard, too. They have big ones in India—the one I saw at the zoo weighed two hundred pounds. We have heard that they are more plentiful than tigers. But I have only ten days to hunt.

In the New Delhi paper I read an advertisement:

YET ANOTHER CHANCE FOR DELHI CITIZENS TO CONSULT DR. ———— FOR

Heart Trouble	Insanity
Nervous Debility	Hysteria
Blood Poisoning	Leucoderma
Digestive Disorders	Fistula

And all other baffling Ailments.

I also saw three columns dealing with matrimonial arrangements. Advertising for wives or husbands, in other words. Am running an ad tomorrow. If the response is good, I may stay. . . .

» «

Phoolsagar Palace, Bundi, India, May 2, 1963, 9 A.M.—We arrived by train from New Delhi last evening and were met at Bundi by the Maharaja's aide, David Singh. David is a soft-spoken, fine-looking young man and the drive in from the city of Bundi was interesting and informative as he pointed out things to us along the way.

This is the dry season and everything is the color of ripe wheat. We saw farmers in the fields cutting and threshing grain in biblical style. Grain is shucked out of the hulls by the feet of cattle who plod around and around tethered to a long pole.

Phoolsagar Palace is new, built in 1947. The Old Palace, two miles away in Bundi, was built in 1434. Bundi's late father's harem are living out their years at the Old Palace.

Phoolsagar Palace is new, built in 1947.

The Old Palace, halfway up the mountain, with fortifications on top, was built in 1434.

We saw the orange flag of Phoolsagar flying from a tower as we approached and soon the whole castle was in sight. It was impressive, to say the very least, with its orange-and-white masonry and orange-turbaned guards at the gates. Peacocks moved regally out of our way as we stopped before a large entrance on one side of the building.

The Maharaja was a pleasant surprise, a well-built and handsome fellow in his early forties. He greeted us in the courtyard and then summoned servants to show us to our quarters and carry our luggage. As each servant came up he bowed to His Highness and backed away. The bow is accompanied by hands held together prayer-fashion against the chest, the head dipping low over them.

The palace completely encircles a pool, the purpose of which, in addition to its beauty, is to help cool the premises. My bedroom is twenty-five feet square with an outside double bed. Off this large room are two dressing rooms and two full baths. On the ceilings of all these rooms are big overhead fans that circulate the warm air.

Another apartment, apparently like mine, is across from me on this end of the pool. Between the two is an enormous sitting room, twenty-five by sixty feet or so. It is filled with luxurious chairs, divans, and tables. Entrance to this room is through a door leading from a porch screened completely by mats down which water cascades, setting up an effective air-conditioning system. The mats are made of twigs woven together into a blanket six inches thick.

The porch opens out on to a courtyard on a slightly lower level than the pool. There is a fountain out here and in the late evenings this area serves as a dining room. Water for the pool comes from a small lake about a third of a mile from the palace. It is lush with lotus flowers and the air above is bright with birds of every kind. "Phoolsagar" means "Flower Lake." We have freshly cut flowers in our rooms every day.

We had a very long cocktail hour last night. His Highness, whom I shall incorrectly refer to as "Bundi" from here on, joined us in the courtyard and we talked of many things, but mostly about hunting tigers. He told us that two tigers, a male and female, had been staying near the palace until two days ago, but have now moved to nearby hills. They prowled around for two weeks, he said. Two days ago the male spent the day sleeping under a banana tree on the creek that feeds the pool—about one hundred yards from the palace.

At 10 P.M. several boys in immaculate white suits with orange turbans brought out a large rug which they spread on the grass. They then wheeled out a handsome dining table of dark, polished wood and set it on the rug. The palace teems with help, mostly male, all in spotless white and turbaned in orange. A stream of them brought out the courses of delicious food in gleaming silver bowls, platters, and trays. Bundi tried to warn me, too late, about one of the dishes passed, and I spent what seemed like an hour in an inferno of red pepper and other hot, excruciating Indian spices before I was at last able to draw a full breath. Dinner ended at midnight. It was a long day for us after an all-day train ride from New Delhi.

2 P.M.—We took some pictures around the palace this morning and also of a contest I had with one of the natives who used his slingshot against my bow.

Sitting on the porch now during the heat of the day. It is cool and refreshing with the water dripping through the mats and the ceiling fans going. Bundi showed up at noon for a brief moment.

Four tiger baits are out. They are checked each morning and I'm keeping my fingers crossed. This evening, I understand, we will go hunting with the car. It is a jeep with a special hunting body.

Breakfast was served in our rooms at 9 A.M.—Slice of papaya, toast, tea, and scrambled eggs.

Bundi's wife is in the palace somewhere, we were told, but she has not been in evidence up to this time. There are a few women working about the grounds, but they are always veiled.

Friday, May 3, 1 P.M.—Lunch was served from a tray in our rooms yesterday and after that we drove to the town of Bundi to photograph a wedding. April and May are the months for weddings in India but only on certain days.

The wedding procession went by us on the street. A very colorful affair with a bride who looked as though she should be struggling with eighth-grade arithmetic instead of getting married. There were white horses, festooned with tassels and ribbons, and one man held a small boy before him in the saddle. The police were very co-operative in stopping traffic for the procession and we had time to get some good pictures. Back to the palace about 6 P.M.

At lunchtime Bundi said he would take the hunting car and shoot a leopard. Just like that.

He told us that four days ago a leopard had killed a camel about fifteen miles away, so after returning from the wedding we went out to check. Bundi has had a man watching the carcass and for three nights the leopard returned to feast on its kill. Last evening, however, he was not seen and there was nothing to do but return to the palace.

The immediate area around the palace is a game sanctuary and on the way back we saw two foxes, a hyena, a gazelle, and a number of blue bulls. We blew a tire en route and did not get back until 11:30 P.M. We had the usual cocktails and dinner at one-fifteen this morning. Finished at 2:30 A.M. and then to bed.

After breakfast today we went to the Old Palace to view and photograph the armor. A fabulous place with walls fourteen feet thick in some places.

The Old Palace is built on a hill on the outskirts of Bundi and served as a fort in those days as well as a residence for the Maharaja. The great main doors are studded wth heavy, deadly spikes to discourage the elephants used in combat, in ancient times, from breaking them down. Inside, besides the interesting armor, we saw frescoes on the walls with colors still bright and beautiful after all the centuries.

We photographed a patriarchal attendant demonstrating a water clock now preserved in the museum. It consisted of two brass bowls, a smaller one set inside a larger. The small bowl, which floated in the water-filled larger bowl, had a hole in the bottom and when it, in turn, was filled with water, it sank. This marked the time space of one hour and was heralded by the attendant vigorously striking a cymbal.

» «

We are sitting on the porch as I write. It is still very hot outside but here it is cool and comfortable.

Strange as it seems we *are* tiger hunting. This is the way it is done. We cannot make a move until a tiger has been pinpointed in a certain thicket. Four baits have been placed and the machans are built and ready. Bundi has taken great pains to arrange for this hunt. My machan (shooting platform in a tree) is in front. Then a machan for the photographer and also one for Bundi who will back me with a gun.

We know at this point that two tigers are on two different hillsides. Bundi has men watching them and reporting their movements. However, a hillside location is not enough. We have to know exactly where the tigers are before a beat is arranged, but even then there is no assurance that the cat will pass within bow range. If he does not, Bundi will shoot him with a gun. I estimate my chances of getting a tiger are about 50 per cent.

This has been a long day. . . . We had lunch in the dining room at two-thirty, after which I took a nap. This evening we went for a ride in the jeep to try to locate cats. No cats but we saw a boar, a sambar, a couple of blue bulls, jackals, civet cats, rabbits, and many species of night birds. We got back at 10 P.M. and I'm sitting out the cocktail hour writing this.

If we had stayed here last evening instead of going out to look for leopards, we might have had a chance at a tiger. One passed a hundred yards from the palace wall at dusk.

Bundi is a good hunter and is doing everything possible to make this a successful hunt.

11:45 P.M.—We are still waiting for dinner. This way of life is necessary, I suppose because of the heat. Since 10 P.M. the courtyard has been comfortable with a slight breeze stirring and the moon shining overhead. The table has been set, out here on the grass, all evening. How they keep food warm and fresh waiting out these uncertain hours, I do not know.

The palace is full of beautiful silver. At every meal I see pieces I have not seen before. We drink beer from silver mugs that weigh about a pound each. These are presentation pieces apparently, with inscriptions that read: To the Maharaja of Bundi from Queen Mary. Or, To His Highness from the Prince of Wales, or from Lord Mountbatten, etc. These oversized mugs have heavy glass bottoms for the purpose, we were told, of being able to see what the enemy was up to during a long, satisfying quaff.

We had dinner at twelve forty-five and finished at one forty-five. In bed at 2 A.M.! The food is excellent. Some dinners are Indian food, eaten with the fingers, and others are English, served with all the formality fitting a palace. All of the meat is game, well cooked and delicious. After an Indian meal two boys, in starched white coats and trousers, appear with a silver basin and silver pitcher of warm water, plus soap and towels, so one can wash up properly after having eaten without benefit of silverware.

Saturday Noon—I learned more about tiger hunting last night talking with Bundi. These tigers do not live in the jungle, although by local parlance this country is called "jungle." There is no tropical jungle except in the southern part of India.

The country is hilly—almost mountainous. The leaves are scorched off almost all the trees at this season and the ground is hard-baked, reddish clay.

This tiger baiting is not so simple as I thought it would be. Most careful preparations go into it and all angles require prudent consideration. First of all an exact spot for the bait must be selected. One that can be seen from a distant hill where natives can watch the tiger's movements with binoculars. Also, water must be provided so that he will not have to leave the area to quench his thirst. The water is carried to the spot by natives and poured into a large stone bowl set on the ground near the bait.

After the tiger gorges himself on the bait he sits by the carcass to keep hyenas, jackals, and buzzards away so there will be something left when he is hungry again. When the sun gets too hot, however, about 9 A.M., he gives up and returns to the nearest shade to lie down for the rest of the day.

It is important to know exactly where the tiger is lying and the watchers on the hillside get this information with their glasses. Word is then relayed by runners, on foot, bicycle, or car, to the palace where preparations for the hunt are made. Up to this point there is nothing for us to do but wait.

Sunday A.M.—Bob and I went with Bundi last evening to check with villagers about fifteen miles east of here to see if they knew anything about tigers in their area. No results, but coming back, about 10 P.M., a beautiful tiger crossed the dirt road ahead of us. We stopped where he had crossed and turned the spotlight into the trees where he sat, partly hidden, for a few seconds before slowly walking broadside through an opening to disappear in the bush again. It was a chilling, though thrilling, moment. Bundi said he was a big one and guessed his length at about nine feet, ten inches.

A forest fire about forty miles away has ruined our chances for the bait in that area. The fire did not burn into the immediate area of the bait but got so close that Bundi thinks it should be moved. Yesterday a small tiger circled one of the other baits, drank some water from the bowl, but did not stay.

The native used his slingshot.

Today I bought a slingshot from a native who gave me lessons on how to use it. They carry them to scare peacocks out of the mango trees.

There are many peacocks all over this area. They have recently been named the national bird. While riding around in the "jungle," it is a strange sight to see this gorgeous bird in a background of baked earth and leafless trees.

Tuesday, 11 A.M.—Early last evening I went hunting with Bundi and shot a large sambar in his personal hunting grounds. There is plenty of game there in a wild, natural state. There is almost no game anywhere else.

The sambar is an animal about the size of an elk, although his antlers are not so impressive. The one I shot was about ten years old, with six points. We saw him first at a distance and Bundi told me where to stand while he put him down the trail by circling around him. The sambar and his harem went by me at twenty-five yards. My arrow hit well. He ran about three hundred yards and was dead when we got to him. It was too dark for pictures, so we went in this morning to do that job.

Bundi and I showed movies last night. He had a professional film of his thirtieth-birthday celebration and some reels of tiger hunting.

10 P.M.—At noon today a messenger came in to tell us that a tiger had been seen at one of the baits. They think it was the big one we saw the other night.

A beat was immediately organized. About sixty natives armed themselves with tin basins, sticks, stones, and even an old muzzle-loading shotgun—anything that would make noise. We had a hasty lunch and then set out on the eight-mile drive. The bait was down in a canyon with water in it and we carefully approached the machans ready there for us. Mine was the front machan with Halmi and camera set up about thirty yards away. Besides Bundi's gun there were at least ten more strung out along the line the cat was expected to travel in front of the beaters. The tiger cannot be allowed to turn back toward the beaters. One or more would surely be killed.

It was hot as hell, about one hundred and ten degrees. The tiger had been observed by the head hunter at the bait at 8 A.M. He saw it go into a thicket to sleep the hot day out. About this time another tiger and two full-grown cubs were sighted on a nearby hillside and this is when the hunter made a mistake. He left two natives to watch the first tiger while he went to investigate the second. Apparently the natives were not too careful and were seen. At any rate, the cat became suspicious and sneaked away and when the beaters came by all that emerged from the thicket were some monkeys and a peacock.

The head hunter was very embarrassed. Tears rolled down his cheeks as he stood at stiff attention while Bundi pointed out the mistakes he had made.

Thursday, 10 A.M.—My arrow brought down a fine blue bull last evening. Everyone was impressed as these bulls are claimed to be one of the toughest animals to kill. They are also about the size of an elk, but with legs as long as a moose. They have heavy, pointed ten-inch horns.

This animal is named blue bull because of his glossy, slate-colored hide. Bundi's head skinner takes care of all the trophies. He has an awesome set of skinning knives which he carries rolled in an old brown cloth. He sharpens them before each job with a stone picked up from the ground near where he is squatting.

We took pictures of Rosie, Bundi's elephant, today. We named her Rosie because of her reddish trunk and forehead. I climbed up into the howdah with David Singh, and Halmi took pictures as we rode around the palace grounds in our rock-and-roll seat. Rosie had a strong leaning for some green leaves on certain trees and nearly dethroned us on one or more occasions, rushing madly under and through these trees. To make up for this, though, she stood patiently while we picked fruit at eye level from her back.

This evening we went to the village where the head hunter lives. The big tiger was back last night and cleaned up the bait, but did not lie down nearby. We have now placed other baits in the area where three or four tigers have been seen.

It is 3 A.M. We have just finished dinner and are going to bed.

I climbed up into the howdah with David Singh.

Friday, 8 P.M.—No tiger news today. I am beginning to get impatient. Life moves so slowly here and tradition governs much of the activity. The heat is almost unbearable and consequently life at the palace is quite different from anything I have ever experienced. One dresses informally—loose-fitting silk shirts and bare feet. And while I appreciate the opportunity to live in a palace, the formalities and delays are hard on a restless spirit. No one ever hurries for any reason. This heat melts me. I have the time, but not the inclination to write other than my notes. We average three baths a day and if it were not for my great inertia I would probably take more.

» «

The Maharaja wants to kill a moose. We are talking about setting up a trip. I hope I can arrange to have him visit us in Grayling. He would bring his son with him, which would set Hannah's young heart a-flutter. Bundi is very co-operative and has the patience and tolerance necessary for the limitations of the bow.

Movies are planned for tonight again. A dinner of wild boar will be served about 2 A.M. I got a shot at a boar two days ago, but missed.

I slept about four hours this afternoon and early evening. The sky turned cloudy today and a dust storm developed. I tried to buy some loafing slippers in Bundi today, but could not find my size, 14. Dinner was at two-thirty and to bed at 4:00 A.M.!

» «

Monday, May 13, 5 P.M.—We're on the train en route to Delhi. Many things have happened since I last wrote in my journal on Friday.

At 10 A.M. Saturday we got word that a large tiger and two smaller ones were feeding on a bait about ten miles away. At 2 P.M. we left for the area.

In the meantime a beat had been arranged for, we had lunch and assembled our gear. At the last minute before getting into the hunting car we took time to carry out an old Indian ritual that was supposed to assure a successful hunt.

Two effigies of tigers, each about a foot long, were outlined in gunpowder on the cement drive. When an attendant touched them off with a match and the "tigers" blazed up in a smoky whoosh, it was up to me, the hunter, to stomp out the blaze with the soles of my shoes to symbolize the way I would soon snuff out the life of a tiger.

This performance was accompanied by excited applause and wide grins on the faces of my audience—mostly a smattering of attendants and servants around the palace as well as the hunting party.

This business, like so many things in this strange country, seemed to me a waste of time. I was nervous about the tiger and felt we should get moving before it was too late. Bundi is a good hunter, however, and he knows more about tiger hunting than I'll ever know and a glance at his placid face assured me that all was proceeding according to rule.

We parked the hunting car in some thick brush and made our way as quietly and fast as possible to the shooting platforms. I was alone in the first machan, nine or ten feet up on the stub of a thorn tree. The mountain rose steeply about a hundred yards from me. Thirty yards on my right, Bundi and Halmi with his cameras were up and ready in the number 2 machan. On my left a third machan supported David Singh. Eight or ten more guns acted as stops at stands beyond the machans. Some were on the ground, some in trees, and two on the elephant. I looked down on a well-used game trail just below me that stretched on to pass under the number 2 machan.

Suddenly out of the quiet we heard the beaters. A great band of fifty or sixty natives forming a semicircle strung out on the mountain and along the sides of the steep canyon walls. Some of them had muskets and some tin pans. All had sticks and stones which they threw or rolled down the steep walls to accompany their yells, whistles, gunshots, and general clamor. The beaters did not advance much but kept up their infernal racket until the whole countryside rang with the din.

We were only about three hundred yards from where the tigers were known to be sleeping and I fully expected them to come out on the trail directly below me. It was a tense time and not one of us took our eyes from the area where it was anticipated the cats would emerge from the bush.

After several minutes of this frozen concentration I caught a slight movement to the right. My breath suddenly choked me as I turned to see the biggest of the cats stealing along the edge of the steep mountainside about a hundred yards away. He started climbing slowly in a zigzag path. It looked too far for me, and I expected to hear Bundi's gun any minute since these tigers must be killed at every opportunity. The only reward the beaters have for risking their lives on these hunts is to see the tiger killed to save their cattle, camels, goats, and themselves. Bundi told me that he would not allow a tiger to escape if it could possibly be prevented.

I watched the cat on the hillside. Several seconds went by and no shot from Bundi. It occurred to me in a flash that maybe he had not seen the tiger and that this might be the only chance I would have.

» «

The arrow looked good but struck into the flinty hillside behind him. He changed ends quickly as only a cat can do and my second arrow hit true and brought on a most blood-chilling snarling and roaring. The tiger spun around a couple of times and then headed straight down into the bush below me. Just as it disappeared into the thicket Bundi's gun went off and I thought, there goes my trophy. I looked at His Highness then for the first time and saw that he was shooting back of me at one of the other tigers that was streaking toward the beaters. I found out later that none saw the cat I shot at, at any time.

The terrible roaring stopped abruptly and there was considerable conversation in their native tongue between Bundi and his hunters. The head man went into the thicket with the big double and found my cat dead.

Now word was flashed to the beaters to advance on the other two tigers who were still in the bush between us. They were roaring and growling and darting about just a few yards from us. When the beaters came within fifty yards the cats had to make a run for it. The one Bundi hit came down my trail like a streak, baring teeth and growling. I shot behind him but Bundi rolled him over with his second shot. The other was shot at several times by the stop guns but escaped up and over the hillside to freedom. I couldn't help but admire its courage and even feel a little thrill over the well-deserved escape.

With all the tigers accounted for the hunters and beaters closed in around the machans as I picked my way down the thorn tree and was led into the thicket on hands and knees. We had to crawl through a tunnel-like passageway because one could not even hack his way through that dense tangle of thornbush with a machete. We came out into a small opening and there lay my tiger between a large rock and a tree.

It was a handsome, average-sized tiger with a beautiful skin. It weighed about three hundred pounds. The arrow had gone through the liver.

We did not stop to look for the arrow since the sun was beginning to drop behind the mountain and we had pictures to take before the light faded.

Bundi's men carried the beast out on poles, the big carcass swaying as if in a hammock. It appeared to be about all the barefooted natives could carry as they shuffled along over the uneven ground.

The bearers were relieved of their burden when we came to an open space, laying the tiger on the ground for pictures. We went through the customary role of congratulations and handshakes, and smiles and admiring glances at the trophy. Bundi was relieved, I believe, to have this over. I feel sure he did not think it very likely that a tiger could be taken with a bow.

Rosie was brought up to admire the dead cat, also. But she showed nothing but disdain, if not anger, at the sight of it lying dead and helpless on the ground. A centuries-deep enmity, no doubt, between tigers and elephants. She made feigning shuffles toward the carcass and even kicked it around a little like a cat playing with a mouse.

After the photographers were through we loaded the tiger on a truck and took it to a nearby village where word had gone on ahead and a small celebration was in readiness for us.

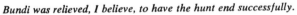

Bundi was relieved, I believe, to have the hunt end successfully.

Colorfully dressed women waited with a drummer to put on a victory dance. The cat was dropped once more upon the ground and the women moved rhythmically around it to the beat of the drum, singing the traditional tiger-kill song, while a hundred or more people stood watching. The women were veiled and carried bowls on their heads filled with radishes fresh from the garden and green onions with long, bright tops. The temperature was well over a hundred and Bundi's offerings of cold beer, limeade, whiskey, and gin from the palace car were gratefully accepted.

Later, in the cool of the evening, when the temperature had nose-dived to ninety degrees, we started back to the palace, traveling through two villages en route. I don't know who sent word but the people here were ready with a celebration, also. The first village had a bagpipe in addition to the drums and dancers. The village chief presented Bundi with one rupee (twenty cents) offered on a towel held in both hands. Protocol called for Bundi to then give the rupee to the chief's wife after which the dancing girls circled the car and Bundi deposited a rupee into the bowl each carried on her head. The same thing was repeated at the second village.

» «

Our train reservations were made for Monday morning. The tiger had been shot on Saturday, so we had only one day, Sunday, to finish our film work.

The killing of a tiger calls for a celebration at the palace too, and this was to be no exception. We showered and rested between 7 and 10 P.M. and then assembled in the courtyard.

Chairs were arranged in a semicircle on a rug spread out before the fountain. We were seated in the center with Bundi, flanked by his aides and department heads.

Several rounds of drinks preceded the entry of three musicians who seated themselves, cross-legged, against the fountain wall at the edge of the rug. A drummer sat down in the center with two very small kettledrums. On his left was a sitar player and on his right a native with an Indian accordion.

Now it was time for the dancing girls. Sisters, aged eighteen and twenty-one. They were the daughters of a former palace dancer we were told.

The girls were dressed in red silk native costumes with long flounced skirts that rippled out over their slim, bare feet as they danced.

The dance went on for more than two hours until even the spectators began to grow weary, entertaining as it was. These girls never marry, Bundi explained to us, but they have gentlemen friends. The elder had a child and the younger was pregnant.

We got to bed at 4 A.M.

The next morning farewell ceremonies took place in the courtyard before we left for the train. The Maharaja was there to greet us and as we began our good-bys, his head servant, followed by five attendants, all in splendorous white with gold buttons and orange turbans, paced across the grass bearing a large tray draped in gold cloth. On the cloth lay a beautiful Bundi dagger. A three-hundred-year-old relic from His Highness' collection of arms. Bundi presented the dagger to me with appropriate words and I was prompted by someone standing nearby to give him a silver coin in turn to assure that "our friendship would not be cut"

A three-hundred-year-old relic from His Highness' collection of arms.

by the gift of the sharp dagger. I was exceedingly pleased to receive this fine token of the Maharaja's friendship.

One of the attendants who had followed the head servant out to the courtyard now stepped forward with another tray on which lay three garlands of golden flowers which were looped around my neck, one on top of the other, as a parting gesture of friendship.

After the final handshakes and promises to meet again, we started out the gate on the way to the train. The militia stood at present arms as the car rolled to a stop in front of Rosie who had been brought up to place still another wreath of flowers around my neck with her trunk.

We had spent eleven days in Bundi. The hunting was far from strenuous and in spite of the heavy social activity and late hours, it was a most unusual and pleasant experience. I have an invitation to come back. There is still the leopard, and a beautiful little gazelle called thinkara that was never there when my arrows got there. I doubt if he ever would be.

EPILOGUE

On the overhead rack, seat row eight, right hand side, Flight 202 Alitalia, is where I left my briefcase when deplaning at New Delhi on our way to Bundi. I missed it just after we had cleared customs, but the plane had gone.

A teletype was dispatched to Bangkok, but the plane beat the wire.

Another wire to Hong Kong, but the plane beat that one, too. Contact was made with the plane at Tokyo, but they reported no briefcase on the overhead rack, seat row eight, on *left* side Alitalia Flight 202.

Another wire reached the plane at Hawaii advising them to look on *right* side, seat row eight, Flight 202 Alitalia.

» «

By this time we had left Delhi by train for Kota turning the responsibility of having the case forwarded to us at Bundi over to Trade Winds, a Delhi customs and brokerage service.

Six days later the case reached me by special messenger at the palace in Bundi. Bill from Trade Winds was $22, itemized as follows:

> Round-trip train fare Delhi to Kota (8 hours each way).
> Round-trip bus fare Kota to Bundi (40 miles).
> Taxi fare Bundi to palace (2 miles). (Taxi is a
> two-wheel, horse-drawn buggy with rubber-bulb auto horn.)

The whole trip would take three days. I have no idea what third-class fare would be.

Chapter 11

MOÇAMBIQUE, AFRICA - 1964

Wednesday, June 3, 7 A.M.—It seems like a sacrilege to say that we sit by an ebony-wood fire as we wait for breakfast this first morning of our hunt in this African autumn. The black ebony is from dead trees and branches dragged into camp behind the hunting cars. It burns with a hot glow. Within the hour we will leave for a forty-mile trip into elephant country, bush roads all the way.

My companions are: Peter Barrett, outdoor editor of *True* magazine, Arthur Godfrey, radio and television celebrity, and Robert Halmi, New York photographer. We have separate missions yet all centered about a common one. Godfrey

It seems like a sacrilege to say that we sit by an ebony-wood fire.

is here for the presentation ceremonies related to his gift of an airplane to one of the African bush doctors near Nairobi. (This will follow our hunt.) I want to kill an elephant with a bow and arrow. Bob will take the pictures and Pete Barrett wants a story of it all.

The group met in Salisbury, Rhodesia, on Sunday, June 1. I joined the other members of the party there, flying back from Nairobi after a three weeks' sightseeing and photography safari with my wife in Uganda and Kenya. We had still to fly on to Beira from which a fifty-minute flight by bush plane took us to the main camp. We are now at Camp Ruark, fifteen miles from the airstrip. The well-known writer, Robert Ruark, has hunted from here on several occasions.

Our hunting country is Moçambique, or Portuguese East Africa, somewhat farther south than the familiar hunting territory of Kenya. The country is rough and game reported to be plentiful. We look forward to this hunt with great anticipation.

The camp is clean and tidy. All the buildings are masonry with thatched roofs. Small bundles of grass are laid overlapping like shingles, making a remarkably watertight and snug roof. Godfrey has the "White House" on a little hill beside camp on the banks of the Save River where hippos grunt all night and crocodiles sun themselves by day on the sandbanks across the river. The clear water is the home of tiger fish, so named because of their animal-like teeth, and we hope to catch some of them while here.

Bob and I share a fine masonry hut and two of the professional hunters sleep in the Apache trailer brought with us for use on overnight hunts. Pete Barrett has

The camp is clean and tidy.

a place of his own where he writes his daily notes undisturbed. Godfrey, in his "White House" needs solitude also to do his daily radio tapes flown to the States twice a week for broadcasting.

The fall climate of Moçambique is bracing and refreshing in the early morning. The nights are cool, around fifty degrees average, and the days are as pleasantly warm as my home in Michigan in September. The grass has begun to brown and leaves are just beginning to turn and fall.

Moçambique is a paradise for game. We have seen almost everything except elephant and buffalo in the short time we have been here. Yesterday, in a little pre-hunt sortie, Bob and I and our Portuguese hunter, whom we call "Fish" (because his name, Amandeu Peixe, means just that), saw hundreds of impala and wart hogs and many, many other species—eland, nyala, wildebeest, oribi, reedbuck, dik-dik, and baboons. My initial shots of the hunt were not noteworthy—over an impala and under a waterbuck. We found a water hole that a great many animals visit and had plans to go back to hunt there today, but word came into camp that elephants were coming to water near a village about forty miles away and we decided to investigate this first.

Noon, Same Day—We are getting lunch and provisions for going after the elephants. I am writing in the main lodge. On the wall opposite me hang two confiscated muzzle-loading guns with inscriptions beneath: EX-POACHER FAIF, NOW GAME WARDEN, and EX-POACHER MAWINGA, NOW GAME WARDEN.

Poaching is a very serious and troublesome thing in Africa. The natives devise effective but cruel snares and traps to catch animals and wildlife officials are using every means to apprehend them. It seems apparent here that some of the offenders are very penitent indeed.

Fourteen natives came by to visit us.

While waiting for provisions I have time to jot down a word about our serenade last evening. Fourteen natives came by to visit us. They had drums and other musical instruments and put on a show that lasted for several hours. Godfrey returned the compliment by entertaining them with his ukulele and he made a short tape for his radio show.

Thinking of the hunt ahead I am reminded that the elephants have smaller tusks here than some of the monsters that loomed up before my camera on safari last week in Uganda. However, Uganda is not open for bowhunting, so smaller ivory will have to do.

Thursday, June 4, Noon—We are stranded in the bush with a broken tie rod on our Toyota, a Japanese hunting car. It was broken crossing a rocky riverbed this morning. Bob and Fish are taking it off to try to make repairs. If they are not successful, we may have to hike the five miles back to camp.

On the way here yesterday an impala and a wart hog jumped my bowstring (heard the twang and were gone before the arrow got there). And last evening I came close to having a shot at a greater kudu. He was a beautiful animal, high at the shoulders, with record horns, Fish said. A kudu bull is impressive with dark, grayish-blue coloring set off by white stripes and long spiraling horns. The two females with him had tawny bodies with very faint stripes showing. Another chance I turned down, was a nyala about twenty-five yards away. I thought his eighteen-inch horns were not big enough. He walked by me while I was making a stalk on a waterbuck. I could regret this later.

The elephant hunt has not lived up to expectations. Natives often tell of an abundance of game near their villages to attract hunters in the area on the chance of getting meat. We missed them by several hours this morning, although we were on our way long before the reported time of passing. We followed them for some hours, but gave up and visited another village. Information here was vague and next to nothing, so we spent the afternoon and evening looking for lesser game hoping to make another try at intercepting the elephants in the morning.

» «

Same Day, 6 P.M.—We returned to camp in the car which Bob, Fish, and six natives had managed to repair. After lunch we went looking for the kudu we had seen. He was there but was wild and out of sight in a flash. I shot low at a fine nyala at about fifty-five yards. Plans are to be up long before daylight tomorrow to try again to find the elephants coming for water. If we do not see them, we will return to the main camp in the afternoon for another try at nyala. Fish says there is a good concentration of them there. On Saturday morning we will return to Camp Ruark to lick our wounds and have a bath and shave.

Our present method of hunting does not promise much success. We drive across country in the hunting car and occasionally come within long bow range of game. At other times I drop off at some cover and our African helpers try herding or I attempt a stalk. The latter is almost impossible because the grass is very dry and noisy. Only once did I have a chance at success in this. A waterbuck had gone into tall grass from the edge of a lake and I had soft, bare soil to walk on. I got within twenty yards, but he was gone before I could draw the bow.

There are few enough water holes and enough game to make blind hunting on trails or at water holes most interesting. But this method of hunting is seldom used here. I am having difficulty selling my hunter on the idea of blind hunting but he is slowly learning the limitations of the bow. This is not to complain as he is most co-operative in every way. All of the personnel here are very pleasant, including the natives, and even the poachers after we took their weapons from them.

On Tuesday we have been invited by the governor, who will be our host, to see a native dance by the people of Zavala, a small coastal village. We will fly there from camp in a government plane. It will be marimba music with the usual drums, I suppose. Should make a good picture.

» «

Sunday, June 7, 8 A.M.—Have just finished breakfast and am sitting by the fire with the low sun warming my back. This is our hunting camp. We came in here last night from the elephant hunt. A big pachyderm died Friday by one arrow. The day was both exciting and exhausting.

We were up at 5 A.M. and on the trail at six. We soon found droppings that were fresh and steaming in the cool temperature. After fifteen minutes in the bush, Savo stopped us and took the two rifles and my bow and laid them on the ground by a tree. Then he took a well-worn, shiny tin flask with a screw top from his pocket and began a ceremony. He took small pinches of snuff from the flask between his thumb and first finger, waving his hand back and forth over the guns and bow before depositing it on a green leaf he had placed on the ground beside them. Each time his hand moved across the weapons he muttered something in his native tongue. He was imploring the spirits of his ancestors to guide us successfully on the hunt, I was told.

On our way again, we soon ran into a reedbuck and immediately after this a herd of about twenty-five buffalo ran off at the sight of us with a great crashing of brush. Unfortunately the elephants were just ahead of this and they also ran off out of sight. We tried to catch up with them walking fast and sometimes running, but it was twelve miles and three and a half hours later before we found them again. By this time the herd had grown in number to about two hundred. This seemed to be the place for this large group to gather for their midday siesta under the shade of trees in the valley.

We were in brush that did not cover us completely and the elephants were lined up, three and four deep, for a third of a mile or more. There were big ones, small ones, and medium-sized ones all moving at a slow pace toward the trees. Downwind from them, we managed to move up to about fifty yards, crouching down and running part of the time. There was a large elephant toward the rear but it had no tusks. Others had tusks which varied in size but nothing too exciting as far as we could see.

Fish, Halmi, and I planned to work in close to the line and pick out the best bull we could find but were suddenly confronted with unexpected problems. Two scouts from the rear of the herd either saw us or sensed that something was wrong and cut out of the line to investigate and get downwind from us. They came straight toward us, big ears extended and flapping, trunks in the air, moving noiselessly as elephants do. Our natives and the head man with a .375 realized the danger and warned us with a low whistle before they scattered into the bush in hopes of finding a tree big enough to climb. Just before they fled I saw the terrified expression on the gunbearer's face and was about to ask him for the rifle but he got away too fast. Fish had his gun at ready as we also took off. Fish had never seen so many elephants at one time, he told us. He is a young fellow with limited experience, although very reliable and a good shot. He is the present champion of trapshooters in Moçambique.

The two scouts in the herd had caught our scent, but how they got the message to the rest of the herd, which ran off into the trees, was one of the marvels of nature that man has no way of determining.

With the elephants out of sight we reorganized our group. The natives held a meeting and came back with the decision: "Too many elephants. We all get killed." So they stayed behind while the rest of us circled again, making sure to stay downwind, and went into the forest. Almost immediately four or five elephants, led by a good bull, came our way. He did not have big tusks but was a large elephant. The bull stopped behind some bushes and we froze beside our cover at the edge of a clearing across from him. The bull's tusks stuck out about two feet. Fish whispered to me: "Shoot him."

I could not shoot him, of course, until he moved from behind the bushes and even then it meant that I had to step out into the open before drawing my bow. Bob was in proper camera position behind me and the suspense was unbearable. In what seemed like an eternity the bull started moving out across the opening about forty yards away. I stepped out from my cover and the bull turned his head to look at me. . . . I am not sure whether he was walking or standing still when I shot. The film will tell the story.

The arrow entered at the elevation I had intended it to, but farther back than I wished. He and the other elephants in his group ran off. We heard more elephants near us and were relieved that they did not choose to come closer. I knew I had a killing shot but did not know how far the bull could travel. We rounded up the natives and sat down to rest away from the trouble area. In about fifteen minutes we decided to take the trail. The natives held another conference and their decision was again "no." Fish was able to convince them after some time, however, to stay with us.

The trail was not hard to follow. There was plenty of blood, but after 200 yards of traveling we heard a sinister, throaty, blowing and a hundred yards ahead an enormous elephant's head showed up over a bush. Again the natives scattered and again we had to reassemble them over their protests about continuing the trail. When the elephant had gone off into the trees, Fish used his most convincing persuasion to get them to come with us. We trailed the bull I'd shot for another two hundred yards and then ran into more elephants.

This time nothing could influence the natives to continue. Besides, we had no water and were twelve miles from the nearest village. The sun was hot, the temperature about ninety degrees. Both Fish and I had blisters on our feet. Savo finally advised us to turn back, saying he would send two men at daybreak and find our elephant.

The village needed meat badly and Fish assured me that they would do this. This is the first time I have ever left a good blood trail, but common sense told me to turn back. We detoured around two more groups of elephants before reaching the village at 3 P.M. Everyone was exhausted and badly in need of water.

Alfredo, the tracker, offered to go after the car four miles away and Savo, who was chief of the village, offered us everything he had. Muddy water from a well-used vessel which we refused. Next he killed two chickens and had them roasted in five minutes. They were still bloody and we refused them also, as politely as we could. He then went into the bush and came back with palm beer. This is the juice of the palm tree and it was full of ants, but we drank some anyway. Our natives accepted everything that was offered and were completely refreshed.

Alfredo got back with the car at 6 P.M. and we fell on the beer, fruit, and bread it contained like hungry wolves. It was dark by the time we started out and getting out of the bush back to the road was a nightmare. Fish steered by the stars. The Southern Cross loomed brightly in the sky. On our way we saw the beautiful African porcupine, a honey badger, and a civet cat in the headlights.

Fortunately for us Walter Johnson, Sr., a seasoned hunter who runs these camps, had arrived at the main camp from Lorenzo Marques and, hearing we were hunting elephants from the lower camp, came down to see how we were faring. This provided transportation and he accompanied us in the morning when we left to look for the elephant. We passed the native trackers on the way and found my bull about 200 yards from where we left the trail. He had died on his belly without rolling over. One tusk was buried in the earth.

When an elephant is down, word goes out to the villages nearby and the entire populace comes to get a share of the meat. Every man has a knife with which he hacks and cuts at the carcass at top speed, hoping to get a lion's share before it is

He died where he fell, without rolling over.

all gone. The women carry the meat off in their woven grass baskets, biting off pieces to eat as they go. It is remarkable to see how fast the enormous hulk of an elephant can be reduced to practically nothing by these meat-hungry people. The natives were happy. Plenty of biltong. We photographed the interesting operation in detail.

I wanted a head mount, so the entire head, trunk, and tusks were loaded into the hunting car. It took fifteen men to do this. The arrow had gone in about twenty inches and did great damage to the liver. Walter Johnson estimated the bull at about four tons. The tusks at thirty-five to forty pounds each.

Dr. Ken Miller from Beaumont, Texas, is hunting here also. He had trained at Harper Hospital in Detroit and knew our family doctor, B. E. Henig, and had also once relieved Drs. Clippert and Keyport in Grayling while they were on vacation. His home was then in Cadillac, sixty miles from Grayling.

Monday, June 8, 10 A.M.—Our car is being repaired so we took another one for hunting this morning. I made a stalk on an impala and got a shot at fifty yards. The arrow went high and sliced along the backbone into the shoulder area. It ran about 400 yards and folded up. He was an old buck with face and neck badly scarred from fighting.

We started back about three o'clock and saw a fine nyala buck going into some

At forty yards a brief opportunity presented itself.

bushes. I got out and had quiet footing for a stalk and then made one of my lucky shots. At forty yards a very brief opportunity presented itself as he was passing out of sight behind a tree. The arrow was away and missed the tree by a scant inch. He ran about 150 yards and fell. The nyala is a beautiful animal and a rather rare trophy.

The natives are perplexed and astonished at the power of the bow. In fact, one of the problems of having them see how animals can be dispatched with this weapon is that they often want to pull and examine it. As a result the handle becomes a bit tacky.

Sunset is at 6 P.M. in this southerly quarter of Africa and sunrise occurs at 6 A.M. It is difficult to get used to seeing the sun in the north at noon.

Godfrey and Pete Barrett came in from hunting today with a giant eland Arthur had shot. It was a beauty with thirty-inch horns, weighing twelve to fourteen hundred pounds.

Yesterday was a lazy day for us. Pete and Arthur went hunting and Fish, Bob, and I took a ride. I did not take my bow. In the afternoon we fished for tiger fish. It was not easy fishing. I caught one about four pounds and hooked another that got away. Godfrey came in with a bushbuck and a nyala with twenty-eight-inch horns.

Tuesday, June 9, 10 A.M.—We're airborne in a twin-engine Piper plane. Godfrey, Barrett, Halmi, Fish, and I. On our way to Zavala to see and photograph the native dance.

We visited briefly this morning with Dr. Miller and his companion, Mr. Buckley, also from Beaumont. They left very early to hunt a buffalo that has been damaging crops at a native village. It also killed one of the villagers a few days ago.

This recovery period following the elephant hunt, while welcome, is really three days lost from hunting. I am sure the native dancing will be most interesting but the days slip by and before long the sun will rise on our departure date.

This is such magnificent hunting country it is disappointing not to be out in the bush in all daylight hours. The rivers by both camps are alive with hippos and crocodiles. We see many of both each day and always hear the hippos at night. Guinea fowl, francolin, and sand grouse, plus a very small quail, are also in this area. Other birds are plentiful, too, and some have gorgeous coloring. Coming into camp last evening we found a beautiful dead "roller" (African jay). Fish's friend, Rui, who was in camp last night skinned it for me. He is a taxidermist and will mount it.

Thursday, June 11—There is so much to do and see here that daily notes are not always possible. The native dance at Zavala was a great show. Twenty-three marimbas and seventy-five dancers. The performance lasted about two hours.

The highlight of this evening, from my point of view, was to be made a member of the Chopi tribe. Chopi means archer and it was therefore fitting that my name should be Chopi. The indoctrination was very interesting. The Portuguese administrator, Saul Rafael, introduced me to their two chiefs and told those assembled of my shooting an elephant. This drew enthusiastic applause and many eyes rolled in my direction.

The setting for the dance was a small amphitheater on a hillside overlooking the Indian Ocean. Seats in a half circle stepped up from the sand floor to pillars that supported an arcadelike, lattice roof.

Following the entertainment we were driven back to the airport where Fish's mother met us with a delicious lunch. Red and white wine, large, very tasty shrimp, crab cakes, deviled crab, crab turnovers, passion fruit, the sweetest tangerines I've ever eaten, and sandwiches and rolls. We returned to main camp at 4 P.M. and were back at our hunting camp at six.

The evenings in camp are enjoyable. Cool enough for a jacket. We sit around the campfire with cocktails and tidbits, swapping stories. Dinners are delicious. Lately we have been having eland liver, beautifully prepared, served in bite-sized pieces. All the meat is game. First we had impala. Then Arthur shot the eland and last came the nyala. This was the best, I thought.

Our vegetables come from a well-kept garden beside camp. Breakfast is a cutlet of meat of some kind, an egg and bacon, all following fruit in great variety. Lunch in the bush is a treat also. Oranges, pears, apples, sandwiches, and slices of tenderloin rolled in eggs and bread crumbs.

The day begins at 6 A.M. sharp when tea is served at bedside by a bright-eyed boy of fifteen or so. Another young man soon follows with a pitcher of hot water which he places on the washstand. Each leaves immediately after his task, closing the screen door silently behind him.

Daylight is just beginning to show with a red glow in the east. Outside, the embers from last night's campfire are stirred into a blaze as we emerge wearing warm jackets to sit around the fire with an extra cup of hot tea.

We talk of various things, interrupted at intervals by the grunting of hippos in the river. Baboons bark and bushbucks snort, accompanied by the songs of birds at sunrise. Walter Johnson, Sr., is the sage of the group and is usually the first to get to the fire. He is about fifty-five years old and has spent most of his time in the bush, and much of it hunting ivory. He says he thinks he has killed close to a hundred elephants.

A half hour of this and we move into the "dining room" for breakfast. This is an open-air, round hut with a conical grass roof. The outside wall rises some thirty inches and is open to the roof above this. Our dining table is about eight feet long. A serving table stands just outside.

An important part of the day's routine is "sick call" when the women of the nearby villages bring their children to Walter Johnson, Jr., for treatment before he starts out hunting. The youngsters have any number of ailments: a thorn in the foot, a reed underneath a toenail, cuts on the body, a "snake" in the stomach, which means a sore stomach, but most of all an eye ailment that could be prevented by more liberal use of soap and water. Treatment is administered from a first-aid kit kept well stocked by departing hunters.

Breakfast is over about seven-thirty and we are ready to start the day's hunt. The engines of the hunting cars are warmed up by the time we climb aboard. The cars are open with windshields folded down over the hoods. Almost the entire country can be covered with these cars and it is difficult (except when far from water) to travel even for five minutes without seeing game.

There are wart hogs by the hundreds, impalas by the thousands, with a good sprinkling of waterbuck everywhere. In lesser numbers are zebra, hartebeest, wildebeest, kudu, nyala, sable, eland, buffalo, bushbuck, reedbuck, forest hog, dik-dik, elephant, and several species of smaller animals not known by me.

The dining room is an open-air hut.

An important part of the day's routine is "sick call."

A good sprinkling of waterbuck everywhere.

Returning from the hunt at night, if game has been taken, we go directly to the skinning area which is, fortunately, beyond the boundaries of our camp. The natives who take care of the camp live here amid skins, bones, skulls, and horns. Strips of meat hang drying on racks in the sun. This is the method of preparing "biltong" and it tastes like dried beef but would be better, I should think, if it were soaked in brine first.

Trophies are admired by the hunters and remeasured, and talk is of record-book minimums which no one seems to know for sure.

Going into camp, young Babunda, the younger brother of our gunbearer, carries the gear into our quarters. If other hunters are back we loiter by the fire to hear their experiences of the day. The cocktail table is set up and appetizers served during the bull session that follows. The chill of the evening comes quickly and during this hour we take turns at the shower, a circular hut with walls of vertical reeds and a pointed grass roof. The shower mechanism is a specially designed bucket with a spray nozzle at the bottom. Two chains turn it on and off.

Dinner is always ready when we finish our cocktail hour, after which we return to the fire for an hour or so and then to bed, seldom later than 10 P.M. We have

Wildebeest and impalas.

screen doors and two screen windows to keep out the bugs. Bob's and my hut has a wide black band around the bottom on which someone has painted pictures of animals with white paint. One is a wart hog with kudu horns.

Yesterday we started out early; tea at 5 A.M., leaving at six for a long trip to buffalo country. We never got there, however. We spent some of the time with two kudu bulls but did not get a shot. Later, on the way, I was able to get within forty-five yards of a fine waterbuck and put an arrow through him. He ran about 200 yards and then went down. I had not realized these animals were so big. This one was nearly as large as a bull elk and had horns twenty-eight inches long. By the time we were finished with pictures it was too late to go on, so we returned to camp.

I was able to get within forty-five yards of a waterbuck.

Godfrey and his group had returned also. We had a fine lunch and later did Godfrey's radio tape in which he directed a round table discussion including the details of shooting the elephant.

» «

Saturday, June 13, 9 A.M.—Sitting on my camera box while Fish and our two natives try to get the Land Cruiser out of a deep washout. It is resting nose down at about thirty degrees. A short time ago we were riding through tall grass at about ten miles an hour trying to locate a big kudu we had seen earlier when, without warning, we nose-dived into a ditch about five feet deep and six feet wide.

I was in front holding my bow. Bob and two natives were in the back. Fortunately for us the windshield was down, resting on the hood. Bob came flying over Fish, bounced off the windshield with his shoulders breaking the glass, and landed headfirst in the ditch with only his feet in sight. His legs were not moving and I thought he had broken his neck.

Peter, one of the natives, rolled over me, over the hood, and out into the grass beyond. Babunda, the other native, cleared Fish, ricocheted off the hood, and joined Peter who was still clutching my movie camera as he flew out of the car. Fish having the wheel to hang on to, kept his seat. Bows, arrows, cameras, and guns were scattered all over the area.

We went headlong into a ditch.

We stopped so suddenly against the vertical walls of the wash that it was like hitting concrete. I am not sure where I landed. I guess half in and half out. I was concerned about Bob. Fish was digging him out and asking all the while of both of us, "Are you hurt?" We had had the wind knocked out of us and at the moment could not speak but, for the most part, except for some cuts and bruises, we came through in good shape. I have a wrenched back and maybe a cracked rib. I can still see Babunda and Peter bouncing and rolling into the grass like footballs.

Peter took the ax and cut a pole about five inches in diameter, sharpening the end like a chisel. With this he dug out the edge of the wash that held up the frame of the car. In about an hour he had the car out. There was only minor damage to equipment and nothing wrong with the rough Toyota except a broken windshield. My camera stock was broken and the rear sight of Fish's rifle bent badly but some blows with a hammer put it back in shape.

Sunday, June 14, 8:30 A.M.—Around the campfire again as the sun begins to take off the morning chill. This is a day off from hunting to do odd jobs of filming around camp. We are photographing Walter Johnson, Jr., and Fish, who live in the Apache trailer we brought with us and are also taking pictures of it packed for mobile use. It is a fine piece of equipment and has been very useful around camp and on trips.

Yesterday after we got the car out of the ditch we continued on, not really expecting to find the kudu we had seen but they were there about a third of a mile ahead. Three bulls, two small ones and a big fellow with six or eight females. They were not too wild since they stood shoulder-high in tall grass and, after several attempts at stalking, I finally got within shooting range of the big one. I had to shoot through grass but the arrow got there and hit low through the ribs, too far back, unfortunately.

Most animals when hit race off at great speed but this kudu merely walked away. I got within range again and hit him in the back leg cutting the femoral artery. He ran just two jumps, walked about 100 yards, and fell to the ground. A fine animal, beautiful fifty-four-inch horns and weighing between five and six hun-

I hit him in the back leg, cutting the femoral artery.

Peter, Babunda, Fish, and I with the kudu bull.

dred pounds. There was not a scratch on his handsome striped hide. I was tempted to have it skinned for a full mount, but decided on cape only for a head mount.

This is without a doubt my best African trophy. An elephant is impressive but not pretty. It had been beyond my fondest hopes to bag a kudu with the bow and arrow but here it was, lying before me, the spiral horns glistening in the sun. There were smiles on the faces of Peter and Babunda and on the face of Fish, a wide grin.

What a country. Such an abundance and variety of game. Two days ago I shot a waterbuck in the rear with a blunt. He kicked out behind as if a bee had stung him as the arrow bounced off. A wart hog reacted the same way from a blunt hit.

The natives are living high with all the game we have killed. We leave pieces of meat at the various villages nearby, a great treat for them.

Arriving at the skinning area to drop off the horns and cape of the kudu, we saw the massive head of the buffalo Arthur Godfrey had shot that morning. The boss, the wide part of the horns on the forehead, measured seventeen inches. The natives will gorge themselves with meat for the next few days.

This early autumn season the Africans gather dry grass and tie it into small bundles, about two inches in diameter, for thatching their roofs. It is also the time to burn grass. They set many fires and I have been amazed to see how soon fresh green shoots grow up again. The animals flock to these areas. This age-old practice of burning grass is both good and bad. The purpose is to make room for new grass, consequently providing food for animals to graze on. This it does. But the fires also kill the seedling trees, so no forests can grow here. Trees would soon cover the grazing grounds, of course, and increase the browse.

The witch doctor did a kush-kush for us today. He bestowed mystic powers on us, my bow, the car, and Apache trailer. He also uttered words of wisdom telling me what I already knew, that I would get more game if I used a rifle. . . . He thought I could not afford a gun.

Monday, June 15, 4 P.M.—We are at main camp. The plane is coming in to pick up Godfrey's tape. This is the first cloudy day. We did little yesterday except take pictures and find a better place to catch tiger fish. Peter shot a good buffalo and this morning also a greater dik-dik and a bush pig.

One reason for coming here today was a hippo hunt that Werner had arranged. There is a shallow, muddy lake nearby with many hippos and crocodiles in it. We were to boat out through the reeds, decayed vegetation, and floating islands of tall grass, to an open area where the hippos were. One boat, the photographer's, was made from a stock tank and carried Halmi and four natives—the latter were the motive power. Gas drums had been wired to the sides to make it more seaworthy.

Our boat was a small wooden skiff that should have been larger for the number of people who rode in it; Werner, Fish, two natives, and I. There were about a dozen hippos rising and submerging. Werner had instructed me in the ways of hippo shooting, so I tried to follow instructions, when a big bull stuck his head out, and shot an arrow into its neck. He dived down and came for the boat beneath the muddy water. He circled the boat at the front end and Werner fired his .458 into the waves with great rapidity. There were quite a few hippos under that muddy water and we had some tense moments expecting the boat to be heaved into the air at any minute.

Halmi was taking pictures and his native crew had bulging eyes. My arrow came to the surface and was retrieved intact. The big fellow I had shot surfaced about fifty yards from us and half swam and half walked at good speed toward the marshy, tall grass. With a great lunge he dived under it and that was the last we saw of him. Everyone was glad to terminate the hunt after this. The hippo was not injured badly as the arrow had hit the thick skin on the back of his neck.

Tuesday, June 23, 9 P.M.—In flight to Nairobi now, sitting with Godfrey and about to have dinner. Have not written for almost ten days and have done little hunting during this time.

When we drove into the ditch in the Land Cruiser I was hurt more than I realized at the time. My back gave me the most trouble. It was not comfortable to ride in the jeep and to hunt; one must ride in order to find game.

As a result my activities were curtailed, although I did get another impala and a big wart hog with fine tusks. The impala was about fifty yards away. He was in charge of a group of does and very busy keeping other bucks away. It was only under conditions such as this that I have ever been able to get within fifty yards of these graceful, restless animals. In these circumstances the buck has a habit of facing away and pretending to ignore one. I saw this also in Uganda with the kob.

The impala was hit in the left hip. The arrow traveled forward into the lungs. He ran about 100 yards. The pig was shot from broadside through the hips. A second shot dispatched him in short order.

We made several early morning starts for buffalo country but each time were turned from our purpose by other animals. As a result the only buffaloes I saw were those we ran into while after the elephant.

A week ago a native in this vicinity was gored by one of these ill-tempered brutes. He was going to a water hole in the evening when a buffalo hooked him putting a horn between his buttocks. The horn came out through the groin. He was mauled badly and not found until the next morning. Some hunters brought him into main camp two days later and Dr. Miller did temporary surgery. The next day the patient was flown to Beira on the plane that came in for Godfrey's radio tape.

On one of our rides through the bush we came upon three natives preparing to wrest some honey from a beehive in the limb of a large tree. Two were adults and one a boy. We stopped to record the operation on film.

The men were making two baskets from green palm leaves. The boy was making a rope, also of palm leaves. After the baskets were finished, they took dried reeds and tied them into a bundle about five inches thick and five feet long and secured it to one end of the rope. Next they lit a fire on the ground and one of the men climbed the tree to a limb above the honey. He carried the palm rope in his hands, lowering the bundle of reeds into the fire until one end was burning and then hoisted it up to the honey limb to rout the bees. While the escapees swarmed all about and over the native, he was stung only twice. After the bees were gone, he used the rope to haul the baskets up and then lowered them to the ground again, full of honey. We thought of course, that the honeycombs would be carried back and shared in the village but the trio sat down and consumed the lot of it on the spot.

One afternoon we had another try at tiger fish going up the river to a large pool. For a while we had a strike at almost every cast. These fish would strike the lure up to four times on a retrieve. About every six strikes, one was hooked. For every three fish hooked, one is landed. Tiger fish are vicious-looking devils and the strongest fighters I have ever seen. They make about four jumps each, some jumps as high as six feet, shaking the lure out of their mouths the while. I believe the fish would take a fly, wet or dry. That would be real fishing. Twice they took fifty-yard lengths of eight-pound line from me and kept right on going.

Another very edible fish inhabits that water—the tilapia. It appears to belong to the bream family and weighs one half to two pounds. Prepared by a good cook it is the tastiest fish I have ever eaten. These fish are speared by the natives; almost never taken on artificial lures. Here again I would bet they could be caught with flies.

Tiger fish resemble bonefish. They have rather large scales and are beautifully colored in orange, silver, and black. I caught one that weighed about five pounds and Fish caught one of about ten.

Tilapia are speared by the men and cleaned by the women.

Surprisingly the river is cold and clear with a loose, sandy bottom. We fished standing in water two feet deep wearing shorts and tennis shoes. A boat would have made things easier.

We never found time to try for crocodiles, although the river is full of them, averaging seven to thirteen feet. I believe a good way to hunt them would be to float the river in a boat camouflaged with palm leaves. One could hunt hippos the same way.

Walter Johnson, Sr.'s tracker, Wanella, wore a sort of skullcap made from a nyala neck skin. The long brisket hairs were parted in the middle and I looked at it covetously for several days before asking Walter to tell Wanella I would like to buy it. The price was fifty escudos and I gladly paid. Halmi, photographing the transaction said, "Put it on," which I impulsively did, only to become host, in less than one minute, to some very unwelcome inhabitants in my hair. I was five days getting rid of them.

The natives here have bows and arrows and use them. The bows are made of local wood, round, in sectional shape and usually have strings of rawhide. Pulling one back about twenty inches the weight is about forty pounds. The next inch it goes to fifty and then to sixty and seventy, but nobody ever pulls it that far. The arrows are bamboo with heads of forged iron. Very deadly heads, but too heavy. The hunters deposit poison, made from pulverized seeds that grow in the area, back of the head on the tang. The arrow is fletched by a single feather tied to the rear of the shaft.

This is good bow country. The grass that will soon be burned provides cover for the game. Even so, shooting distance is seldom less than forty yards. If game were scarce it would be difficult for the bowhunter here, but game is not scarce and sooner or later a fine trophy can be had.. Total bag for the bow on this hunt: elephant, kudu, nyala, waterbuck, two impala, and two wart hogs. No wounded animals were left.

If I remember correctly, Godfrey's bag was: buffalo, eland, kudu, nyala, sable, waterbuck, impala, bushbuck, reedbuck, zebra, wildebeest, wart hog, and baboon.

Pete Barrett, who hunted only a few days, bagged a buffalo, nyala, bushbuck, oribi, and zebra. Pete looked over many kudu, trying to get one with sixty-inch horns but never saw one that big.

Arthur Godfrey did some bowhunting during the last few days. He claims there are many wart hogs suffering from pneumonia brought on by the strong breeze of his passing arrows. Wart hogs are expert at jumping the string but are second to impala in this respect. The latter can jump so gracefully that from my seventy-pound bow they are long gone when the arrow gets to them.

This country is easy on arrows. While there is much grass due to burning, there is no turf. I took forty-eight arrows on this trip and am bringing forty back with me.

Before leaving the main camp we placed our marks on the white wall of the lodge which is customary for departing clients. Pete Barrett wrote his name and underneath it, "TRUE." Halmi wrote his name underneath Pete's and added, "NOT TRUE." Godfrey came up with a zesty "A. Godfrey, EX-GAME WAR-DEN, NOW POACHER." I left an arrow firmly imbedded in the cement wall above my name. I hope I will see it again next year.

» «

The following is an interesting letter sent to Pete Barrett by Dr. Miller who sent a copy to me.

Dear Peter:

I intended to give you a ring when I came through New York Monday to say "hello" and see if you had arrived home safely but was delayed in customs and my plane connections became too tight to permit a call. Also, Werner had said that you were interested in the native that was gored by the buffalo and would appreciate a follow-up report. I checked on him when I came through Beira and he had made an uneventful recovery and was about ready to return to his village good as new.

We had a terrific elephant hunt in the Limpopo concession the weekend you left. I got two seventy-pounders in three days but damn near had to walk a hundred miles out of the bush. We were hunting on the Rhodesian border near where the Elephant River enters Mozambique in extremely rocky, mountainous terrain. We were a hundred miles from base camp and had gone cross-country over the rocks many miles in the jeep when we knocked several holes in the oil pan on the rocks and lost all of our oil. We were stranded without oil, overnight gear, or food as we had planned to return to Spike Camp that night. Fortunately, late in the afternoon I killed a big elephant. The next morning we had the natives butcher the elephant and we rendered the fat and got about eight gallons of "elephant oil." We plugged up the holes in the crankcase as best we could, although we were still losing oil at a steady drip and started out of the rocks at sundown. Every few miles we had to add oil and that night it became so cold the oil turned to lard. We would pack the oil spout full of lard and of course the motor heat would liquefy it. Finally, we made it back to base camp in the wee small hours, tired but at least not footsore. The moral of the story is: "in case you run out of oil, just shoot an elephant."

It was a great trip, a great hunt (including Copenhagen and Paris) and last but not least—an unexpected pleasure to meet you, Arthur, Fred, and Bob and enjoy your fellowship on Safari!! Please give them all my best regards when you see them.

Cordially yours,
Kenneth T. Miller, M.D.

NAIROBI

June 25, 1964—The safari is over. Godfrey, Halmi, Barrett, and I got back to Nairobi two days ago from Moçambique. Pete and I spent the day together, making notes and seeing the town. Godfrey and Halmi went flying with Dr. Mike Wood (a bush doctor who received an airplane, to help in his work, from Godfrey) on his rounds of native patients and to witness and photograph surgery in the field. Peter left for New York that same evening.

Yesterday morning the official presentation of Godfrey's plane to the African Research Foundation was made. Jomo Kenyatta could not be present, as had been planned, so Dr. Njoroge Mungri, Minister of Health and Housing, accepted the plane and made a speech during the colorful ceremonies and band music at the airport. A luncheon at the airport concluded the festivities and, following this, we all flew in the new plane to Lolkinyei, a Masai village where one of Dr. Wood's mobile units was in operation. Here were more ceremonies—a dance by Masai warriors, etc., was included in the well-arranged plans for our arrival.

The weather was rough for landing and once the plane was on the ground it was immediately surrounded by the impressive, tall warriors with their long spears and intricately braided hair. They made a striking picture in ocher-painted bodies and Masai necklaces. The new white plane soon bore many red imprints of their fingers. There was much handshaking beginning with the chief who wore an overcoat and felt hat. Next in importance was the head moran (warrior) who was highly decorated with more beads and more paint than anyone else.

It was agreed that in return for the dance staged in our honor, Dr. Wood would take the chief and head man for a ride in the plane. This he did, buzzing the group several times. After they landed the chief stepped out on one of the wings and told his subjects about his experience in a plane for the first time. "It was easy," he said. "We went up and we came down."

After this speech we went to the mobile hospital van which was fully enclosed and equipped to do major surgery. It was staffed with two doctors and a nurse who administered periodically to the needs of the Masai tribe.

While we watched, the doctor pulled fourteen teeth in as many minutes. The patient would point to the tooth that hurt, the doctor yanked it out and laid it in the hand of the sufferer. I wondered sometimes if "a tooth in the hand was not worth two in the mouth." Teeth are prized for decorative purposes on strings around the neck. They suffered the extractions stoically with no sign that they felt pain.

Warriors had gathered from three different villages, one of them quite nearby. The huts were in a circle and shaped like loaves of bread. They are constructed on a lattice of woven sticks plastered with cow dung. This is woman's work.

African society is well advanced from ours in that the women do all the work. The Masai warriors do nothing but stand around talking with each other or visiting other villages. If they see a girl who inspires them, no problem.

The weather became more threatening as the warriors went into their dance— really three dances, since each of the three groups performed separately. They

There was much handshaking.

moved mostly in a snake-dance sort of formation and at each skip-step a low, guttural, two-tone sound was emitted unlike anything I have heard before. There was no music or drums.

These warriors have remarkable physiques most of which could be observed in detail since their only garment was a strip of brick-red cloth hanging over one shoulder. They carried long spears and a polished stick. During the dance the pointed iron butts of the spears were stuck firmly into the ground in a circle.

One of the doctors had spent many years in Masai country and could speak the language. He said that he had seen them throw these spears through buffalo and rhino. This again proves that, as with arrows and bullets, when there is weight, great velocity is not needed. These are the people who formerly group-hunted lion with shields and spears. The government frowns on this method of hunting but Dr. Wood says sometimes a warrior takes on a lion singlehanded and comes to him with serious injuries from fang and claw.

The Masai are proud and fierce, with great integrity, we were told. They were eager to talk with us and I felt that they were extremely disappointed when we were unable to understand them. Godfrey asked the doctor if the natives were not terrified and confused when one of them was anesthetized for an operation. The doctor replied, "Sometimes they say, 'Look, he has killed him.'"

"But what do they say when the patient is revived?" asked Godfrey.

"They say, 'Now the damn fools have brought him back to life,'" the doctor said.

The dance had gotten nicely underway when the rain came, two inches in two hours.

Godfrey stayed in the van where he had been making a tape with the chief, a group of warriors, and the medical staff, while Bob and I, together with Dr. Wood, took refuge in the Land Rover. Some of the warriors who had been dancing simply stood there, their yellow-red ocher grease shedding the rain as if they were covered with duck feathers. The women, however, took off for the village to take advantage of the rain on their piles of cow dung, which would now be pliable and in condition to smear in the cracks on the roofs of their huts.

There are many flies around a Masai village. There is no sanitation. The cows are herded inside the circle of huts at night leaving a perfect breeding ground for insects. The huts have no windows and the door is low, allowing for a creeping entrance only. It is dark inside and the smoke from the cooking fires tends to discourage visitors as well as flies. . . .

About four-thirty in the afternoon the rain subsided and the rear doors of the van were opened to get the exchange of presents over with so we could return to Nairobi before dark.

Arthur presented the chief with a blanket and had some tobacco and red ocher for the warriors. He told them what fine people they were. The chief thanked Mr. Godfrey and told him to tell his people back home how poor the Masai tribe was and to send more presents.

It was unfortunate that the weather spoiled the dance before it had reached the frenzy stage and spear-throwing contest. We were also to have seen the spectacle of taking blood from cattle and were told that the Masai rarely eat meat or vegetables. Their diet is a curdlike cheese mixed with blood from the cows. They are handsome people. They lead a promiscuous existence and have problems with venereal disease and eye ailments. They do not bury their dead but simply take the corpse out to the bush for the hyenas. Old people about to die are often taken out to be disposed of in this way before death occurs.

Upon leaving, our take-off from the short, muddy, and rough airstrip was nothing less than miraculous. The rain was still coming down and, inside, the cabin fogged up badly. We had intended to go to the Amboseli Game Refuge for the night but decided to return to Nairobi instead.

Yesterday we flew to Laitokitok, a government district center where the ARF operates an eye clinic. From here we flew to Dr. Wood's farm for lunch. The farm is one of eight situated on the slopes of Mount Kilimanjaro. A very interesting place with, among other things, a thousand acres of wheat from which he takes two crops a year.

We had a delicious lunch and then flew to Amboseli Park where we were driven around by a warden. We saw a great deal of game and got some fine footage of a cheetah and her four offspring less than a month old.

Saturday, June 27—Arthur is behind with his radio tapes and decided to stay at the hotel and catch up. Bob and I were picked up early and taken to the airport where Bob took off with Dr. Wood in a Cherokee on an emergency call to a village north of here. Bob wants to photograph the operation scheduled there.

Bill Bunford, two pilots, and I departed in a twin Aztec for Lake Rudolph on the northern Kenya frontier. We planned to photograph the Turkana tribe who wear no clothes. We also wanted to fish for the giant Nile perch some of which weigh as much as three hundred pounds. Dr. Wood and Bob were to join us there following the operation. We ran into bad weather, however, twenty miles from Lake Rudolph and were forced to return to Nairobi. During most of the flight we had been only a few hundred feet over this wild north Kenya country. We were forced to fly at that altitude by the low ceiling and intermittent showers.

Habitation was sparse. We saw only occasional villages, with clusters of small huts about which natives stood staring up at the plane. Our twin engines gave us a feeling of confidence as we stared back at the glistening spears by their sides. Bill said this was a remote area we were flying so low over and that the natives were savages and known to be head-hunters. I asked if there were any arms aboard the airplane and the answer was no. Later I asked Dr. Wood if he carried a gun on his flights into the interior and he also said no. I think I would prefer to have a gun to stand off someone seeking my head.

The doctor and Bob were late coming back and when we made contact with them by radio we learned they were bogged down in a muddy field and may still be there as I finish these notes in my hotel room at 6 P.M.

Later—They came in just as I finished writing. We had dinner together and then to bed.

Sunday, June 28—An invitation from Jack Block, owner of the New Stanley and Norfolk hotels, to visit his farm fifty miles from Nairobi in the Rift Valley was readily accepted. In the party were Mrs. Block and Alma and Stan, entertainers in the Grill Room at the hotel.

At the farm we were joined by Mr. Block's brother and his wife and Lady (somebody). We had a fine lunch underneath some yellow fever trees and visited an adjoining farm belonging to Mr. and Mrs. Francescan Bizletti. Their place is known as the Marula Estate of Naivasha.

Both of the Bizlettis are animal lovers. They have a beautiful large, full-maned male lion and two females in a sizable compound backed up against a cliff. In another cage Mrs. Bizletti was playing with two younger lions. She invited us to enter the cage which we did but declined her offer to join in the play.

The show-stopper was a four-year-old female cheetah named Tula. Mr. Bizletti was with her and invited us in. I loved the cat. She was not at all timid and rubbed my legs and licked my hands, purring like an idling motor as I stroked her fur. She appeared to weigh eighty or ninety pounds and is capable of running sixty miles an hour on long, loping legs. A fine pet. A species that has never been known to attack man.

This concludes the African part of the trip. At 1 P.M. tomorrow we leave for Rome. We have had a busy time in Nairobi. Because of Godfrey's African Research Foundation activities, there has been a full schedule and never an idle moment. I am hoping for a few days of uninterrupted rest in Rome before joining Mrs. Bear in Copenhagen.

The show-stopper was a cheetah named "Tula."

Chapter 12

KISPIOX RIVER - 1964

GRIZZLY HUNT

KISPIOX—STEVENS LAKE BRITISH COLUMBIA

Friday, September 18, Noon—Have just finished making camp. The white tent looms up like a full moon against the dark spruce background. We're in a clearing along the Kispiox River—a muddy-trail mile from the south end of Stevens Lake.

Wally Love and Kolbjorn Eide arrived here on horses five days ago to get things in shape around camp. Jack Lee met us at the airport in Smithers and Bill Wright and I flew in to Stevens Lake in a Beaver plane with nine hundred pounds of food and gear.

The original purpose of this hunt was to make a bow and arrow grizzly hunting film for ABC's "Wide World of Sports" program and we have equipment for a crew of ten. Unfortunately, ABC found their schedule too tight and had to postpone their participation until next year. Our aim now is to follow through with the plans I made with Jack Lee and Bill Love when I left last year—to make a grizzly hunting film.

There are many films of hunting brown bears and pictures of brown bears catching spawning salmon but none, to my knowledge, of grizzlies. This is what we hope to get. Camera platforms have been erected at popular grizzly fishing sites located on a stretch of river where we saw twenty-three different grizzlies last fall.

Bob Halmi was to accompany me on this hunt as photographer if the ABC plans fell through and as co-ordinator if ABC's plans materialized. He was prevented from doing this at the last minute by illness in his family. This was just a few days before leaving home, so in desperation I called my friend "Jolly" Bill Wright in San Francisco who is a bowhunter and knows how to operate a camera. To my query by phone, "Bill, do you want to shoot a grizzly?", he replied, "When do we leave?"

As a result we are now here putting finishing touches on our comfortable camp. We have a twelve-by-fourteen tent made of white, eight-ounce canvas. The sidewalls are five feet high so that all of the floor space is usable. An oval-bodied sheet-iron stove, with the pipe going out through an asbestos patch in the roof, provides heat and keeps our clothing and gear dry. Poles running full length inside the eaves keep the tent standing firm, and nails driven into them make hanging space for clothes and cooking utensils.

A double-deck bunk takes up a three-by-seven-foot space in one corner. An-

Our camp in a clearing along the Kispiox River, a short mile from Stevens Lake.

other double-decker in the opposite corner would still leave space for comfortable living in the tent. Hanging from the ridge inside are cotton-tape loops supporting slender poles from which are hung the lanterns, drying boots, and clothing. Across the back near the stove, we have arranged benches of hand-hewn boards from an old Indian cabin nearby.

Great spruce trees fence the west side of the clearing and from this area the trail leads to Stevens Lake. Signs of an Indian campsite, sheltered under the branches of a tree, are visible at the edge of the clearing. Pieces of equipment hang from the tree—traps, pots, and pans, a shovel, saw, and ax. Leaning against the tree is an iron-shod sled.

Wally and Kolbjorn have bridged the small creeks with fallen spruce trees and a fine dock greets us when we reach the lake. Two boats with small engines are tied at the dock for the trip up the lake to Grizzly Creek. We went up there last evening and stayed until dark. Caught some Dolly Varden and left them on the point to see if bears were in the area.

Jack and Bill came up here early in August to enlarge the photography platform we used last year and built two more overlooking favorite bear-fishing spots. Wally and Kolbjorn sat in one of them the evening before we came and saw three grizzlies come down to the river, walking under the platform en route. The bears caught and ate some fish and then returned to the hillside by the same path.

We saw no bears last night, although we stayed late and did not get back to camp until after dark. But Kolbjorn and I, from our platform at the mouth of the creek, enjoyed watching a loon teach her lone offspring to catch fish. The water was clear and we could see them swimming beneath the surface with great speed. The mother caught small fish and gave them to her little one after they both surfaced. An eagle was there also, scanning the river for fish and, just before dark, three mergansers came by.

Before going to the river last night a bull moose appeared in the woods along the trail. Bill and I spent several hours trying to catch up with him, to no avail.

There are sockeye salmon in the creek by the hundreds and the coho (silver salmon) are milling around the mouth of the creek.

Bear signs are few compared to other years. Perhaps because we are earlier the bears have not yet found this banquet site. It was ten days later when we came last year but we have time, and hope to see many grizzlies.

Saturday, September 19, 10 A.M.—Jack Lee and his wife, Frances, got in last evening at seven o'clock. They came upriver from Hazelton, bringing nine horses and another tent as well as the rest of our supplies. This makes a total of twelve horses contentedly grazing on the grass in the clearing. The cook tent is set up and everything is in order. We plan to go up the creek right after lunch.

Sunday, September 20, 8 P.M.—Searching along the creek yesterday, there was nothing of note until we got to the upper end of creek ✕2. From there, looking across the connecting pond to creek ✕3, we saw two bears on a log. We made a stalk and Bill was close to shooting range when I cracked a twig trying to get him lined up with the bear for pictures. The bears made off and we did not see them again.

Photography platform ✕2 is not properly located. This is the hottest area on the creek—I shot a grizzly here two years ago. We have decided that a cluster of spruce trees on the opposite bank would support a platform better and offer an unrestricted view of more river including the log across the water.

Kolbjorn felled a large hemlock across the creek from the north bank and did a fine job dropping the top at the point where we'd build the new platform. We cleaned it of all branches and now have a bridge for ourselves and a log from which the bears can fish. It is about a foot above water and is not likely to go out in high water as the stump will hold it on one side and the rocky point on the other. We soon had a fine spacious platform built on the spot and trees were cleared for a good view of 180 degrees. We also cleared brush along the shore.

At platform ✕3, we felled a "bear log" also. Bears like to walk logs and frequently jump at fish from them.

Monday, September 21, 10 P.M.—Kolbjorn suggested last evening that we should check the creek where it leaves Swan Lake to see if bears are feeding there. This is where we camped two years ago. We should also check the creek on

Bears like to walk logs.

the northeast side of the lake, he said, leaving no stone unturned in our search for bears. Why he would suggest the tough job of dragging the boat across two ridges in order to do this only attests to the quality of guiding services offered by Lee and Love, Outfitters. Wally helped Kolbjorn with the boats, about a half mile of tough going, but we found no bear signs, although there were plenty of fish in the short creek.

Motoring to Falls Creek up the northeast side of Swan Lake, we found an abundance of fish and bear signs but we saw no bears. As in other years the wind was blowing straight up the river and our presence could be detected before we got there. Our plans, when we hunt it again, are to put ashore in a bay beyond the creek, circle to hit it at its upper end, and come down with the wind in our face.

We left the boat at the lower end of Club Lake and hunted down the creek toward Stevens Lake. We saw the two bears again at the end of creek ⌗3 but they either heard or winded us. We cut across the ridge and returned to camp in our second boat.

Tuesday, September 22, 9 P.M.—Having made so much noise dragging the boat over rocks and left so much man scent on the creek, we thought it advisable not to hunt there again for a day or two. We wanted to check some creeks about ten miles up the Kispiox and this seemed like a good day to do it. We used the horses for the trip today. Kolbjorn and Bill checked one creek while Jack, Wally, and I looked the other one over. Not a fish on either one and consequently no bears. Bill shot a ruffed grouse on the way home.

Wednesday, September 23—This was the test day. The photography platforms had been built since August and renovated last Sunday. Up to now, one week, we have not done any serious hunting—all has been make-ready work. Today would determine if we had made the proper plans and had been wise in the selection of hunting spots.

It was raining as usual when we left camp at nine this morning. Every day for a week we have had some rain in variable degrees of intensity. There were both moose and bear tracks on the muddy trail. The bears had been at our docking site and bitten holes in two of our plastic gas cans.

It was still raining as we climbed into the photography platform. It never let up, in fact, all day. With camera on tripod, covered with plastic to protect it from the rain, we sat down on chunks of timber to wait for whatever action was to come.

The platform was not big enough for four of us and Wally and Kolbjorn tossed a coin to see which one would leave and investigate platform ⚒3 for reports on the activity there. Wally lost the toss and moved on to the next location while Kolbjorn stayed with us.

At twelve-thirty, two beautiful silver-and-black grizzlies came out just thirty yards upriver on our side. I felt sure these look-alikes were from the same family. The one I took to be a female, and who also seemed to be the boss, looked as if she would weigh 175 or 200 pounds. The other one probably 225 or 250.

They walked straight out on a log and were not concerned about the changes we had made in the landscape by clearing the brush and building the platform. For the next hour they caught fish and ate many of them. They explored the river all the way down to the lake but came back to do most of their fishing near our site.

They accepted the new log bridge without question and one of them came across to a spot just ten yards from us. At one-thirty the larger bear started walking up on our side until a gust of wind gave him our scent and he fled to the bush warning his companion with a bear-talk "auk, auk." At this signal, the smaller bear rushed into the brush also.

They came back at about five o'clock and stayed for an hour or more, walking logs, lunging for fish and splashing around. They seldom caught a live fish but seemed content to eat dead, spawned-out fish they found on the bottom in the still water. We exposed 550 feet of film this afternoon.

Wally's report on platform ⚒3 was as follows: When he reached the spot a dark brown bear of between 350–400 pounds was in the river. It spent ten minutes looking suspiciously around before eventually leaving the river of the far side.

Near noon two smaller bears came in and fished, he said. Only one of them caught anything and they left after a short time. At one-thirty they were back again, staying about ten minutes, doing a little haphazard fishing.

Thursday, September 24, 3 P.M.—Rained hard all night and until just a few minutes ago. We decided to stay in camp and thoroughly dry out all gear and grease our boots. The camera equipment took a severe wetting down yesterday. I hope the film stayed dry.

A lone Canadian goose circled the clearing at camp this morning and set down near the ruins of the Indian camp. Jack, Wally, and Kolbjorn are cutting a "go-devil" trail to Stevens Lake. A "go-devil," Jack says, is a wide, skidlike sled drawn by a horse. This is to save backpacking from the plane. The horses have been moved to a fresh grazing ground.

We have had rain almost continuously since we came. Probably a total of only six hours of sunshine. The sun is out now as I write and it looks like we might get a break.

The Kispiox has risen about two feet in the past two days. This is good since there is a great concentration of sockeye and coho salmon, at the bottom of the canyon, waiting for more water to get them through the falls and rapids. We are anxious for them to do this as we need a fresh supply of fish on the creeks.

Same Day, 8 P.M.—A new outlook on life since the weather cleared up about 3 P.M. today. Much hustle and bustle! Wood cut and piled high and Frances is three pies ahead. Bill and I did some practice shooting and took pictures around camp. We hope this weather will hold out for another day or two.

Friday, September 25, 5:30 P.M.—Bill, Wally, and I are sitting in platform ⚓2. We have been here since 9 A.M. and have not yet seen a bear. Kolbjorn is alone at ⚓3 to record events there.

It was clear and cold last night. Stars were brilliant and there was a heavy frost this morning. The first of the season. The sockeye salmon have greatly diminished in numbers and this afternoon the first school of coho went upstream.

Although we have not seen any bears, we have been entertained by the antics of other wildlife. We saw a hooded merganser, for instance, devour salmon eggs by the hundreds. He swam just below the spawning fish, gobbling up the orange eggs as fast as they appeared. A golden eagle sat for a long time on a stub nearby, and across the river a kingfisher used a branch as his catapult to dive for minnows. We plan to stay until about seven-thirty if the light holds. These last two hours could be the best time.

Same Day, 8 P.M.—A little after 6 P.M. a small sow and three cubs, two black and one silver, came in to the creek below us. They scrounged about along the shore picking up bits of fish left by other bears. Then they crossed on our bear log and snuffed around just below us for a while before moving upstream, crossing back on another log and moving downstream toward where our boat is tied. Kolbjorn is about due to meet us there. He might find himself rather busy.

The bears were in sight for about forty minutes and gave us an excellent show. Mama had her hands full keeping in touch with the three hungry little fellows. Several times we heard her calling "auk, auk" to them.

By 7 P.M. we felt that the bears had cleared the area. My guess was that they had met Kolbjorn and run off. But not so . . . !

Wally was the first to go down the ladder. Bill was handing him gear. I looked across the river and there were two of the cubs near the end of our log. Wally scampered back up and we stayed up until seven-thirty before making our departure. When we got to the far end of our log bridge there were the bears again, about thirty yards up in the bushes. We sneaked out without disturbing them and found Kolbjorn on the ⚒1 platform. The family had been under and all around his perch. They had even investigated our boat before wandering off. Kolbjorn had seen the same group earlier from blind ⚒3. He also saw a male bear and a sow with a yearling.

Sunday, September 27, 1 P.M.—Sitting in blind ⚒2 with Jack and Bill. Kolbjorn is in ⚒3. We have been here just an hour. A beautiful day with no rain.

We decided to make a fishing picture this morning since the light was so good. This was done at the mouth of the creek where we always seem able to catch Dolly Varden trout.

Three Dollies and a rainbow trout made up our catch of the morning. One of them is now suspended from a string on a tree across the river—the string

Bill Wright caught a Dolly Varden.

stretching over to our blind. We hope to have fun with a bear by raising the fish just beyond his reach. We'll see.

There were no bears here yesterday. As usual it rained most of the day but we have now erected a canvas roof over our heads which keeps off some of the rain. Back at camp a bull moose spent several hours in the brush, Frances said. He came within twenty yards of the tent and she also saw him at close range when she went to the river for water. Jack thinks there is probably a cow nearby also.

Tuesday, September 29, 6 P.M.—No bears showed at either blind on Sunday, although Kolbjorn saw one briefly on the upper creek. The bears have us confused. There is not nearly the action of other years.

Yesterday we intended to hunt Falls Creek on Swan Lake and before leaving thought it would be wise to check the creek banks here at camp. This we did and found tracks of a sow and cub and also a third, larger track.

A plane came in to our dock on Stevens Lake this afternoon. It was the fisheries men here to take sockeye specimens from Falls Creek and to travel from Swan to Stevens lakes by rubber boat. This interfered with our hunting, so we went fishing for steelheads on the Kispiox instead. No luck at this but Bill and I caught enough Dolly Varden for a fine meal.

This morning Bill and Kolbjorn went up to spend the day at #3 blind and Jack, Wally, and I cut a new trail to Stevens Creek where coho are now spawning.

Thursday, October 1, 5 P.M.—Am in our tent alone. Warm and snug while the wind bombards my cozy retreat with a heavy downpour. This morning we built another photography platform on Stevens Creek overlooking the coho spawning. We do not expect to get action there immediately. The fish are still running up the creeks and many are gathered at the mouth of Swan Creek waiting to swim upstream for the last activity of their lives.

They are beautiful fish. Since leaving salt water, they have lost their silver sheen and now, after swimming a thousand miles upstream in fresh water, their backs are dark gray, their sides show streaks of red, and their bellies reddish-pink.

We have caught several at the mouth of Swan Creek where they still retain their fighting spirit, making gyrations and jumping out of the water. A month from now they will be dead or dying. Their offspring will return to these waters another year to repeat the cycle of reproducing their kind.

Yesterday Kolbjorn, Bill, and I spent the day between blinds #2 and #3. It was raining and a rather cool day. We quit early and were catching Dolly Vardens at the mouth of the creek when two bears appeared on a log at blind #2.

We made our way up there but could not see them, so we crossed the log and climbed up into our blind. We saw one of the bears almost immediately, in the brush twenty yards away. Five minutes later another bear walked directly under our blind and went to the river to pick up pieces of discarded fish. The sockeye spawn is about over now.

A second, and larger, bear walked up to our ladder and looked straight up at our three peering heads before turning to walk away. We got some pictures of the group at the edge of the stream.

Jack, Wally, Kolbjorn, and Bill left at 3 P.M. to hunt and photograph from the blinds on Swan Creek. I decided to remain in camp to do chores, get cleaned up, and catch up with these notes. I am without doubt the most comfortable of our group, with the wind and rain howling outside, but I dislike the idea of missing any action the others might run into. The grizzlies seem to think only of their stomachs, not of weather.

From here on this will be a hunt with less emphasis on photography. We already have seven hundred feet of grizzlies in action on the creeks. Much of the footage is close-ups of fishing and eating fish. Any fair-sized bear is target for an arrow from now on.

We have not been able to find any trace of the giant bear I have been looking for in this country for four years. The inroads of civilization could have pushed him farther north or he may have died of old age.

The bear situation is definitely different from other years. This year there are sockeyes in all of the creeks and the bears are roaming. Almost every day we see one to three grizzly tracks on the trail from Stevens Lake to camp. They are digging skunk cabbage and eating water-lily roots along the shores. Some are still cruising the creeks picking up odd fish. The bears we have seen lately seem reluctant to get their feet wet and prefer to walk the logs or shore. A week ago they took delight in sitting in the creek to eat fish rather than carry them ashore.

Friday, October 2—The group got in late last evening. They had a stormy, wet trip but saw three grizzlies on the east shore of Stevens Lake. As we went up the lake this morning we saw where they had been eating water lilies.

Wally and I are settled down in blind ⚔2. It is 1 P.M. Bill and Kolbjorn are up at blind ⚔3. We tossed a coin for position last night. It is raining off and on and the light for pictures is not good but there is no wind and the temperature is moderate. I got cold at about two-thirty, however, and suggested that we go down to the boat and see if we could catch a fish or two. Also, I had shot a blunt into a stump across the river and wanted to put a few drops of anise oil on the feathers. In the event a bear came along and sniffed it, it would make a fine picture. As it turned out, pulling in a rainbow trout, I glanced up the river and saw a grizzly on the side our blind is on.

Wally and I debated the situation and decided the bear would work upstream and we had better try to get back to our blind. We kept a watch across the river and when nearing our log bridge we saw the bear take a dead fish into the brush to eat it. We quickened our pace, crossed the log, and climbed up into the blind. We were no sooner up than a bear came out on a log downstream on the side we'd just left!

This blind is about 300 yards from the mouth of the river where we tie the boat. We walk on a bear trail to reach it—the trail varying from ten to twenty yards from the water. The riverbank is fringed with alder. We had unknowingly passed this bear coming up the trail to the blind. Now we had two bears before us. One was about 200 pounds and the other larger. They were nervous and kept testing the air with noses held high. The big one crossed the river and joined the first one on the far bank.

Together they went downstream, walking logs and searching for dead salmon, and then worked their way back up and approached our position very cautiously. The small one came up just below us on the far bank. He picked up a dead fish and went up the hillside. The other went into the brush also, possibly sharing the fish and taking a nap since it was forty-five minutes before they came back again.

This time they were even more cautious and came to the creek thirty-five yards away, looked the area over for a few minutes, and then went upstream toward ✗3 blind where Bill and Kolbjorn were watching. Final departure was just before five. I had exposed about 150 feet of film and would have shot the larger bear if he had obliged by sniffing my arrow. Both were nicely colored. Silver and black.

Saturday, October 3, 3 P.M.—There was no further action yesterday at blind ✗2.

We checked Stevens Creek again this morning but the coho are still not there in any great numbers. We had a lazy midday at camp taking pictures and getting organized.

This is the best day we have had. Not a drop of rain so far and the sun shining brightly. Jack and I are in blind ✗3. Bill and Kolbjorn in ✗2. Only six sockeyes in sight from our blind. An eagle just caught a fish a hundred yards or so away.

About three-thirty we heard a bear on the wooded hillside about 100 yards down the river. At four-thirty the grunt sounded if it were directly across from us and just now, at five-thirty, we heard it again. "Auk"!

Sunday, October 4—Sitting on a hillside near Stevens Lake. Jack, Wally, Kolbjorn, and Bill are building platform ✗5 at a point where a log crosses the creek. Above and below this are several spawning cohoes.

Last evening from blind ✗3 Jack and I saw the two biggest bears we have seen this year. Bill and Kolbjorn saw nothing from blind ✗2.

We decided to build this blind last evening at dinner. In building the last blind we had used all available supplies of spikes, rope, and wire, and hardware was now a prime problem. We scrounged around camp this morning reclaiming some spikes and nails from the deserted Indian cabin. We took every other rope from the tent and some large nails that were used for hanging things inside. Searching further, Wally and Kolbjorn took the boat to the end of Stevens Lake to an old oil-research camp where we had seen odd pieces of plywood, two-by-fours, and nails and spikes.

Hunting toward the new blind site, Jack, Bill, and I found thirty feet of ✗9 wire that Indians had used for a grizzly snare. This was a good find although it took some doing to untangle it. Jack and Bill worked at it while I went on. Several times I heard something ahead of me but supposed it was Wally and Kolbjorn. When I reached our destination I waited for Jack and Bill to catch up. Bill came first and we crawled through the alders to the edge of the creek. Downstream on a log were two fine grizzlies. We had just passed this section but could not see the creek through the brush. We immediately backtracked to Jack who had also seen them. They were fine male bears. The first big ones we had seen this close. One looked to be about 350 pounds and the other 450.

They went downstream on the far bank. We stole down our side and took a stand near the end of what appeared to be a well-traveled bear log crossing the creek. We did not have long to wait. On the other side the bears passed the end of the log and started up the hillside. At this most opportune moment two cohoes made mighty splashes just above the log.

The bears had had no luck fishing and this temptation was too great. The smaller one turned and came walking straight across the log in our direction. I was backing Bill for pictures. When the grizzly was twenty yards away he started to draw his bow and I started the camera. It sounded like a bulldozer in the stillness of this British Columbia forest. The instant the camera started, the grizzly flipped over like a cat and clawed up that log getting back to the far side. Bill had only a snapshot.

To shoot a grizzly with a bow is task enough as it is necessary to get very close. To shoot one with a bow and make a film of it is quite an assignment and we failed on both.

Monday, October 5, 4 P.M.—Happy Birthday. This is for my wife from whom I am always separated on this date since she had the misfortune to be born in hunting season! Wally and I are up in the new blind. It is quite an establishment perched on a hillside about thirty feet above the river. We have a plywood floor and a roof of drooping branches against which my back rests while sitting on a section of log we use for chairs.

We finished the blind last night about seven o'clock. The front of the platform is supported by two spruce poles about ten inches across at the small ends. These are cross-braced and support two horizontal logs that are spiked and wired to the trees behind us. Two-by-fours on edge span the logs and plywood is nailed over all.

For photography this is the ultimate. The creek is wide and slow at this point. Apparently the cohoes prefer this milder current as there are about forty directly below us. It is a clear day. We got here at eleven this morning. Bill came with us and spent an hour photographing the fish and an eagle perched on a tree nearby. He then went down to join Kolbjorn and watch for bears at blind ⅗3.

During the platform building yesterday, Bill cut a trail in from our docking place. This makes a better approach since now we won't have to follow the bear trail along the river. Our new roost is a delightful place. We experience great contentment sitting here waiting for nature's show to begin. Birds and fish are the preliminaries to the production—darting from tree to tree or splashing in the bright water below. Suspense hangs heavy as the day quiets into evening and the grizzlies, for whom all living things yield right-of-way, may approach quietly to this spot.

Perhaps not tonight, however. In hunting there is always the element of luck to be reckoned with. We may have disturbed this area too much yesterday. Or perhaps the grizzlies hankered for a taste of skunk cabbage and went off in another direction. But as the day wanes our chances increase, although the light for photography decreases. I would like to photograph these two big grizzlies. Up to now I do not have pictures of big bears. I would also like to shoot the big one and would do so if he presented himself after my film was exposed.

We must leave here at seven o'clock, although there is shooting light until almost eight. It takes twenty minutes to walk the new trail to the boat and another ten minutes by boat to the mouth of the creek where we pick up Bill and Kolbjorn. From there it is twenty-five minutes down to the end of Stevens Lake. It will be dark when we get there and the trail to camp then takes another twenty minutes. We usually have dinner about 9 P.M.

Tuesday, October 6, 3:30 P.M.—There are rainbow trout in the creek. The water is crystal clear and we see them lazily finning below the cohoes, hoping for

an egg or two to drift by. While watching them yesterday I saw them rise to a
rare fly and decided that our new perch would be a good place from which to
photograph some fly fishing. Some of these trout should weigh two pounds. There
are whitefish also and they will take flies.

Another clear day and Bill manned the camera while I whipped the water with
a fly. A good trout took it the first time but he also took my ✳12 Adams fly. I
was using a 4X tapered leader from which I cut off about eighteen inches to get a
heavier tip. After this they refused the ✳12 and I changed to a ✳16 Palmer tied
fly. With this I caught three trout. The whitefish would have none of this fly.

We had lunch in our tree house and then Bill and Kolbjorn took the bear trail
over to Falls Creek to see if cohoes are spawning there.

The sockeyes are gone, their spawning finished. The bears and gulls have
picked up all dead fish and pieces. Blinds number 1, 2, and 3 are finished, as
cohoes do not spawn in fast riffles as sockeyes do. This is the only coho spawning
area we have found so far. Most of them must spawn in the lakes between the
creeks.

Unless Bill and Kolbjorn find cohoes in Falls Creek we are limited to this spot
and to the blind on Stevens Creek. There are cohoes there and another attraction
also. Jack brought an old horse to that spot—one destined for the glue factory.
Five days ago it was laid to rest on the offriver side of the blind. It is only about a
third of a mile from camp and we visit it every morning. We have seen a very
large bear track on the trail from Stevens Lake not far from the bait. Jack had
been clearing the trail and we discovered that the bear had walked the trail
behind him.

Our hopes were at highest pitch, therefore, as we went in for a look this morning. The big fellow had taken the trail to the bait, left droppings this side of our
crossing log, crossed the log, and followed our trail to within fifty yards of the
bait. He had not touched it, however. The wind might not have been right or perhaps he was too cautious to go straight to the bait the first time he saw it.

We have two chances now besides still-hunting. That blind and the new one we
are in now. Both are prime spots and both have good-sized bears in the area.

The bears did not show last evening. They were here, however, between the
time we left and when we got here this morning. I had erected a "bear detector"
on the log. Some alder branches placed so they would be brushed off if a bear
passed. They were gone this morning.

Thursday, October 8, 3 P.M.—Jack and I are in blind ✳3. There are a few
cohoes spawning about sixty yards from us. Bill has to leave Saturday. With no
takers of the bait as yet, we discussed the problem of getting a bear since only
blind ✳4 remains hopeful. It seemed best to man it night and day, so yesterday
morning, Bill and Kolbjorn packed sleeping bags and food. Wally went along to
help Kolbjorn portage the small boat back from Swan to Stevens Lake.

Wally got back last evening and told us that the bears were along the river
when they got to blind ✳4. He left and did not know the outcome.

Jack and I hunted all the way down Stevens Creek yesterday. Wet bear tracks
on a log indicated they had been made recently, although we did not see him. We
saw various other tracks, too, including those of the big bear.

We have had clear weather for the last three days. Yesterday was almost hot.

Today is cloudy and warm. We checked the bait and hunted the creek again this morning. Nothing to report except that there are still more cohoes.

Wally left by horse for Hazelton this morning to arrange for a plane to come in Saturday for Bill. Bill has had no luck yet with the bears, so he and Kolbjorn spent last night, also, in blind ⚡4. His time is running out.

Jack and I decided we were wasting our time on Stevens Creek and that we would go back to blind ⚡3. We have some Dollies and a coho for bait.

With hindsight we realize that if we had known earlier in the hunt that sockeyes would fade so fast, we could well have gotten some average-sized bears. We thought it more important to get pictures at that point, however, since that was the first object of the trip. The sockeye run has been early. Last year we left here on the fifth of October during the height of the run. This year we should have arrived about September 1.

We have noticed another change from other years—there have been no mad sows nipping at our heels, roaring and huffing and puffing. Nobody has gotten "treed" yet. Rather a dull hunt in this respect. I had half hoped we might meet the big black mama again that was so intent on doing us in last year.

In spite of bad luck in bagging bears up to now we have added much to our knowledge of fish and bears and other wildlife. The coho salmon, for instance, prefer, in fact, insist on, slow water in which to spawn. Some even spawn in the shallows of lakes. Reaching the spawn area the female is attended by a large male who guards her fiercely against all aggressors. He chases them away with gusto, even biting at a tail if one gets too close. While he is chasing an offender, some lesser one who has been lying below will rush in behind his back.

There are Dolly Varden, rainbows, and whitefish to observe and the mergansers, robbing spawning fish of their eggs, are a study of continuing interest.

We are sitting out, you might say, a period between spawns. The cohoes are still very active but from observation at blind ⚡5 the grizzlies have not yet caught a fish. Their frustration has been accented by loud roars following desperate lunges and splashes.

We heard a bear roar another time on the hillside across the river from where we are now. A few days later, we went over and found where a bear, presumably a boar, had killed and eaten a cub.

Friday, October 9, 3 P.M.—Jack and I are in blind ⚡3 again. Got here at 9 A.M. to find the two Dollies we'd put out for bait gone but the coho still here. At noon we hiked up to visit Bill. He was sitting in blind ⚡4 counting cohoes. Kolbjorn had gone to camp for food. They have not seen any bears. This is a last-ditch stand for Bill. His last evening. I plan to stay another week. There is more to learn here.

The scarcity of bears now could mean that they have had enough fish and are tapering off to a vegetable diet in preparation for hibernation. My thinking is that they will be back on the river, however. At this point, twenty-eight different bears have been sighted. It would seem that there have been enough bears seen to complete both the photography and the trophy, but only four of these bears have been of trophy size and these were reluctant to offer themselves as targets at a respectable distance.

Saturday, October 10, 9 A.M. **In Camp**—Jack and I left the blind at six last evening to have a look at our bait before dark. Fished a bit at the creek and caught a good Dolly for lunch. Pictures at camp today. Bill leaves this afternoon and we need more pictures around camp before he goes.

It was almost dark when we carefully approached the bait last night. Barely visible beyond the carcass stood a very large bear, probably twenty yards away. Jack said that he was facing us. We could see the dead horse as it was behind a rise in ground. Almost immediately, from the brush below, a small cub shinned up a tree fifteen yards from us. It made a great racket breaking dry limbs as it climbed. The big one remained quite still.

Seeing a cub we knew there was a sow there. However, the big one looked too large to be a sow. At any rate the place took on an unhealthy atmosphere. It was too dark to shoot accurately with a gun and a charge seemed imminent. I could think only of getting out of there. When we were 100 yards away we heard a menacing growl.

Jack and I discussed the big bear and decided it had just happened on the bait scene after the sow and cub got there. We were strengthened in this theory when we heard ferocious growling and snarling for half an hour about midnight. We could hear them all the way to camp. We have no stomach to get involved in this family squabble and will not go to the bait tomorrow. By the next day the big one should be master of the situation and he is the one I want.

Wednesday, October 14—Bill was supposed to have left on Saturday. We had a lazy morning. Bill packed and Jack and I hunted Stevens Creek and sat in the blind. The plane was due in between four and five in the afternoon. At 3 P.M. it started to rain and really came down. Ceiling was at the treetops. There would be no plane that day.

Jack and I went to the bait again Sunday. We got there at 2 P.M. and around four o'clock two small grizzlies came in and had a feast. It was too dark and quiet for the camera. They filled their bellies and went off down the river. We stayed until dark but no more bears came.

On Sunday night the rain stopped. Bill's plane came in at 10 A.M. Monday. It was a welcome sight, bringing supplies to take us off the rice diet we'd been on for two days.

Monday afternoon Jack and I hunted Stevens Creek and found good bear signs and a few places where grizzlies had caught and eaten fish. It appears they are working the coho run now. At five-thirty we went to the blind and in no time heard twigs crack on the ridge above us. A fine five-hundred-pound grizzly walked out of the bush and made straight for the bait. He lay down with his rear half behind a tree and tore at the meat with fang and claw. I lost no time getting into position and ready but was reluctant to shoot because while he was broadside to me the shoulder blade was sliding back and forth over his rib cage as the front leg worked like a piston clawing the bait.

Waiting a minute (which seemed like an hour), something suddenly went wrong and the bear was up and off in an instant. I shot him in the rear as he headed off. The arrow seemed too far back but we learned later it had cut the femoral artery. He roared and spun around twice breaking the arrow off against a tree. I had another arrow nocked and waiting and this one went through the

The grizzly head and skin filled the packboard.

lungs. He started off with a jump or two, walked a dozen steps and lay down. In half a minute the heavy breathing stopped and he was dead.

All of yesterday was spent in skinning the bear and taking pictures. We concluded that he had been one of the antagonists of the night before and that the fight must have been a stand-up affair since his chest was badly bruised and bloodshot.

Today we took pictures in camp. The bear skin, laced to drying poles, made a good background for campfire scenes. In the early afternoon Jack and I went to the bait blind. When we got there, a year-old grizzly popped up a good-sized hemlock tree where he was hidden from us by some limbs as we got into the blind. We have noticed that bears seem to prefer the rough bark of hemlock for climbing over the smoother bark of spruce or balsam.

We were quiet for half an hour and by this time the bear seemed to forget about us and came down to have a little snack at the bait. He was very jittery, however, and kept looking about, more afraid of other bears, we thought, than of us. I have never seen a more nervous bear. He would shin up his tree again whenever his imagination got the better of him, puffing and grunting all the way. He was a beautiful silver-shouldered fellow, well filled out, with a white patch on his throat and chest. We estimated his weight at about 125 pounds and named him Junior. After he left there was no more activity that day.

Friday, October 16—Our last day in camp and a combination of rain and snow falling steadily. This hunt has been extremely fruitful for studying bears and photography. The first part of the hunt was devoted to this end. With the sockeye spawn ending earlier this year and the grizzlies showing little concern for the cohoes, our trip could have ended without a kill if it had not been for the horse Jack brought in for bait. Hibernation could be just two or three weeks away, depending on weather, and having had their fill of fish the bears seemed to crave red meat. The horse filled this need.

Mike Nolan, a Yukon outfitter, says that grizzlies are very even-tempered animals; always mad. This is not entirely true, although a sow with small cubs is apt to have a short temper. On this hunt we saw only one sow with a small cub and we were not sure it wasn't a runt from last year. Aside from this one, all the cubs we saw were born in February of last year. At this age the mother more or less sheds responsibility.

Last year, hunting the same area, we encountered many sows with small cubs. One kept me up a tree all night huffing and puffing below.

In addition to the twenty-eight different bears we saw during the first part of this hunt, we saw thirteen more at the bait. Two of the bears were only ten feet away, two were twenty feet, and many were less than twenty yards from us.

During four seasons that total three months of this type of hunting, I have reached certain conclusions that can apply at least to the bears of the upper

Making notes of the day's activities.   *Hemlock and spruce country.*

The fisherman is determined.

Precarious footing.

Kispiox in the fall of the year: their eyes are very poor, their nose is not as good as I had expected, but their hearing is the best.

Our last week was not without its thrills. The camp was about four hundred yards from the bait and the area was a beehive of cruising, hungry bears.

The trail from camp to the landing at Stevens Lake paralleled the creek and many times, making the trip over and returning about an hour later, we found bear tracks over ours in the mud on the path. We found tracks only forty yards from our tents and often heard the roaring and growling of bear fights nearby. We developed a habit of watching out of the corner of our eye and Jack began packing his rifle when tending the horses a quarter of a mile away. I almost felt uneasy carrying the name of BEAR!

Chapter 13

MOÇAMBIQUE - 1965

A number of friends, having read my field notes on the hunt here the year before, wanted to make this second trip into Portuguese Africa with me. My reasons for going back again was to do a film of hunting the Cape buffalo, an animal that had eluded me last year.

Frankly, I had a profound yearning to have another hunt in that great country and the filming provided the excuse to go there. Had I known that I would be so fortunate as to bag both a buffalo and lion, I would not have needed an excuse.

June 3, 11 A.M.—A tire is being repaired as I rest, with my back against a tree in the warm sun. This is the first opportunity to write notes since we reached camp three days ago.

There are eight in our party. Bill Wright, San Francisco; Dick Mauch, Nebraska; K. Knickerbocker, Virginia; Robert Munger, Michigan, and I from Michigan. In addition we have two photographers from New York, Robert Halmi and Zoli Vidor. Also a writer, Jim Crowe, from the Detroit *News*.

Wally Johnson, Sr., is my guide. Our outfitters are Moçambique Safarilandia which is directed by Werner von Alvensleben.

Yesterday we began our prime project of filming and shooting a Cape buffalo. With a carload of camera gear we started for buffalo country at 8 A.M. About ten miles from camp a native stopped us to say that a lone bull buffalo was terrorizing his village, chasing people and destroying gardens. Besides this they were badly in need of meat. He told us the buffalo spent his days in the thick reeds along the river. We went to have a look.

We ran into a group of natives there who were operating and sampling the product of a palm brewery near their camp on a riverbank that dropped down to the reeds. These reeds, with stems like bamboo stalks about a half inch thick, covered the flats for a third of a mile. At the moment the buffalo "was there" according to one of the natives who pointed down into the thicket about sixty yards from their camp. Calling it a "camp" was a generous term. All we could see were reed sleeping mats and a bow but no arrows. Walter suspected the natives had had a little too much palm wine but he decided after some hesitation to give it a try. Frankly, none of us were too eager to go into those dense reeds and push a buffalo around—particularly one that had been chasing people. The native did not say whether anyone had been hurt here but we knew that a lone buffalo in a

With a carload of camera gear we started for buffalo country.

village about three or four miles away had killed five people so far this year and was still at large.

This place did not look good for photography but the natives said there were clearings in the reeds where we might get good shots. We did not know that this particular buffalo had been caught in a snare that had injured his foot. The wire had caused it to swell to twice its normal size and the walking surface was raw and bleeding.

We went down into the reeds with some apprehension, with one of our natives, Luiz, carrying my .375 rifle. Walter recommended him as a good man and handy with a gun. It seemed wise, considering the close work necessary for pictures, to have two backup guns.

Walking into the reed jungle with buffalo trails crisscrossing our path we heard the buffalo about twenty yards away and took the trail. Making our way as quietly as possible we heard him pass us several times as he circled. After about half an hour of this, all of us beginning to feel more and more like buffalo bait, we decided it was too risky and started back to the car. The two brewery fellows were ahead, followed by the native with my rifle. Wally was next, just ahead of me. The rest of the party were strung out behind.

Suddenly from a small rise on our left there was a thundering of hooves and great crashing of reeds. The only warning we had was the buffalo's grunt just before he started toward us from not more than twenty feet away. His charge was directed at the natives ahead of us who immediately melted into the reeds, including the man with my rifle.

Up to this time the animal was charging blindly and did not see us. We had not seen him either, but when he hit the trail just ahead, he saw us. Wally shot from the hip as the buffalo crashed our way, head low and traveling with the speed of an express train. It was a lucky shot breaking the neck with a deadly hit over the lowered head. He dropped ten feet from us. A very auspicious start so early in the hunt.

Action soon started for the rest of the party, too. We were dispersed in several different camps. Bill Wright had Walter Johnson, Jr., at Camp Panzila. Their target was elephant. Dick Mauch went with them to do the photography and Jim Crowe to write the story. The rest of the group are hunting from the main camp.

» «

June 5, Saturday A.M.—An hour ago I killed a fine buffalo with one arrow. We have seen many buffaloes these past few days but have had many failures. Transporting camera equipment through the brush is difficult but when sound gear is added one becomes almost immobile. Each time we seemed to have a good set up something happened to prevent a shot.

This morning was different. We were slogging through the brush in the Toyota in an area purported to be good buffalo country. It was fairly open. A small scattering of bushes and an occasional thicket, broken here and there by dongas or creek bottoms that were heavily timbered and brushy.

Suddenly I got a glimpse of a buffalo going through the thicket. We circled the spot and found tracks going out into the donga. Wally told Luiz (pronounced "Louise") to take his rifle and track them. (There were two bulls we were sure.)

We found him dead 300 yards away.

We needed time to get over on the other side and had just arrived when out they came straight for the car. The bigger bull was antagonistic and kept trying to ram the car. Wally, at the wheel, was skillful at dodging and maneuvering, but one charge, followed by an ominous grunt, exploded directly toward the side of the car. Wally swerved again, barely in time to avoid the massive head three feet from us.

This mechanized bullfight took place at a speed of about twenty miles an hour. It was all we could do to stay in our seats during the short turns and rough lurching of the vehicle. And there was one near casualty.

Juca, one of the natives, was sitting in the back holding a camera and rifle when one of the buffaloes made a charge from the right and hit the car near the back. The charge jolted the rear end, shoving it over about three feet and ripping off the spare tire. The impact threw Juca overboard and to the ground. Wally stopped immediately but Juca bounced up and started to run—camera and gun flying through the air.

At the same instance I jumped out on my side of the car and got an arrow on the string as the buffalo galloped past headed for the bush. He was quartering away at about thirty-five yards when the arrow hit, going into the rib cage. We found him dead 300 yards away with green paint from the Toyota ground into his horns.

Our main camera was damaged in the fracas, so Wally took Zoli into camp to make repairs. This was the greatest excitement so far, with a trophy to satisfy the most ambitious hunter. But no pictures.

June 7, Monday, 5 P.M.—We are now hunting from Camp Ruark. Moved here this morning and have just returned from a few hours of tiger fishing. We did not have much luck, although Knick and I hooked several and landed one. The best fishing was at a pool where we hesitated to fish because of hippos. One carries a gun when fishing in this area, both for crocodiles and hippos.

In all of yesterday's hunting we did not see a buffalo but this morning we got action. Soon after starting out we stopped at a nearby village to inquire. The man we talked to called to his wife to ask if there were buffalo tracks in the garden. She said "Yes, they have already been in this morning and were in the garden last night, also." They were sure we could find them either in the high grass nearby or in the hills beyond. We cruised around in the grass but found no buffaloes, although there were plenty of places where they had bedded down.

We then moved into the hilly country and located two bulls in a heavily brushed creek bottom. Wally sent Luiz in on the track with a rifle while we went around on the other side hoping to be in the right place when they came out. We were not that lucky. They evaded us and crossed some flat country, taking refuge in more thick brush. We circled again on foot this time and again the buffaloes escaped, although we were within twenty yards of them. We tried circling again for the third time after seeing them go into a wide creek bottom and again hoped to be in the right place when they came out. I was in position up front with Wally and the two cameramen some distance behind. Luiz was moving along the track and it was not long before we heard grunts from mad buffaloes.

Expecting action momentarily we were tense and nervous when a series of snarls and deep, throaty growls came out of the bush. We thought this was the buffalo until Luiz came out yelling, "A wounded lion, boss; he charged me but turned off." He also told us the buffaloes had charged him and then went out the same side they came in.

The charge failed because Luiz was on a high bank that the buffaloes could not climb. "I'm not going back in there unless you go along, boss," he concluded, and it was entirely evident that he meant it.

We questioned Luiz about the lion and he told us it had a crippled back leg that looked as if it had been caught in a snare. We went cautiously into the bush to look but failed to find any trace of it. We gave up on the buffaloes, also, since they were out of sight and this was not good country for photography.

We seem to be having more than our share of excitement. This has been the third buffalo charge we have been in on and today there was a crippled lion thrown in as well. Buffalo hunting is a very specialized business. The procedure goes something like this: We usually inquire of the local natives on the whereabouts and habits of buffaloes in their area which they have to know in order to stay alive. We learn where the buffaloes water and that it is usually early in the morning. They leave for the bedding ground just about daylight. We follow their tracks in the hunting car through thick brush, shenatzi, about six feet high. The bush is broken up by ravines or dongas, some of which are difficult to cross with their dense trees and thorns. In any of these places, which might be within a mile to three of four miles, we can expect to find buffaloes hiding from the hot midday sun.

Besides the natives, another source of information are the tickbirds or buffalo birds that ride on the backs of these animals looking for ticks in the hide. These birds leave the buffaloes in the evening and return in the morning. With careful scanning of the skies we can see them searching for the herds. When they drop down and pinpoint the buffaloes, we can abandon the tracking and make straight for the spot.

We find them resting in the shade in thick cover. Sometimes they are standing and milling around as we approach on foot, trying to get close enough for a shot with bow and camera. We have gotten close enough for a bow shot many times but the thick brush usually spoils any chance for pictures. Sometimes the buffaloes leave at the sound of the car approaching and the sight of a herd of fifty or a hundred buffaloes thundering across the open is a magnificent one. When this happens, the tickbirds leave the buffaloes and follow them in the sky. We race across the rough country, crashing everything in our path with the Toyota, in an effort to reach the next thicket ahead of the cloud of dust and circling birds. As a rule the herd wins the race and we are faced with another stalk.

By the end of the day we are scratched and torn by thorns and return to camp to repair the damage to cameras and equipment and ourselves. An average day produces at least two flat tires from thorns or sharp pieces of wood that pierce the casings. The beatings the Toyotas take is unbelievable.

June 14, Monday—This past week we have lost three hunting days because of poor light for photography. I spent those days alone in a blind at a water hole with the long-lens camera making a film record of birds and animals. Reading back over my list later, it hardly seemed possible that there could have been so much activity.

Wart Hogs	105	Kudu	3
Monkeys	28	Zebra	7
Baboons	176	Mongoose	1
Nyala	49	Saddlebill Stork	3
Impala	72	Ground Hornbill	3
Wildebeests	28		

The most interesting event seen during this time at the water hole was a mock fight between two nyala bulls. They never really got down to business but circled each other endlessly with bushy tails held erect and the hair along their back and manes standing on end. They moved in very slow motion threatening to lock horns at any minute, and often did, crashing horns together and butting their heads with a resounding smack.

Four more days of hunting buffaloes finally came to a conclusion yesterday. Early in the morning we drove to the village of Conjone, a brother of Peter, who was our tracker last year. Peter has been promoted to "keeper of the animals."

Conjone, or actually his wives, operate a farm of sorts. The main crop is sugar cane from which alcoholic spirits are distilled on the premises. At this writing, however, there is a shortage of liquor at Conjone's holdings. We were told that the reason was that Conjone took a fancy to one of Chief Maringa's wives and was sent up for trial. The wrath of Maringa, who is also the medicine man proficient in Kush Kush, was so aroused that he burned Conjone's current crop of sugar cane.

Conjone got some satisfaction out of the affair, however, when it was decreed at the trial that his three months' jail sentence could be served at a time convenient to Conjone!

Our first sight of the philanderer was eye catching. He was dressed in cowboy boots, khaki shorts, an ornately decorated jacket, and a stiff-brim felt hat, pinned up on one side, Australian style. Despite his taste in dress, he was wise in the ways of buffaloes. He knew where they were at any hour of the day. Right now, he said, there were several bulls bedded down in the tall grass just beyond a patch of corn that would have been knee high if the buffaloes had not eaten it.

Conjone seemed glad we had come. Besides the crop trouble, his people had not had meat for quite some time, he said, as he hopped on the back of the hunting car to accompany us.

We drove through high grass that was too dangerous to hunt on foot. Two bulls were flushed out which we pursued from bush to bush but finally lost. Conjone directed us across country where he said a large herd would be standing, drowsing, in the noon heat. We flushed a lone bull out of a cool, brushy creek bottom but he eluded us and got away. Conjone said that this bull usually hung around on the outskirts of the herd and suggested that we go back and try again.

His buffalo know-how was confirmed when we came upon a herd of about sixty in the heavily brushed creek bottom. They were reluctant to leave this refuge and milled about as we jockeyed for position. There were quite a few bulls in sight, and some opportunities for shots, but never in the right place for pictures. We worked with them half an hour until they left and went into another cover, which we circled for some time and then finally came upon the situation we had been looking for for two weeks.

A good bull with a cow stood in a small opening as we approached. When I emerged in the open they just looked at me from about forty-five yards. The bull had his ribs exposed, standing broadside. I held up my shot until I heard the camera running and then released the arrow. It went into the rib cage and both buffaloes wheeled and went back into the bush. After the rest of the herd left the area we tracked my bull 250 yards where he had fallen. It was a thrilling and satisfactory episode and we feel sure of good pictures as well.

June 16, Wednesday—Yesterday and today were spent entirely with the camera to obtain cuts needed for the buffalo-shooting film. One more day will complete this sequence. Following this we hope for a few days of hunting without the handicap of cameras.

Last Sunday, Knick went to join Bob at Camp Inhalauguene. At the same time Wally, Jr., with Dick and Bill, came to our camp. They are still with us. Dick has a wart hog and a fine nyala.

June 18, Friday, 11 A.M.—Yesterday we did some early morning filming and then went to a tree platform near a water hole we had found last week. Luiz climbed up with me to spend the night. We had food, blankets, and the big camera. It looked like a promising place. A profusion of lion, elephant, buffalo, and many lesser species left tracks in the area.

This was my first night at a water hole and I'd expected some night action with the full moon but there was none. Luiz told me this morning that he had heard an elephant splashing below but did not wake me. I can see the big tracks now as I sit in the blind writing.

We kept a list of the animals seen from this blind until pick-up time at 3 P.M. the following afternoon. We got some excellent footage of a herd of fifty or more buffalo that came in for water about eight-thirty this morning. It is interesting to note that buffaloes barge right into a water hole while other animals come in warily.

Our list at this place included:

Wart Hogs	32	Baboons	132
Impala	131	Kudu	12
Buffalo	110	Monkeys	27
Ostrich	4		

June 19, Saturday—Up in my platform at water hole ⚡1. I got here at eight o'clock and flushed a herd of twelve wildebeests. The weather is cloudy and the light is not good. After dropping me off here, Wally, with Bob and Zoli, continued toward water hole ⚡2 to place a lion bait near the platform. There are many lion tracks around the water hole in that area despite the fact that this is not particularly good lion country.

A pride of lions was within 100 yards of camp three nights ago and, this morning as we were about to leave camp, someone told us that a lion had killed a wart hog about five miles in the direction of main camp. It is agreed that we all meet for lunch in the main camp on Sunday. This will be the first get-together of the entire group since we arrived on June 1. We may decide to stay together in the main camp for our last week here.

The most winning personality in camp is Wally, Jr.'s boy, Tisus. A native chap whose job is to keep the car clean. Wally says he is eight or nine years old. At any hour of the day he greets us with a flashy, ivory "good morning." We heard the story of how Tisus happened to be in camp.

Wally was driving along a bush road one day when this little fellow flagged him down.

"What do you want?" Wally asked him.

"I want to work," Tisus answered him.

Wally was impressed by this direct approach and told him he would be back next week and they would talk it over. But Tisus was not to be put off and said stoutly:

"I want to work now."

Wally told him to get his blanket and climb aboard. He has proved to be an excellent hand, young as he is, and I predict he will be prime minister someday.

June 20, Sunday—Everybody gathered at the main camp today according to plan. We started in early to catch the plane coming in for Jim Crowe who was leaving. We needed the plane for pictures. Later in the morning we did more camp scenes and by noon our group of five hunters was assembled, each with stories to tell of his experiences. Summing it all up, hunting has been good. The group has collected an amazing number of trophies.

After this break in the hunt we decided to go back to separate camps after all. Dick and Bill with Wally, Jr., went back to their camp while Bob and Rui decided to try for elephants. Knick and his hunter, George, went back to the camp where they had been hunting and the photographers and I elected to stay in Camp Ruark as we have additional filming to do here as well as a fishing sequence.

Werner von Albensleven has also arranged a hippo hunt. If time permits we will do this near the main camp on Friday or Saturday as we all gather for the flight out to Biera Sunday.

June 23, Wednesday—We have spent two days on the fishing sequence and gotten into some good-sized tiger fish. No luck with either the lion or leopard bait. Game is so plentiful that they seem to prefer, and can easily kill, their own. We finally finished our picture yesterday. This film has taken more time than previous ones as we are producing, technically at least, a much better film, shooting from script with sound. This leaves me a little over three days to try for a lion.

We moved back to the main camp last evening. This morning after checking our bait we stopped in at Camp Ruark. Dr. John Vasco of California, who was staying there, had shot a lion the evening before. His professional hunter, Ken Fikes, told us they had found a buffalo that two lions had killed and they had built a blind near the spot. The lions, both males, had come in at dusk and Vasco had killed the smaller of the two. The other lion stood them off and refused to let them claim their trophy, so they had to go back and pick it up this morning. The party brought in the head of the buffalo the lions had killed. It was a monstrous old bull. We saw the carcass later. It was an awesome sight, ripped by fang and claw.

June 24, Thursday—Last night was one to remember. It began in the afternoon when we went to the spot where Dr. Vasco killed his lion. It was a rocky

We caught some good-sized tiger fish.

creek bottom with banks six feet high on one side and twelve feet high on the other. Ken's blind was about forty yards away on the low side. Some natives, attracted to the place by vultures, were cutting meat from the carcass but ran off when they heard the car. Between the vultures and the natives there was not much left. We decided to freshen the banquet and added a waterbuck.

We then moved the blind to the edge of the bank about twenty yards from the bait, adding more brush to help keep the lion out in case things went wrong. Thorn branches were placed along the front in the event he might come for us when my arrow hit.

With luck the lion would come to the bait while there was still shooting light. If not, depending on how hungry he was, he might come in later and be there at daybreak. Ken had given us each a blanket. We ate our lunch leftovers and were still and quiet by 4:30 P.M. At five-thirty the lion was there. We heard him crunching bones. He saw me rise up and was off before I could shoot.

He was back again in the dim light of five forty-five, one eye on the meat and one on us. He knew we were there. This time I was more deliberate in getting into position but he still saw me and was off, hesitating a moment on top of the far bank. Perhaps I should have shot then, but I was not sure of my accuracy in the poor light at that range.

We did not see him again, although he prowled the area until an hour before daylight, roaring and growling at half-hour intervals. Two other lions were answering in the distance.

It was a harrowing night, not much sleep. Next morning we found his tracks twenty feet from our blind.

The lion had two counts against us. His companion had been shot the night before and now we were keeping him from food.

We went back the next night. This was a two-blanket night and we now had sleeping pads. The lion came in at the same time. I raised up and he streaked up the far bank. I had a feeling we would not see him again and shot. The arrow struck home. He let out a grunt and increased his pace to melt into the bush. We sat quietly wondering who would make the next move. I heard Luiz click the safety off his rifle. In about five minutes we heard what I thought was the lion's last gasp and said to Wally:

"I think he is dead."

Wally agreed. But Luiz was not sure and warned us:

"Be careful or he might be upon us."

So we tried to settle down for the night. Everybody got cold and at midnight we built a small fire. I believe the temperature dropped to about forty-five degrees. At daylight we took the trail and after about 250 yards I found my arrow in five pieces. There was quite a lot of blood where he had lain and a faint blood trail from then on. Luiz and Juca did a marvelous tracking job, trailing him for four hours, about five miles.

Then we saw him running across an opening. I remarked to Wally that he seemed to be in good shape, was not shot in the body cavity, and appeared not to be hurt too badly. Wally agreed and so we abandoned the trail. We might have gotten him but he would have had to be gunned down.

June 30, Wednesday—The clan gathered at main camp Saturday. Halmi had a cable from New York advising him of his wife's illness and he left Saturday morning. The rest of the group were spectators at a most unusual hippo hunt. Werner had arranged this in the muddy lake near the airport. It was a haphazard operation not without excitement. We had tried it last year and were happy to conclude the hunt alive.

This year would be different Werner said; everything had been arranged. Two make-shift boats were lashed together for photographers and extra fire power. Wally, Werner, and I set out in a small skiff powered by a six-horsepower West Bend motor. We towed the "raft" and started after the hippos who were there in numbers, about sixty in all.

Hippos look so pudgy, fat, and round that few people realize their speed both in water and on land. In water they are a tough antagonist because one never knows where or when they will surface. A skiff can be crushed like an eggshell. Men, who consider it routine to face lions, buffaloes, and elephants, hesitate to take liberties with these monsters of Africa's rivers and lakes. A large bull weighs five thousand pounds and has a head three feet long.

We got into them soon and the largest bull was enormous. I shot an arrow into his neck and he submerged. We got into the whole pack then, water swirling all around the boat. We could not find the bull but did retrieve my arrow. After a half hour's search we saw him standing on the shore a couple hundred yards away. We went after him and at thirty yards he came for us full speed. I don't know who fired the first shot. He was coming fast through three feet of water. The shot turned him and he veered off passing us at ten yards. He either submerged or sank. We cruised around for a half hour. Werner said he was dead and would float in about three hours.

Right after lunch word came that the hippo was dead. We set out with ropes and gear to drag him out on shore.

This proved to be more than we'd bargained for. The great hulk lay in three feet of water and two feet of mud. Wally and I went out in the skiff carrying rifles to fight off other hippos if necessary. Dick went along to film the operation.

The dead hippo was 100 yards from the marshy shore. The closest we could get to the waters edge with the Toyota and winch was 150 yards. Our job was to tie a rope under his big teeth to connect with a rope from the car. About a foot of the hippo's back was exposed, his head was in the mud. Wally stood on his neck but was unable to get the rope in place.

The cheering section on shore tried hard to help. Natives stood expectantly, knives poised and mouths watering, anticipating a feast of hippo meat. Someone called advice from the bank:

"Tie the rope around his tail and maybe you can roll him over."

We succeeded in this finally and gunned the motor, but the carcass did not budge.

"Use more slack rope and take a long run at it," someone else shouted.

There were spectators on the other side of us also. About sixty hippos stared balefully from the muddy pool that was not more than 400 yards in diameter. They had gathered uncomfortably close to watch the operation.

We pulled out plenty of slack rope, about fifty feet. Mistakenly the rope was fastened to a cleat on the foredeck rather than aft. Wally opened the throttle wide. We shot away and cheers went up from the shore. They were short-lived, however, since unfortunately we were not in line with the hippo's tail when the rope tightened. The hippo didn't give, the rope held fast to the tail, the nose of our boat snapped sharply around, and we capsized.

Three feet of water, two feet of mud, and sixty hippos grunting expectantly and, we were sure, a thousand crocodiles gliding unseen beneath the surface toward us!

An unpleasant predicament all around. We retrieved the guns and cameras by searching in the mud with our feet. The West Bend motor had to come off the boat and be laid on the bottom of the pool while we uprighted the skiff and bailed it out with a hat. We put the motor back on the transom and climbed aboard.

Dick and I each grabbed an oar but Wally wanted to try the engine first, so we humored him, tongue in cheek. To our surprise, three pulls and he got a sputter. Two more, a short spurt. Another pull and we were headed for shore.

"Bloody good stuff you make in America," Wally said over his shoulder.

We went to camp, had a bath, got into dry clothes, and then went back to the lake.

The hippo, about two tons of it, had just been winched to dry ground and now a hundred natives were on hand to share the meat. After an hour there was very little left of the carcass.

Sunday morning everyone left but Dick and me. We decided to stay an extra week, succumbing to lion or bush fever; I don't know which. Dick went after leopards and Wally and I together with Luiz and Juca left main camp and reached Camp Alvis Delima just at sunset.

It took us three hours over dusty, rough African roads. We came here for lions since others of our party reported seeing them here and hearing them roar at night. We heard them too, early the next morning. We tried to determine, by studying tracks, where the greatest concentration was and then put three lion baits out and one for leopard.

A native and wife stopped by the camp today looking for meat, or that failing, the wife would give haircuts since she owned a pair of scissors, which made her a barber. We declined but thanked her anyway. The husband said there were lots of lions around his village.

"They keep us awake roaring all night," he said.

» «

A week later.

We have just finished such an exciting hunt that I'm afraid another sleep-out episode with the lions set down in this journal will call up suspicions that I am stretching the truth. It is the bow that brings on these situations. With a gun my hunt would have been over quite some time ago. The first lion seen would have been shot that first night, the buffalo sequence over in less than a week, and we would be on our way home. But the range limitations of the bow brings one of necessity so close to game that sometimes the response is uncomfortably enthusiastic. . . .

Last Wednesday night I had the thrill of a lifetime. A hippo coming head-on beneath the muddy water, to crush you and your eggshell boat, is a hair-raising thing to live through. Or dropping a mad, crippled buffalo at ten feet is a heart-stopping experience. Or a screaming, towering elephant at close range should certainly be the most terrifying. Yet none of these experiences, exciting as they are, lasts more than a few seconds. The thrill I had this past week, however, continued for six hours! It was like this.

Wally, Luiz, Juca, and I drove to Alvis Delima camp on Sunday afternoon. We stopped at a village en route and picked up a native named Paulo who, Wally said, had been a snare poacher of the worst kind before they converted him into one of their best game wardens.

"He knows this area like a book," Wally commented. We found Wally, Jr.'s boy, Tisus, at the village also. He had been given a few days off and was visiting his father and the rest of his family. I had previously given Tisus some candy done up in cellophane wrappings and I gave him some more now which he shared with his smaller sister. She looked at the candy appraisingly for a few seconds before popping the whole thing in her mouth.

Tisus, who can speak some English along with his other accomplishments, regarded this "uncivilized" lack of knowledge in our presence with embarrassment and then said sternly:

"You gotta skin it first."

Monday we roamed the country looking for lion tracks and scanned the skies hopefully for circling vultures that would pinpoint a lion kill. Tickbirds lead us to buffaloes but it's the vultures who tell where a lion has made a kill. If we were lucky enough to find a carcass not entirely consumed, the lions would be back. We would then add fresh meat to his larder and hope for the best.

No kills were found, although we pursued even a single vulture unmercifully, hoping for a clue. We did find an area where there were many lion tracks, however, and here we shot a wildebeest and dragged it behind the car in a wide circle before chaining the carcass to a tree. We built a blind about twenty-five yards away and spent Monday night in it. Just at sunset a lion roared about half a mile away and another lion answered from the same area. A hyena laughed and a leopard barked in the distance. As the night wore on two civet cats came in, to fight over the bait, but no lions appeared.

We traveled farther on the next day until we found a spot well sprinkled with the tracks of large lions. Two wildebeest were shot, one of which we dragged around behind the car to lay a scent trail. That done, we chained both carcasses to a lonely tree eighteen yards from a thicketlike circle of trees about twenty feet in diameter. We planned to build a blind here if the lions found the bait. Wildebeest are almost always used for lion bait in this area where there are thousands of them. To take them for bait may seem like wanton killing but, when one considers that the lion would kill them for himself anyway, the odds are about even. Lions appreciate bait either fresh or in any stage of aging—up to several weeks. . . . We keep away the vultures (who find carrion by sight only) by covering it with leaves and branches.

Sleeping in camp on Tuesday evening, we heard a lion roar nearby and then a leopard barked. We checked our first bait early Wednesday morning and found that the civet cats had been back but no lions. At the second bait we were happy to discover that two large lions had been feeding on one of the carcasses. A discovery like this is sensational in itself. Only some great turn of events would prevent their coming again in the evening.

The big cats will come in silently to within eighteen yards of my arrow. If we are lucky, they will come early while there is still shooting light. They could also come in very late with the possibility of being on the bait for morning light.

Another sleep-out now. This one with great anticipation. We went back to camp for blankets and food and returned in the afternoon to build our blind. No attention need be paid to the wind since lions, like leopards and tigers, have very poor noses. Luiz, Juca, and Paulo began clearing out the inside of the circle of trees. We planned to drive the hunting car inside and use it as part of our barricade. The three men chopped and grubbed at the undergrowth and bushes while the rest of us got everything in readiness for spending the night in the blind.

A wild shriek from Luiz stopped all operations while everyone rushed to see what was the matter. Backing away in all haste, he pointed to a python coiled up on the ground. The snake had been hiding under a clump of bushes that Luiz was chopping out. There was time to get a blunt-headed arrow through its head which took care of that problem. It would make a fine trophy I thought, coiled as it was when Luiz found him. We looped twelve and a half feet of python over the limb of a bush nearby and went back to our work of building the blind.

Looking back now I reflect that this could have been called the "Night of the Python," the "Night of the Big Fright," or just—"Nightmare." One thing I am sure of is that it was a night I will never forget.

As we cleared the blind we piled the brush around the edge as a circular fence, providing a limited measure of security but no obstacle at all if a lion chose to leap over the top.

There were just two trees large enough to climb, one on the bait side where Wally and I would be, the other opposite us where Luiz, Juca, and Paulo would spend the night. The tree on our side was a thorn tree that offered poor possi-

Twelve and a half feet of python!

bilities for climbing. The men trimmed their tree to make it easy to climb. This made it easy for the lion to climb also, if the emergency arose. The car was camouflaged with brush on top and on one side.

An hour before dark we ate a snack and stretched out on our blankets. We had three .375 caliber rifles with us. Wally lit his pipe and studied the situation. He decided that our side of the blind looked thin and that a lion could look right in and see us.

Luiz said, "Boss, the way you two snore he don't have to see you."

After the sun went down we were lying flat, silent, and motionless. The hour was five-forty when we heard a sudden crackling of bones, which gave us a jolt since we had not heard anything come in. My sixty-six-pound Bear Kodiak bow laid at my feet, an arrow nocked on the string. I eased to my knees, keeping low, and got into shooting position. The light was poor but good enough—eighteen yards is not far. There were two lions, both males and both of them saw me.

Lions are fearless at night and it is difficult to remember that they can see as well in poor light as we do in the daytime.

Both cats stopped feeding. One almost broadside, facing me slightly, and the other one behind him staring at me head on. I felt an urgency to shoot quickly. The light was too poor to see the path of the arrow or where it hit but there was no doubt that it did strike home when no time elapsed between the hit and the first vicious snarl. Both lions sprang up and the back one shot off to the left. The hit lion, growling and snarling at every bound, curved toward us and then swerved away to the left also, passing very close to the blind.

His roar was earsplitting. The reason he changed his course and did not continue his charge, we decided, was because his partner made a beeline out and he didn't feel like tackling us alone.

The lions gone, there was complete silence except for the whispered speculations of Wally.

"Where did you hit him?"

"I don't know," I told him. "Right behind the shoulder I think but I can't be sure how high or low."

There was silence for another ten minutes. Ten ears straining for the slightest sound. It was dark now. There is not much twilight in Africa.

We were not long in learning where at least one lion was. A shattering roar rattled the very leaves of our blind, the walls of which now seemed so thin they would not keep out a rabbit. One of those lions, maybe both, were out there twenty yards away in the black night.

A wounded lion is not to be trifled with even in the daytime. We could only guess that this was the wounded one hell bent for revenge. He must be sitting out there in the dark, studying our leafy barricade, and selecting the best spot to leap in and land on the greatest concentration of human flesh. I clutched my .375 and Wally and Luiz held theirs. All safeties off. If he came in, our first sight of him would be his silhouette against the faint light of the sky.

Lying half slouched against the thorn tree I covered the area behind Wally who was facing me. He covered the area behind me and Luiz took charge of his end of the compound. If the lion came in, we would be lucky to get a shot off in time, luckier still to hit him, and nothing short of a miracle to get a killing shot. In any case we would have a lion upon us, dead or otherwise.

There was another mighty series of prolonged roars and snarls. Still from the same location, followed by a deadly silence both in the blind and out in the darkness.

I can vividly remember all the details now—a week later. Nobody said a word or laughed or coughed or cleared his throat at any time. I remember asking myself: What Am I Doing Here? My insurance company had told me before I left for this trip that they would reduce my rate by five dollars a thousand if I quit this crazy business. Now for the first time I began to see the sense of it.

There was another half hour of agonizing silence. Then a lion, a half mile away, gave the low half purring, half moaning get-together call that lions do. Another answered from somewhere. In the safety of camp I had found this interesting but out there that night it made the hackles on my neck stand up like porcupine quills. My legs were cramped and stiff. It was cold but no one so much as touched the corner of a blanket to relieve this condition. The tension in that blind filled the air like dense fog.

I began to worry, seriously now, how long the natives could stand it, or myself and Wally for that matter. And as if to test us, another roar like the vibrating, bone-shaking blast of an ocean liner.

Luiz suddenly broke down. It was eight-thirty by the luminous hands on my watch when he crept over to Wally and whispered:

"Boss, Paulo is mighty scared, says he's going to climb that tree."

"You tell him to keep still and quiet." Wally whispered back fiercely. "If he tries to climb that bloody tree, the lion will be in here on us before he can get one leg up."

Luiz knew from experience with the boss that Wally was holding him responsible for what Paulo did.

We waited even more expectantly after this stirring around in our blind, quietly done as it was. And as if to remind us again of the situation, another terrible roar and snarl came from outside. For another hour no one allowed himself so much as a satisfying deep breath.

The night was getting cold. The temperature must have been down to fifty and each roar of the lion seemed to send it down an additional degree. At nine-thirty Luiz risked Wally's wrath, his job, and everyone's safety by inching over to our side of the blind once more.

"Boss, I can hear that lion tearing flesh. I think he feeding on the dead lion."

Wally made no reply but we all listened intently and following another raging blast from the dark, I, too, could hear the ripping of flesh and clicking of teeth.

This was an electrifying development. For the first time we had a valuable clue. It was highly unlikely that a wounded lion would be eating anything and a lion that was not wounded would certainly be less of a problem to us. With indescribable relief we put our guns on safe and I quietly slid my aching muscles down into a prone position on my back.

The sky was beautiful. The Southern Cross made a brilliant display in the velvety night. A large bright satellite raced across the heavens. The moon, in its first quarter, was due to appear at midnight. We waited eagerly for its light.

At ten o'clock Luiz whispered again.

"Boss, that lion out there is tearing up the skin of the dead lion. It won't be any good. Maybe if you fire a shot it might scare him off."

This brave show from Luiz didn't fool anyone. Luiz was worried about his own skin.

Wally asked my opinion. I thought it was worth a try. If the lion was bent on doing us in, it might be better to have the showdown now rather than later when our reflexes would be less keen from loss of sleep and the cold.

The streak of fire and the boom of Wally's big gun was comforting but only for a split second. The defiant reply from out in the darkness was the longest and loudest series of snarls and roars we had heard so far. And the silence that followed was ominous.

These outbursts continued at about fifteen-minute intervals. I thought of the possibility that my trophy was being ruined. Lions will eat another lion carcass Wally assured me. I knew that bears consume their own kind. Was the agony of this long night going to go unrewarded. The thought of losing my lion made my skin feel icy cold.

There was one hopeful angle to this, however. It didn't seem likely that the hit lion would have dropped in that short distance. Unless struck in the head, neck, or spine, animals usually run 150 to 200 yards after being hit with an arrow. I grasped at the possibility that the roaring lion was eating the dead python hanging in the tree rather than my lion. Wally said, "Could be." Luiz said, "Maybe."

At eleven forty-five, right after another screaming roar outside the blind, Luiz pronounced his ultimatum.

"We go home or we *all* going to climb that tree."

Wally considered this for a few minutes realizing, I'm sure, that the small tree could hardly hold all three natives anyway. He asked what I thought of making a

We found the lion two hundred yards away.

break for it in the car. It had never occurred to me to try to get away in the open hunting car but now that he'd mentioned it it seemed like a brilliant idea. Any risk seemed less than being pinned down in this blind.

We took nothing but our guns. It was difficult getting into the car quietly with all the brush and branches we had piled over it for camouflage but we felt an urgency that made anything possible. The car started at first try. Wally switched on the lights, gunned the motor, and we bulldozed through our barricade with a burst of speed that almost threw us out on the ground.

Fortunately the country was open and fairly flat. We raced out for two hundred yards and then made a tight circle sweeping our backtrack with light to make sure we were not being followed before heading for camp.

Early the next morning we returned to the battleground. The lion had eaten part of the python but the loss of that trophy seemed trivial compared to the relief of finding my dead lion two hundred yards away. The arrow entered low, back of the foreleg, and pierced the heart.

It was a beautiful lion and I felt very fortunate to find it intact after the hours of suspense during the night. A full-grown male, weighing 460 pounds and measuring ten feet in length. Hung up in camp he reached far above my head with the tail touching the ground.

Dropping Paulo off at his village on the way back to camp with the lion, he had just one final remark.

"Boss, next time you stop by and ask me to go lion hunting, I say, 'No thank you.' "

» «

Moçambique Safarilandia are fine outfitters operating in a great game area. This part of Africa has a delightful climate at this time of year with an average day temperature of about eighty degrees. The nights can be as cool as forty-five degrees. This is the dry or winter season and there are practically no insects and no rain. Werner von Alvensleben directs activities and manages the operation in a most businesslike way. Seven professional hunters, totaling a great many years in the bush, are at the service of clients.

Should you book a hunt there and happen to draw Wally Johnson as your professional hunter, he may ask you if you want to hunt lions or hippos. If you have insurance problems, perhaps you should say, as Paulo did, "No thank you."

Field notes are written where and when.

Chapter 14

POLAR BEAR - 1966

Five hundred miles by air north of Fairbanks, Alaska, lies the Eskimo village of Barrow—the largest Eskimo town in the world, boasting twenty-one hundred inhabitants. It occupies a small segment of Point Barrow, which juts into the Arctic Ocean 350 miles above the Arctic Circle. The most northerly tip of Alaska.

Twice in previous years I had hunted polar bears from this point. Both times I had failed to get a bear with a bow and arrow. Bob Munger of Charlotte, Michigan, was my hunting companion again on this trip.

In this third attempt we made arrangements with the outfitter to camp out on the ice pack and hunt from motor sleds instead of planes. The location chosen was the mouth of the Coleville River, in Harrison Bay, 150 miles east of Barrow.

The American Broadcasting Company would film the hunt for their "American Sportsman" series. Cliff Robertson, cinema star, would hunt with a rifle and I would hunt with the bow. We had much to learn. . . .

The hunt began late in the season when we hoped to miss extreme cold weather.

During the winter the Arctic Ocean is almost covered with ice—usually referred to as the ice pack, and correctly so. Not the smooth sheet of ice we find on a frozen lake or river but a jumble of broken pieces, many of incredible thickness and breadth, scattered about or piled in ridges many miles long.

The action of wind, current, and tide may break a great chunk apart and drift it out into open water. Later this island of ice, that could be many square miles in size and up to five feet thick, might start back to its original source again by a change of elements. Its velocity will be slow but the tremendous energy behind its millions of tons meeting shore ice results in such awesome grinding and churning that pieces are tossed about like feathers. Pressure ridges build up like small mountains and the whole thing is welded together by the excessive cold until the wind changes again and the sequence is repeated.

Walking around on this frozen ocean is like traversing small valleys and climbing up mountains. This frozen salt water is not brittle as frozen fresh water is. It is somewhat rubbery and milky in color. In very old pieces, however, the salt has settled to the bottom leaving the ice a clear, cold aquamarine blue. It is from this ice that we get our drinking water supply.

The ice pack is mysterious, challenging, beautiful, and moody. It permits few errors in judgment. . . .

Walking about on this frozen ocean is like traversing small valleys and climbing mountains.

April 13, 2 P.M.—The plane from Chicago had a group of priests who were traveling with The Most Reverend Joseph T. Ryan, Archbishop of the Diocese of Anchorage. Consequently, the plane was met by the governor and senators plus a band, so we had a royal welcome here in Fairbanks. Hope to be out on the ice sometime tomorrow.

April 15, Friday—We met the ABC crew in Fairbanks on Wednesday and got here to Point Barrow by DC-3 charter plane last evening. . . . Waiting for the bush plane now to take us to Colville River where the guide and outfitter, Bud Helmericks, lives. It will take three trips to get us all out. Burr Smidt, Cliff Robertson, and I are going on the first flight. The film crew is griping about the weather.

Barrow has changed from when I was here three years ago. Motor sleds replacing dog sleds and motorbikes replacing bicycles. Main Street is rerouted for two blocks because of abandoned vehicles half buried in the snow. Kids noses are still running. . . .

The bank, opened when we were here in sixty, has burned twice. Natural gas has replaced coal and General Telephone has dial phones in many places.

We are renewing acquaintances with local people. The hotel is full of guides and hunters. Ninety-three bears have been taken to date. Also a number of wolves. Snow sleds are spelling the doom of caribou, wolves and wolverine, as they travel faster than the animals can run.

The movie at the local theater last night was *A Thousand Clowns*. The theater is converted to a dance hall when the movie is over at midnight.

The hotel is filled with guides and hunters.

Whalers around town are gathering gear since a whale has been reported offshore.

I talked with Helmericks by radio last evening. Everything in fine shape, he says. Expect to have camp established out on the ice in about four days. Robertson has to leave on the twenty-sixth, so the first bear is his.

Later, Same Day—We are still delayed by bad weather. The small plane can't take us until it clears. The hotel lobby is crowded. Some tall stories going around. . . .

April 16, Saturday—We left the Top of the World Hotel in Barrow by a Beaver plane on skis. It was late afternoon before swirling snow, reducing the Colville River area visibility to zero, let up. Our first sight of Bud Helmericks' home reminded us of a lonely lighthouse squatting in a vast expanse of space, a never-ending sea of white. The ocean ice pack was to the north and the prairie sloped gently south to the Brooks Range of mountains fifty miles away.

The home is fitted with modern conveniences. A diesel generating plant churns night and day while a radio transmitter sputters its messages.

Burr, Cliff, Jerry Kaligeratos, and I, together with some of our gear, made the 160-mile flight in two hours. We will sleep here tonight.

April 17—Bud and his son Jim took us out to the ice camp this morning by bush plane. Two of our tents had been erected the day before but a bear had come through and ripped some canvas. One tent was partly down and both were torn. We sewed them up with a bag needle and thread. The rest of the camp will consist of more Thermos tents. Two Prairie Schooner types and two Giant Thermos Pop Tents. We will put one tent inside another for extra warmth.

April 18—Bob Munger came out from Barrow today with one thousand pounds of camera, film, and gear. The pilot set the plane down on the ice beside camp. Another load of the crew is expected later today if some engine trouble with the plane clears up.

April 19—The Beaver was not repaired so Mike Scott, sound man, and Steve Goldhor, cameraman, chartered George Thele and Joe Vanderpool who are Polar Bear guides, to bring them from Barrow in bush planes.

Our cluster of tents is about forty miles out on the ice pack. This is about the limit of what the natives call shore ice which is not expected to break up for another thirty days or so. Leads (open water) will be opening up farther out, however.

A mountain of ice, about thirty feet high, fifty feet wide, and three hundred feet long, rises immediately behind our camp. This serves two purposes—one, a windbreak, and the other an attraction for bears. Deep, hard-packed snow has drifted around the edges of this outcropping and seals, wanting to hide their breathing holes, come up underneath this snow. When it is time for young seals to be born, the mother enlarges the holes with her teeth and claws until it is big enough to allow her to emerge completely and make a den in the snow nearby, which serves as an escape in times of danger. The young seals are kept in this den until they can go into the water and learn to swim.

The polar bears are completely aware of this routine and prowl the ice packs sniffing for seals. If the camera and sound men had been here the first day when the bears came through, they would have had a great opportunity for pictures.

Another purpose this large ice pile at the campsite serves is to provide our water supply. Some of the large chunks are many years old and the salt has completely settled out of them. With a steel tent stake and hammer we can flake big pieces off and melt them down over our propane gas cookstove.

One of the eight-by-twelve Prairie Schooner tents is used for the kitchen and dining room. It is heated by the cookstove fed from a small propane gas tank. Another eight-by-twelve tent is heated by an oil burner. The two Giant Pop Tents are heated or, I should say, partly heated by catalytic heaters burning white gas. In one of these Bob and I sleep. Because there is so little space, most cameras and gear are left outside covered with a tarpaulin. Our lowest temperature to date was eighteen degrees below and the highest eighteen degrees above.

We arrived here on the ice, which is five to seven feet thick, on Friday. Today is Tuesday the nineteenth. No hunting has been done, since our outfitter has had three other clients who will not finish until tomorrow. In the meantime, we have been shooting camp scenes and getting acclimated.

In the afternoon we had a card game.

Wednesday, April 20—The label on a bottle of wine we had for dinner last night read SERVE AT ROOM TEMPERATURE. This brought on some reflection since it had to be thawed before pouring.

Yesterday was a beautiful day. It was snowing but the wind was mild. The temperature was ten degrees below at early morning and up to ten above at midday. We spent the morning shooting film and in the afternoon we had an archery contest, a card game, and hiked around on the ice pack.

This morning we shot film again. Helmericks still has a client and they are out now to get him a bear. Jim Helmericks is in camp with us, doing the cooking. He is repairing a landing strut for his plane that sits on the ice nearby.

We have soaked a burlap bag of fish in seal oil with which Jim, with his snow sled, had made a drag trail around a three-mile circle here. We hope a bear will pick up the scent and amble into camp.

Thursday, April 21—Bud flew in this morning. He advises us that he has hired Dick MacIntyre with his 185 Cessna to replace Jim and his broken plane.

This is good news. Mac is a good pilot and has good equipment. He might be of great help in locating bears. Another day of shooting film. There is much trouble with camera equipment in these low temperatures.

Friday, April 22—Helmericks flew in at ten-thirty this morning to say that MacIntyre developed engine trouble and had to turn back to Fairbanks. . . .

More film work. Mac radioed that he would be in tonight and this is none too soon as Cliff must leave on the twenty-sixth.

Bud and Cliff and I flew over the ice for two hours today trying to find bear tracks. The number of tracks was encouraging—some just three miles or so out.

Our problem is to find seals for bait. This is not likely to happen until a lead opens up. So far there has been no open water. The temperature last night was twenty degrees below zero. The high today was twelve degrees above.

Writing my notes is difficult. Our sleeping tent is too cold. The camera tent is full of equipment and the cook tent, where I am now, is crowded and heavy with cooking and gas stove fumes.

Sunday, April 24, 6 P.M.—We are weathering a storm. It was twenty below last night. It is twelve below now with a twenty-knot wind. Impossible to remain outside for long. A card game is going on. There are seven of us in this eight-by-twelve tent. The oil burner keeps it fairly comfortable.

Three bears passed by camp a few miles south sometime yesterday. I found the tracks on an exercise hike while waiting for Helmericks to come in. We then flew for two hours, Bud, Cliff, and I, and saw many tracks—quite a concentration of them just two or three miles north of camp. No open water that we could see.

Bud came in about noon today bringing fuel and groceries. Cliff has been staying at Bud's house the last two nights. MacIntyre finally got in last night but we can do no hunting in this weather.

The snow is blowing in and drifting around the tents. We have put up snow walls (blocks of snow) for a windbreak. Bob and Mike have been building an igloo in odd moments but the storm put an end to that.

The main reason we need Mac's plane is to get Cliff a bear. No one can guess as to when this gale will stop but when it does we will go out and do the job. This will wind him up and his part of the film will be finished.

In our plane hunts to date we have seen many tracks and ordinarily one just follows the track until he comes to the bear. Unfortunately, there has not been enough snow for tracking. We can see the tracks now only where snow has drifted up against an ice pile. What we need is snow without wind so we can see bear tracks in the open. The weather is colder than it should be at this time of year. Bud says they had three days straight of sixty-five below in early March.

This hunt is a great hardship for the camera crew fresh out of New York. Bob and I had a general idea of what conditions would be since we have hunted up

We need snow without wind so we can follow tracks.

here before. Burr Smidt, ABC director, is doing a masterful job in keeping harmony, however, and everyone is being a good sport to the best of his ability. There are four days left for the ABC crew.

Cliff's bear will have to be shot in the next two days. If weather permits. It will take another day to film his kill and departure. This will leave five or six days for my show, none of which has been shot. We will start with arrival, assorted camp shots, snow sled pictures, etc. When this is finished, the ABC people will probably leave and Bob and I will finish the film.

I am determined to kill a bear without the use of a plane. It is not that we have been neglecting opportunities to do this to date but the elements have been against us. Only two seals have been sighted up to this point. The weather must be warmer before they will come out on the ice to sun.

Helmericks is not much help in figuring out my problems of bow versus bear. But in these nine days I believe I have learned how to do it—but we need seals.

Wednesday, April 27—I am three days back on my notes. It has been very cold. Usually twenty below at night and yesterday ten below all day with a fifteen-knot wind. It is 5 P.M. now as I write this. We have just come in from five hours of flying.

This was an exceptional day in temperature—plus twenty-four at noon. We were able to stay on a bear track for half an hour because the temperature softened the snow and tracks could be seen better. But it was not quite good enough. We tracked a good bear for almost an hour but ran too low on gas and had to return to camp.

Cliff was supposed to leave yesterday but canceled a TV contract and is staying tomorrow also, for what is to be his last day. He could possibly extend this by an additional day as he is very anxious to get a bear. If we have snow without wind, we could get Cliff a bear in half a day.

Jim got a new strut and left for Fairbanks today to have the wing tip repaired. Bob is taking over as cook. We don't object to Jim's departure as it makes one less for our crowded quarters. It is not likely that he will be back for a week or ten days.

On Monday we sighted an ugrug (bearded seal) sunning on the very edge of the ice beside open water. Bear hunting was not good because there was no tracking snow, so we decided to have a try at him.

We landed both planes a mile and a half from the seal and did a stalk; Cliff and I and Steve with his camera. We were lucky to get to within a hundred yards and find cover behind a chunk of ice.

I had my camera running on long lens with the seal centered. Steve was wider and back of Cliff who successfully shot the animal.

Yesterday we hunted all the way to Barrow, gassed up there and hunted all the way back. We saw no bears.

Because of this warmer weather I feel confident, for the first time, about the hunt tomorrow. Some snow would guarantee success but warmer temperatures would be almost as good. Most bear signs are near camp. They are cruising this so-called shore ice sniffing snowdrifts for seal dens.

It is difficult to write. I am in the cook tent and everybody is talking. Have just finished a rundown on my part of the ABC show. As I have said, nothing at all has been done on it except to outline the script. If Cliff does not get a bear, we have prepared a double ending. It will be a good film even without a bear. The ugrug hunt was terrific.

Mike and Bob are still putting finishing touches on the igloo. Eskimo men put one up in just a few hours. Our contractors worked two days. . . . It stands fifty yards from camp, flying a yellow towel from atop a staff. We call it "Camp Yellowbird."

Since we are outside the continental United States, we are preparing a charter to become eligible for foreign aid which is badly needed.

Jim and Bob dug a fishing hole today. The ice was seven feet thick and, when they broke through, water rose so rapidly that it threatened to swamp the tent where Burr lives. A hastily improvised dam of snow is holding the water back temporarily. We have caught no fish to date.

Thursday, April 28, 7 P.M.—It is hard to believe that the temperature was eighteen above at 7 A.M. After the cold weather we have had, it was like a heat wave.

We went flying at nine-thirty—Cliff's last day. I had great hopes for good tracking snow.

While tracking might have been better, apparently the bears could not stand the heat wave and were not moving. We could find no fresh tracks but there were quite a number of seals out sunning.

Back in camp at 3 P.M. Cliff took off with Mac for Fairbanks and home. Temperature in camp at noon was forty above.

We were surprised to learn how quickly one can get acclimated to the cold. Twenty above is almost hot. I sat on a snow sled outside a half hour ago and shaved very comfortably in that temperature.

We finished Cliff's show with no bear.

» «

Mike and Steve have been fishing through the hole Jim made. Meat bait brings up small shrimp.

Tomorrow we start production on my show. Ours is to be a snow sled hunt. Bud has been detailed to bring in seals for bait. We are finally in business.

Friday, April 29—Another beautiful day. Twenty above at 7 A.M. and up to forty at noon. I can understand how Eskimos can get used to cold weather. I was quite warm in a light outfit.

We shot fifteen hundred feet of film today. All of it traveling with the two snow sleds. What great machines they are.

We have a new campsite, a big, blue hunk of ice that rises about forty feet above the ice pack. It has straight walls on two sides and is about fifty feet square. We will pitch our tents tight against one wall. This will be our hunting camp. It is a half mile from main camp where we are now.

We will lay trails both north and south from the hunting camp (bears here move east and west) by dragging seal or seal oil scented bags for about ten miles each way. When seal blubber is available we will put a scent in the air by burning the blubber twenty-four hours a day.

Bud flew in about 11 A.M. with groceries and then went seal hunting. He came back at 3 P.M. without a seal.

Saturday, April 30—The fifteen hundred feet of film we shot yesterday was all on snow sleds going across the ice and past picturesque places and over and

We shot 1,500 feet of film yesterday.

through drifts and piles of ice. The snow sleds are SKI DOOS made by Bombardier in Quebec and have eight-horsepower four-cycle engines.

I tow a freight sled which is about twelve feet long, loaded with all kinds of duffle and with a thirty-inch target at the very back. The duffle is covered by two caribou skins and the whole thing is lashed down by ropes.

It was twenty above again at 8 A.M. We set up camp at the west end of our big ice cube—two Thermos Pop Tents and a sled garage and blind made of blocks of snow. From this blind we hope to shoot a bear if, and when, we can lure one into camp.

We shot film of building the camp, shooting the bow, cutting snow blocks, and erecting the snowhouse. Bud came in at 3 P.M. with a seal which lies about thirty yards from our main camp. We will not get to the serious business of baiting a bear until this preliminary photography is finished.

Burr has asked Bud to charter a flight out of here next Wednesday, which means we have three days to complete all photography. It will take this long to complete everything except the kill.

After Wednesday, Bob and I will be alone. By that time we will have more seals we hope and will drag the skinned carcasses each day to lay fresh trails into camp to a bait anchored within bow range of our tent.

On it I will try my strategy that has worked so well on black bears—a wire from the bait that leads to a bundle of tin cans inside our tent. The tents have no windows but the rattle of the empty cans should alert us.

We will hunt with the snow sleds also and may do some scouting with the plane while hunting seals. I think we have a perfect location—a big bear track through here before camp was set up, a bear in here to tear the tents the day before we arrived, and one sighted a half mile from here two days later.

It is not possible to do our bear hunting job at the main camp with the ABC crew there. Too much activity. A generating plant running constantly to charge batteries and just too many people, generally speaking.

With all other scenes shot before the crew leaves, it will be up to Bob and me to come up with the key footage.

As an additional incentive to bring bears within bowshot, we will cook the seal blubber 'round the clock on a catalytic heater. With all of these things going for us, sooner or later a bear should wander our way.

Sunday, May 1, 9 A.M.—The temperature was twelve above at 7 A.M. A fog closed in and now it is snowing, reducing visibility to about 200 yards. We cannot shoot film. Bob, Burr, Simon, and I have had breakfast and are pondering what to do. Jerry, Steve, and Mike are still sleeping and there seems to be no need to wake them. Bob and I thought some of doing a little scouting for bear tracks with the sleds but decided against it as we might not find our way back to camp.

I don't believe I have mentioned Simon Ned in my notes. He is an Indian from Allakaket about 400 miles south of here. He does not know what tribe he belongs to but there are about twenty families in his village. He works for Wein Airlines which makes three flights a week into the village. The landing field is about a quarter of a mile away and Simon's occupation is taking the mail from the airstrip to the village. In his spare time he hunts, traps, and fishes. He owns one of the three snow sleds in the village. The rest of the families still have dog teams but all wish they had sleds which cost about $900 here. Simon also works for Bud about five weeks each fall in a commercial fishing venture.

Simon is forty-three years old and stands about five foot eight. He weighs 150 pounds and has six children, one of whom perished, along with his dog team, when they broke through the ice on their way to hunt caribou last fall.

Bud brought Simon in to help around camp. His chores include climbing the pile of ice to scan the area for bears the first thing every morning, bringing in ice for water, and washing dishes.

Bud got news by radio that Jim had reached Fairbanks with his damaged plane. He does not know how long it will take to repair it. It is doubtful if he will get back before the hunt is over.

In the meantime, Bob is doing a good job taking over the cooking. I tried to help with breakfast yesterday. The bacon turned out fine but trouble developed with the pancakes. They would not rise—only turn brown. I fought this for half a dozen unattractive samples, heavy as lead, with everybody offering suggestions. Burr said the batter needed lard which was added. No improvement. Bob said it needed eggs. No better. Finally after I had been replaced as cook, it was discovered that I was using Gold Medal cake flour instead of pancake flour. My replacement seems permanent.

Sunday, 8 P.M.—Bob and I made a snow sled survey today. We went east about two miles, then south for the same distance, and had intended to enlarge our circle but the fog cleared and we came back to camp to shoot film until 5:30 P.M.

We now have about everything needed for my film except the bear. All kinds of shots for almost any kind of eventuality. The light faded at five-thirty today. Usually we can film up to about eight-thirty in good light.

In the Arctic at this time of the year, we have daylight until about 10 P.M. and fair light through to about 2:30 A.M. when the sun comes up in the northeast. It slices down at an angle in the northwest and a sort of presunrise glow covers the north all night.

There are seven of us in the cook tent now. Five of them playing Black Jack and Bob is cooking. The battery-charging generator chugs outside and supplies current for the 150-watt bulb that hangs overhead.

Jerry has been sculpturing a polar bear from a large piece of ice that rises up about a third of a mile from camp. His tools are a machete and a pick. The bear is about life size and is beginning to look good.

Since it is Sunday, Bud does not come out to camp today.

Monday, May 2, 10 A.M.—Very thick fog this morning and not clearing. Twenty-two above at 8 A.M. Visibility was about two hundred yards. This is tantamount to a "whiteout" and one nevers knows where one's footing is. He could stumble into a drift and fall on his face. Or, equally perilous, a step could drop him six feet into a crevasse.

We ran into this condition in late afternoon the last day we flew. We had landed to gas up from cans carried with us and, while there was no fog, we could not determine exactly where the snow surface was. A rather sticky situation. We noticed this yesterday also, in late afternoon, when we finished filming. We stumbled back to camp like drunks.

Complacency is called for on this hunt but it is not always easy with no bear in sight and time rolling by. Card games help pass the time but there is only today and tomorrow for the ABC crew. It could actually be a week before they went out, however, if the fog holds out.

Tuesday, May 3, 8 A.M.—The fog cleared yesterday and we shot the last of needed film except a moonlight scene planned for midnight, but fog again prevented this. High yesterday was forty-seven.

Bob and I slept in the igloo last night just for the hell of it. Not much different from our tent except for the thought of impending disaster if it collapsed on us.

There is very thick fog now and not much to do. Bud has not been here since Saturday, although we expect him today if the fog lifts. Yesterday when it was clear, we could see the heavy fog bank to the south near shore.

I did some research yesterday on the bear-baiting business. We cut off the top of a five-gallon gas can and filled it half full of seal oil and set it to boiling over a heater outside the tents. Bob and I then went off downwind about one fourth of a mile to see if we could pick up the scent. We certainly could. It was almost as pungent as at stoveside. I am pleased with these results and am sure a bear could tune in on it from ten miles out. We will cook seal blubber, too. But this will come later when there are less people here. Too much activity now for a bear to come in.

Same Day, 8 P.M.—Absolutely nothing accomplished today except several walks in the fog. Bud and Jim flew in a half hour ago and brought some supplies. Jim's plane is repaired and he will be with us from now on, we hope. Bud expects the weather to clear tomorrow so that Wein can come in to take the ABC crew out. That will leave Bob and Jim and me from here on out with Bud flying in from shore occasionally.

I feel that we will get a break on the bears. We have to. This hard luck just can't hold. They were here and will come again.

We have two fine shows finished except for the kill. My snow sled sequence should be a good one. And Cliff has the ugrug to spice his up. Cliff said he would come back if conditions improved. In spite of the weather I am optimistic. Tomorrow the blubber pots will burn fiercely.

Wednesday, May 4, 7 A.M.—Weather not good. Visibility almost zero. Temperature is thirteen above and wind strong at fifteen to twenty knots an hour. Bob is cooking breakfast. The rest of the crew is not up yet. Just Jim, Simon, and I who are waiting patiently.

I have only praise for our Thermos tents. The Prairie Schooner, of which we have two, does everything that could be expected. It is shaped like a covered wagon, eight-by-twelve, with six and a half feet headroom. The tents are double, one inside the other. This cook tent takes a beating but stands up very well.

Jim and Simon sleep here. A three-burner propane stove stands inside the door and piled high, on both sides, are cartons of groceries.

The tents are pitched on eight to ten inches of snow over the ice. Some pieces of ⅜-inch plywood, brought out on the sled, make a floor, covering the rear two thirds of the tent. Between the back sleeping area and the kitchen, a moose hide, hair side up, serves as a rug and blotter to swallow up bits of food and small objects dropped by the dwellers. It has been estimated that the rug will yield a small fortune in poker money after this hunt.

Between the traffic and heat from the stove, a depression down to ice depth has developed just inside the door. Corrugated cartons, added as they become available, are used to build it up but tracked in snow melts on the cartons and we have instead a basin of paper pulp.

Another tent of this type, heated with an oil space heater, houses our sound man and assistant cameraman as well as the camera gear. Burr and Jerry live in a double-wall A tent heated with a space heater also. Bob and I sleep in a double Pop Tent. We have a catalytic heater to keep the chill off.

Thursday, May 5, 11 A.M.—Nothing whatever happened yesterday. A strong wind from the west held and the plane could not get in. I took a long hike looking for tracks but did not really expect to find any since they drifted over immediately in the wind.

About 10 P.M. last evening the wind went down but the snow continued. This morning when we woke up it was eighteen above, the wind was down and visibility was better. Spirits are higher now. It is possible that the crew might get out today.

I circled camp about two miles out after breakfast in beautiful tracking snow. The ride on the snow sled was exhilarating. No bears but white foxes have found a bag of fish left at our picture camp and had a feast.

I did some practice shooting. A great day to be hunting. An inch of tracking snow all over.

2 P.M.—Still a beautiful day. Forty above. Shot a seal two miles from camp. Weather is clear. We hear a plane. It seems likely that the crew will leave and I can get this off to mail.

May 6, Friday—The ABC crew got off at four-thirty yesterday. The Beaver plane was to come back today for their gear but it is still sitting on our airstrip as this was another foggy day.

The first thing we did after they left was to move camp—and none too soon. The hole Jim had dug to fish through was slowly flooding the area. Tent floors had melted through the snow down to ice. A bad situation. In Arctic camping tents should rest on snow, not ice.

We now have three tents instead of five. They are pitched on about three feet of snow (drifts that we leveled off), about 100 yards from the old campsite.

Bob and I have an eight-by-twelve, double-wall Prairie Schooner with an oil burner. To get this double canvas we simply erect one tent inside another.

Jim and Simon occupy a similar tent that is heated by a three-burner propane range. This is the cook and dining tent also. Between these two tents we have a Giant Thermos Pop Tent, not heated, that serves as storage for items that can stand freezing.

This morning we put the finishing touches on our new camp and shot a seal about a mile away. He was lying on the ice beside his hole. After skinning it, we dragged it behind the sled back to camp and then around an area three miles east, four miles north, and three miles south. Tomorrow we will extend the north trail to about ten miles. Open water is about fifteen miles in that direction.

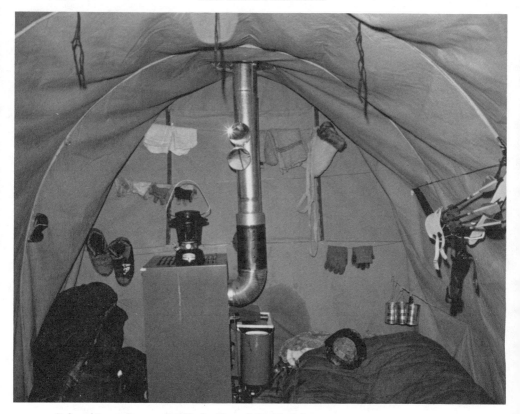

Bob and I now have an 8 × 12, double-wall Prairie Schooner.

Last chore today was to lash a seal down to an ice anchor about eighty yards from our tent and run a wire from it to a stake inside, on which we have hung some empty tin cans (our alarm system). Also the five-gallon gas can half full of seal oil and blubber was set on the heater atop an oil drum to give off scent continuously while we are here. Between the scent and the drags we hope to lure a bear into camp and to bow range. Temperature was twenty above today with an east wind.

Saturday, May 7—High today was twenty-eight and low eighteen. Bob and I dragged a seal behind the snow sled for ten or twelve miles today. About as far as we could go. Beyond this was very rough ice. We climbed on top of an ice pile but could not see open water, although a low cloud indicated water in that vicinity.

Eight or nine seals were lying by their holes but all had carefully selected their locations in flat areas where there was no cover to stalk up to them. Under the right conditions they can be approached to within seven or eight hundred yards with the snow sleds. If we had a child's sled with a frame covered with white material at the front, I believe we could get very close—lying on our bellies and propelling the sled with our hands and feet, watching through a peephole.

The Arctic seal must endure many interruptions during his sleep and sunning periods. At intervals of about one minute he raises his head to look quickly around. It is between these alert periods that one has an opportunity to squirm closer. The seals average about a hundred pounds each and have a layer of blubber two inches thick under their skins. The blubber is a beautiful, translucent pink that settles into clear oil after standing for about a month. This seal oil is used by the Eskimos for heat and when condensed makes a very succulent "dip" for almost any food they eat. Jim says it makes an excellent salad dressing. We shall see. . . . The liver is extracted from each seal for our own use and Jim has promised a fine feast of steak from the one we shot yesterday.

The frozen carcass of a Barren Ground caribou lies beside our tent and the skin provides a warm rug for inside. Our larder, besides roast and stewed caribou meat, consists of frozen steaks, chops, and fowl, canned goods, plus flour, macaroni, beans, etc. All water is melted from an abundant supply of salt-free ice stacked up in a pile fifty feet high beside camp.

We have two snow sleds in camp of the type that are replacing the dog team in Barrow. They will go almost any place except over the roughest ice and use about a half gallon of gas per hour. In addition we have a towing sled to haul supplies brought out from Bud Helmericks' headquarters at Colville River Delta. This sled is about thirty inches wide and twelve feet long. The runners are shod with $\frac{1}{10}''$ thick iron about three inches wide.

Sunday, May 8—Temperature is twenty. Very little to report. Heaviest fog yet. So thick it was difficult to travel with the snow sled although Jim and Simon managed to follow our drag north and found fresh bear tracks coming toward camp on our trail. If the bear had been nearby, they would not have been able to see him because of the fog and they hope they did not frighten him so he won't come back.

This has been a long, dull day. The wind changed to the southwest and late this evening snow began to fall. The heaviest snow I have seen in the Arctic.

Monday, May 9, Morning—Temperature twenty. A brisk wind all night, with snow. It is still blowing and snowing now but the sun is shining and visibility is boundless. This is the first sun and clear weather we have had in ten days.

Bud came out at noon but there will be no hunting today. Wein is expected here for the gear and Bud will have to meet the plane in Colville and lead him out to camp.

We have to stay in camp also, since there will be three barrels of gas to unload from the plane. Nothing can be planned definitely in this country. One is entirely dependent upon mechanical equipment and the weather. Bob flew back to Colville with Bud, to have a bath and spend the night. My turn next time.

At 9 P.M. Jim, Simon, and I dragged the seal north to the end of our trail. We got back at 11 P.M. through fog so thick we could barely make out our trail. It was ground fog, however, and we could look up through it and see blue sky.

Tomorrow is the beginning of the season when the sun does not dip below the horizon. I took a picture at 11:30 P.M.

Tuesday, May 10, 5 P.M.—Temperature thirty. No bears came in last night nor did the Wein flight come in today. Bud and Bob have not showed up either. There was a brilliant sun this morning but at noon a wind of about thirty knots sprang up. Much drifting of snow and again poor visibility.

Jim and Simon went seal hunting. We need a fresh one for our drag. They were caught in the blinding snowstorm that hit our tent like pellets of ice. Jim had an unsuccessful shot at a seal.

First thing this morning I circled camp about two miles out to see if any bears had been near—no tracks. I then opened up our drifted-in path from the tent to my shooting stand overlooking the seal bait and the one leading to the photography position. Here a camera, prefocused, rests on a tripod protected from the elements by a white sheet.

Next I repositioned our heater and cleaned up the inside of the tent, adding more hanging arrangements for drying clothes. Took a Ski Doo and did some photos of ice formations and icicles. Tended the scent pot. Did some practice. Took a nap.

Bob and I sleep in a double Pop Tent.

Wednesday, May 11—A beautiful day. Bud and Bob came out at 10 A.M. and we left immediately for hunting. I flew with Bud and Bob went with Jim.

Fifteen minutes out we saw a bear walking along beside a pressure ridge. This was the first bear we had seen for twenty-five days and it was quite a thrill. Bud asked did I want to try for him and the answer was "yes."

Fortunately we had sighted him at a distance and he did not see the plane, so we flew west on the ridge until we found a place to land several miles ahead. We then made our way back along the ridge on foot toward the bear to a spot that offered good possibilities for ambush, hoping the bear would continue on his course.

I found a place on a pile of ice where I would be out of sight if he came by on my side and high enough to shoot over if he came through on the other side. Bud and Bob found cover about twenty yards back of me to cover any action with the cameras.

We waited for an hour and a half, cramped and uncomfortable and cold, before we spotted him coming about a half mile away. He showed up dark against the bright snow, shuffling along in an aimless way with his mind on a good seal dinner, I suppose, as he investigated piles of ice and cracks in the snow.

At first he appeared to be coming straight by at close range on our side but at about 400 yards he swerved away from the ridge and seemed to choose a course through rough ice that would put him a 100 yards away as he passed me.

I had to make a decision. It seemed best to move out in front of him, which I did when he went out of sight behind the ice. The others moved with me and we again found cover with the cameras back of me as before.

The bear came into sight very quickly. Three hundred yards, two hundred, one hundred . . . coming on a course that would pass me at twenty yards or even closer.

But the wind was not good in our new position. At fifty yards his nose went into the air and he stopped to look toward us. Not sure, but suspicious, he turned sideways looking our way and sniffing. Having been charged twice before on other hunts and at closer range than this, I felt sure that he was trying to make up his mind whether he should come for us or run off, so I rose from behind my cover and released an arrow.

It looked good all the way. Immediately a red blotch appeared, close to the shoulder. He went down in the loose snow, recoiling from the hit and snapping at the arrow while lying on his side. Then he was back on his feet like a cat and took off on the double over the pressure ridge and beyond about a hundred yards where he went down again in some rough ice, this time for good.

A handsome trophy—a bear with ten gallons of seal oil in his belly. What a relief. After twenty-five days of bad weather and tough luck we get perfect conditions and went out to bag a polar bear just twelve miles from camp. We should have a good film.

» «

May 12, Thursday—With good weather forecast I thought I should wire ABC to ask if Cliff would be interested in coming back as he had said he would.

Bud talked to Wein on the radio to inquire if we could go to Barrow on their Thursday mail flight. They advised that they had canceled the flight because of engine trouble, so Bud and Jim flew us in here at 11 P.M. I am sitting in my room in the Top of the World Hotel writing these notes.

Friday, May 13—In Barrow. Nothing of hunting news to report. Waiting for word from New York to see if Cliff is coming up.

This is a Barrow I have not seen before. Spring is here and black gravel is beginning to show on the streets in places but the snow sleds zip right through them just the same.

As we flew in yesterday we saw clouds of eider ducks over the town and the ice beyond. The natives are shooting them as they fly over the leads near where their whaling camps are set up.

A whale was taken here last Monday. It was about thirty feet long. We are trying to get some muktuk to take home.

I bought a kayak for the museum. I think it is the last one in town. We saw it on the roof of a shed and asked the owner if he would sell it. He said, "What were you thinking to pay for it?" I said that I was thinking of a hundred dollars. He said, "I was thinking of $125."

I paid him and made arrangements with Wein to crate and ship it. Simon is getting me an Indian-made sled and Jim has given me a pair of Indian-made snowshoes. Am dickering now for a mastodon tusk about nine feet long.

Saturday, May 14—George Thiele came in last evening from Fairbanks for the weekend. We had quite a reunion. We had hunted polar bears with him in 1960 and 1962.

We saw the sun at midnight tonight. There is good light here now, full twenty-four hours of the day. We can shoot pictures at any time.

Heard from ABC. They advise that Cliff is anxious to come back.

Sunday, May 15—Trying to get back out to camp but the weather is not good. Cliff wired that he will be in Friday. As soon as we can get out to camp we will do some seal hunting, fire up the blubber pot, and make a last-ditch stand to get a bear in to bait.

We have looked at enough Eskimos, have seen Barrow in all of its moods, and have escaped being run down by snow sleds. Arctic Research beat me to the draw on the mastodon tusk. They bought it for one thousand dollars.

Tuesday, May 17, 8 A.M.—We are still in Barrow and not too happy about it. If we have to be weathered in, we would rather be out in our camp on the ice. Bob, Jim, and I are the only ones in the hotel. Talked to Bud yesterday by radio. The weather was not good there nor here. It was snowing and visibility was poor.

Things look somewhat brighter this morning. There are still some snowflakes in the air, but we can dimly see the sun which means that the overcast is thin and might burn through.

10 A.M.—Bud is here. We're going back to camp.

Later—Had some trouble getting Jim's engine started. Temperature twelve. A pleasant flight to Colville. Saw many caribou, a snowy owl, and a flock of brant. In Barrow we saw snow buntings.

We made a stop at Bud's house and had tea and cookies. Then on to camp at 3 P.M. We saw quite a number of seals on the way back and since we need bear bait Bud took his plane and Jim the snow sled and went hunting. Both were back at 6 P.M. with five seals between them.

We had roast caribou for dinner, skinned the seals and went to bed. It is warmer here on the ice than on land.

Wednesday, May 18—Thirty below. Bob and I dragged a seal carcass about twelve miles northwest this morning. This is about two miles farther than we have been before. We crossed a fresh bear track about ten miles out. It was a small one. I made a stalk on a seal and missed him three times at 300 yards with a .244 rifle. . . .

Jim made a drag about eight miles northeast and shot two more seals, so we have plenty of bait.

We all got back to camp at 2 P.M. and finished up the roast. A misty rain has turned to fine snow and now another fog is setting in.

We have six seal carcasses piled in the bait area. Bob thinks a bear might gorge himself to the point of immobility and be an easy target.

We find seal hunting quite interesting. The seals lie in the sun on the ice with their heads close to their breathing holes. These holes are small at the top all winter, when the seals stay under the ice—just big enough, through six to eight feet of ice, for their noses to poke through for oxygen.

In the spring, about the first of May, they enlarge these holes until they can flip out on the ice for sunning. At the slightest sign of danger they disappear back down the hole and out of sight. Their sleep is never uninterrupted; we never saw one that did not raise his head about once a minute to have a look around. This takes about five seconds and since the head is down only about a minute, stalking a seal is tedious business.

One needs a good, accurate, flat-shooting gun, preferably scope mounted. The seals are usually some distance out on smooth ice where there is little cover for either man or bear to make a stalk. This is where the small sled I mentioned comes into the picture.

We fastened a piece of plywood about two by three feet, vertically, at the front of the sled. It is covered with white cloth and has a peephole for watching the seal as one propels the sled with his hands, lying flat on his belly as we did as kids. Propulsion is turned on during that minute the seal is sleeping and turned off immediately when his head comes up. With care a seal can be approached to within a hundred yards in this way.

Sometimes the seals are found within range (up to 300 yards) of a piece of ice that offers cover for a stalk. It is not practical to shoot beyond this range as they must be hit in the head or they will slip down their holes and disappear.

On smooth ice we can usually run the Ski Doo, carrying the small sled, to within a half mile before beginning the sled work.

We have been hunting the common hair seal. They weigh between 80 and 150 pounds. Their diet is almost entirely of shrimp and they must eat very well as the blubber under their skin is about two inches thick.

Thursday, May 19—We have been plagued with bad weather. Bob and I made the north drag this morning. We traveled first through a fine mist that iced our dark glasses and then turned to snow which made it difficult to see our trail on the return strip.

Unless one experiences them, it would be hard to imagine the problems an Arctic "whiteout" creates. Flyers must avoid them, if possible, since they cannot tell how far they are from the snow or ice during these storms. Landing, of course, is the greatest hazard of all and many planes have been lost during these times.

On the other hand, while walking, one cannot tell if a snowdrift is two feet up or is a depression two feet down. Patience is needed in the Arctic. What can't be done today is for tomorrow or even next week.

This afternoon we packed the foldboat and tents at the ice-cube camp and hauled them back to the airstrip. We also took some pictures.

At four o'clock the weather cleared and Bud flew out to camp saying he had a garbled telegram for me. None of us could make out the message, so Bud suggested that we fly over to a DEW line station about twenty-five miles or so away and call Barrow for confirmation on its contents. Bud said that over his transmitter there was so much static he could only make out something about Cliff Robertson.

The men at the radar station were extremely surprised to see us. "Who are you?" "Where did you come from?" "What do you want?" "How did you get here?"

I have not had a haircut in two months and my whiskers bristled over my face, so I kept my hat on knowing I did not look much like an upstanding citizen. When I told my inquirer that I had been camping in his front yard twenty-five miles out on the ice, hunting polar bears with a bow and arrow, it was almost too much, and there seemed to be a question in his mind whether to have us shot on the spot or quizzed considerably further.

He finally allowed me to call Wein at Barrow but nothing else. I explained to the girl in the Wein office that Helmericks could not understand the telegram they had sent out because of static on his radio and would she please read it to me from there. Yes, she would, just a minute. . . .

Ten minutes later she was back and said she couldn't find the telegram. I then told her to wire ABC in New York and ask them to send another telegram stating whether Robertson was coming back and when.

Our host at the DEW line station accompanied us out to the plane, wanting to make sure we had arrived in one, as we said, and to check the number Bud had given him. Nonetheless, we wondered how efficient our Distant Early Warning system is. We had flown straight in front of their screen coming in and had, for five weeks, been flying twenty-five miles north of their site.

We were back in camp at 7 P.M.

Friday, May 20, Noon—Twenty-six below. Wind twenty knots. Thick fog this morning but clearing now. We have done nothing so far today except have breakfast and visit in our cozy tent. If Helmericks comes out we will plane hunt on the way into Barrow to see if Cliff comes on the 6:30 P.M. plane from Fairbanks. We can hunt on the way back also. In fact we can hunt all night now, when the weather is good, since there is daylight around the clock.

Evening—No word from Bud. The weather is not good. Bob, Jim, and I made the seal drag north again. A bear had hit our trail about three miles from the far end but went the wrong way.

On the return trip we put the skinned seal carcass on the sled and Jim carved it all the way back to camp dropping off chunks of blubber at intervals close enough to keep a bear interested.

At 8 P.M. I made a new drag trail northeast for about twelve miles. Did not see a track and was back at ten-thirty. No word from Bud.

Saturday, May 21—A beautiful day. The sun was shining brightly when we got up. We expected Helmericks early. He came out at eleven-thirty.

To keep busy we strung the bear hide up on a vertical pole, using the foldboat double paddle to stretch out the legs. It looked fine hanging there between our tents and we took several pictures.

Bud reported a radio-phone talk with ABC who inquired first if Bob and I were all right and then said that Robertson could come back on Monday evening if this were agreeable with us. Bud told them to send him along.

To keep busy we stretched the bear skin aloft.

Sunday, May 22, Evening—Today was a complete washout. Fog so thick it was not safe to venture out even in the Ski Doo. Bob and I tried it, starting on the northwest drag trail, but a snowstorm developed and we had to return. We took some pictures and had fried chicken for dinner at 9 P.M.

SUMMARY

Cliff Robertson came back Monday evening and stayed two days. We had no hunting weather during this time so there was nothing to do but wrap up the hunt. We did not have one hunting day in the last ten. Fog, fog, fog.

On several of these days we could have used the plane but we cannot see tracks without sunlight. I had hoped to get some bear pictures for the film.

Except for the bear sighted when we were setting up camp we saw only one bear in six weeks—the one I shot.

In reviewing the hunt certain conclusions seem obvious, although other factors, unknown to me, may have influenced the movements of polar bears during the six weeks we spent on the ice.

In the period between April 15 and the 20, eight bears passed within half a mile of camp. We saw one of these. The others were identified as seven different bears by their tracks.

No one disputes the fact that food and weather are the two chief elements that influence the movements of animals. Food is the most important and the food of polar bears is seal. Almost nothing else.

Ice covers the ocean in the Arctic at the time seals give birth to their young. Newborn seals cannot swim for several days, so the mother must make arrangements to overcome this problem. She locates her breathing hole underneath deep snow that has drifted against the side of an ice pile. At this hole, which she enlarges before the young are born, she digs a den in the snow, undetectable from topside, where she hopes her baby will be safe from the inquisitive nose of the polar bear until the family can go down into the water to safety.

Not every young seal survives these first critical days in spite of the mother's caution. The polar bear has a powerful nose and spends his days sniffing around the ice packs trying to locate a den and dig it out. We saw signs of his success in these efforts now and then.

I believe this seal birthing period ended a few days after we set up camp since the bears shifted their hunting activities to the leads that were opening up about fifteen miles north of us. I feel sure we could have had success in baiting bears if our camp had been nearer open water.

Camping on the ice pack is a unique experience. It can be done safely if the location is selected with care. It can also be more or less comfortable if one knows how to camp under these conditions. And while we were not successful, I am convinced that bears could be baited into camp by dragging seal carcasses behind snow sleds. One must be warned, however, that during the latter part of the season, when the ice is beginning to break up, it would be possible to be swallowed up by the sea through one misplaced step.

Another time, I would locate camp farther out on the ice nearer open water. The line between shore ice (which is ice that does not break up until the spring thaw) and the shifting ice floes farther out is quite clearly defined and does not change much from year to year, so with care a camp could be relatively safe farther out. The inexperienced would do well to hire an Eskimo who knows the ice. Otherwise one could be isolated on an ice floe and wind up as a guest of the Russians.

The entire hunt could be done with snow sleds but to avoid the almost endless fogs we encountered, one should be there in the early part of April, although temperatures as low as forty below zero could be experienced at this time. Also some method for preheating the sled engines would be necessary at this time of year.

Seals would be more difficult to find at this time also but if one purchased two or more in Barrow, before going out on the ice, it would be sufficient to lure bears into camp.

In addition to the seal drags, the blubber pot should burn continuously. This puts out a potent incense which, I am sure, can be picked up by a bear five to ten miles away in a proper wind. Our pot setup was trouble-free and operated twenty-four hours a day without attention. The flat-topped catalytic heater burned white gas and had a twenty-four-hour tank capacity. It sat on an empty oil drum and, to conserve heat and protect it from the wind, we covered it with a corrugated carton in which we cut a hole large enough to accommodate an open-end five-gallon gas can holding a small quantity of seal oil and blubber. These heaters burn at a uniform temperature—just hot enough to heat the seal oil or blubber to the right temperature. They require attention only once a day.

From such a location only snow sleds would be needed to hunt bears, either by tracking or by cruising around sweeping the area with binoculars from atop ice

Refueling the blubber pot.

packs. This would be the ultimate in sportsmanship with either a bow or gun but, because of the hardships and the long time it takes with this method, I feel sure that most polar bears will continue to be located from planes. In 1967 polar bear hunting will be done under the permit system as a protective measure. Permits will be limited to the number of bears to be harvested.

Aside from man, the polar bear has only one enemy—the killer whale. In the water the bear is an agile and graceful swimmer but easy prey for these whales. Sometimes he comes out second best in an encounter with walrus, too, but in this case, he is the aggressor.

The Eskimo hunted the ice bear in two ways—with dogs or posing himself as a seal. In the former, while traveling along with his dog sled, a bear is sighted, and the dogs cut loose to bring the animal to bay. Then, amid a great bedlam of vicious dogs, snarling bear, and yelling humans, the Eskimo hunter advanced with his spear, bow and arrow, or later, his gun, and dispatched the bear.

Their even more daring and spectacular method was a sort of decoy game where the hunter spread himself prone upon the ice to simulate a seal when a bear was seen in the distance. He dressed in dark clothing and wiggled his feet like flippers and raised his head at frequent intervals to look around as a seal does. The bear would start stalking close like a cat after a bird, while the brave Eskimo carried on with his seal-like antics. Natives in the Arctic who have hunted this way told me that the bear could be counted upon to make his final rush from about fifty feet and just before this hazardous period the shot had to be made.

In the meantime, the resourceful polar bear will continue as master of the ice pack. He will prowl its white vastness and capture enough seals to grow big and strong and enjoy a happy existence where almost all other animals would starve. His keen nose and sharp eyesight, coupled with a fast left hook, serves him well and man, invading his realm, will never know whether he is the hunter or the hunted.

Chapter 15

ASIATIC BUFFALO, BRAZIL - 1967

Marajó Island lies in the mouth of the Amazon River. It is flat and big, more than a hundred miles wide and long. Cattle country, its elevation is only a few feet above sea level. On the mainland lies the city of Belém. The country is Brazil on the continent of South America.

We had arranged for this hunt well in advance. Our outfitter had mountain-lion dogs imported from Arizona. It was to be a hunt for jaguar—El Tigre, as he is known there.

Monsoons sweep the country in January. We were to hunt two weeks beginning in early December.

Several days before our departure date a cable announced that the heavy rains had already come, that the island was almost inundated, the dogs could not follow tracks. There was an alternative, the cable said: We could hunt Asiatic buffaloes.

These animals, known also as water buffalo, had been imported by ranchers more than a hundred years ago. They believed that, being at home in wet country, these animals might do better than cattle.

The program was not successful. Many buffaloes escaped and went wild to become exceedingly wary and elusive, a menace to the rancher, and with its bad temper and great horns, a worthy trophy.

Our hunt for these beasts was different from any I'd ever had before. Life in this Brazilian jungle, subsisting mainly on what small game we could come up with, was a most interesting experience.

New York, Barbados, Port of Spain, Georgetown, Paramaribo, and on to Belém, Brazil.

December 6—Shirt-sleeve weather and nine out of ten cars in this city are cabs madly trying to run down pedestrians whom they seem to regard as the lowest form of life. It has been said that those hit are lucky to be killed because those who recover face a lawsuit for damages to the cab!

We got in late last night and were met by the outfitter, Richard Mason, an Englishman, twenty-nine years old, about six foot two and with hunting experience here and in Africa. Took a cab to Vanja Hotel. Fortunate to have an air-conditioned room. Continental breakfast in hotel this morning—hard roll and coffee—sightseeing and to the zoo and botanical gardens later in the day.

Repacking gear to reduce total weight. Must go light as trip to hunting grounds on the island (after short plane flight from Belém) is three hours by horse and bullock, through mud, into the swamp where the buffaloes are. No chance for jaguar. Too wet.

We leave for the island at 8 A.M. tomorrow. Belém is a very old city. Mostly one-story buildings and almost all of them need paint and repairs. People are small in stature and many remind me of Mexicans. They are very pleasant and nobody is in a hurry except the cab drivers.

The outfitter says don't wear your camouflage clothing until we are out of town or the natives might think another revolution is starting.

Saturday, December 7, 7 P.M. In Camp—What an evening. Temperature just right and a gentle breeze bringing a cacophony of sounds from the swampy meadow beyond the open-thatched hut we are sitting in. Howling monkeys chattered noisily in the trees just before dark and now the night voices have taken over.

We flew to this island of Marajó this morning and landed at the home of a "cowboy," sending a note ahead in a tin can, to be dropped by our plane at a ranch about five miles farther on. The message announced our arrival with instructions to bring the horses.

We left there at 2 P.M. and got into camp at six. Bob Munger, my hunting partner, and I rode horses while Dick, the cowboy, and our tracker rode bullocks (Brahma bulls); two other bulls packed in our gear.

We traveled almost entirely through marsh, either open or wooded, in water up

We landed at the home of a cowboy.

Two Brahma bulls packed our gear.

to three feet deep. The temperature was about a hundred between showers and the trip seemed long.

Our tracker, a mixture of Negro, Indian, and Portuguese, lives here with his wife and two small children. Dick says that he is a great woodsman. One of his many talents is calling in monkeys—considered edible here.

We must get up at three-thirty tomorrow morning in order to be about three miles from here by daylight.

Sunday, December 8, 5 P.M.—Left camp at 4 A.M. and headed north through swamps and forests by the light of a full equatorial moon. The swamp consists of meadowlike open fields or head-high brush and grass, but everywhere it is wet and there are no trees. The water varies from ankle- to knee-deep as we travel along buffalo trails.

The forest, on the other hand, is not so wet and is even quite dry in some places. The trees are chiefly palms of many varieties, all growing together in somewhat of a jungle. A great many of them have trunks covered with thorns. Here also we walk the numerous trails of the buffalo. We look for fresh tracks and follow those of large bulls. The trackers slip their feet into a burlap sling which enables them to shinny up palm trees to spot buffaloes ahead. I was impressed by the number of tracks and by the great size of them. They must certainly be a larger animal than the African Cape buffalo.

Our tracker's name is Raimundo. He is about thirty years old, five feet tall, and might weigh 130 pounds, but very strong and agile. Before Mason hired him he

*Raimundo shinnies
up a palm tree
to see buffaloes.*

was making one dollar a month as a cowboy but had not been paid for two years. Top wage is four dollars a month.

I use the term "cowboy" loosely. They do not resemble our roping men of the West. Rather they are small of stature, sometimes ride bareback, clad only in shorts, and always barefooted.

Raimundo's wife is our cook. She looks to be about twenty years old. One of the more modern aspects of life here is their conception of marriage. Couples just start living together.

These people have no religious facilities nor any medical attention. Generations of them have never been off the island.

Raimundo leads the way as we start to hunt. Mason is next with a .375 over his shoulder. I follow with Bob and the camera behind me. Beniditto brings up the rear, toting a .404 and water bottles.

These buffaloes are tough, we are told, and sometimes charge on sight. We hope Mason is a good shot.

It was hot after 8 A.M. and we saw no buffaloes at all. Back to camp at twelve-thirty where we had lunch, a shower, and a nap and it is now 6 P.M. Bob is a hundred yards away, shooting doves and parrots for our dinner.

Monday, December 9, 6 P.M.—Bob and I rode horses to the hunting ground today instead of walking. Yesterday's jaunt was tiring, sloshing in the mud and water. The ground is very uneven where the buffaloes have churned it up. We got a late start, 5 A.M., but ran on to good tracks in about three miles. Followed a good bull on foot into the forest and sneaked up fairly close but the cover was thick and he crashed off before we saw him. Took the track of another bull then and ran on to him in some very thick cover. He was only a short distance from us and we could hear him splashing, but we never got to see him.

Starting back on horseback about noon we struck still another track. Tied the horses and tracked again as far as a small water hole in the bush where we

An alligator was sunning on the far bank and I shot him.

Raimundo, Beniditto, and Dick gather palm leaves.

The 'gator is laid in a tightly woven basketlike nest.

The 'gator in his
cocoon, slung on
Raimundo's back.

stopped to rest. An alligator, about five feet long, was sunning on the far bank and I shot him.

We gave up the buffalo since he was with some cows. Back at camp at 4 P.M. Bob shot nine doves and three parrots last evening. We ate the doves for dinner at 9 P.M. This evening the bag ran heavy to parrots. The natives love them.

We have no other meat. Tomorrow evening it will be alligator for dinner. (There are no crocodiles, by the way, in South America.)

Our water is from a surface well here at camp. All of the island is flat and there is no runoff nor the smallest stream. Rain water is not absorbed by the earth. It simply lies there until the hot sun takes it up.

We carry plastic water jugs on the hunts but have learned that drinking too much bogs one down uncomfortably. Half a lime, from a tree near camp, satisfies the thirst. Back in camp, completely dehydrated, we drink quarts of water flavored with lime juice and sugar and spiced with a finger of gin or rum. One's system seems to absorb all of it to make up for the day's loss.

Our feet are always wet—a good workout for the new hunting boots we are testing. Coming back to camp evenings, we remove our muddy boots, dump the water out, and set them outside the tent. They are never dry by morning due to the heavy dew—but wet clothing is no problem—it is comforting in this temperature.

Tuesday, December 10, 5:30 P.M.—Total bag for the day: one monkey. We rode again to the hunting area, about three miles. Tied the horses and found a track which we followed for about two hours, but our quarry left the country. It was the same one we jumped yesterday according to the trackers.

We spent the rest of the day building a platform near a group of mud wallows in the forest. Will leave it for a day or two and then spend a night there. We had parrots, rice, and canned peas for dinner. The 'gator was good last night. White meat that tasted something like king crab.

Wednesday, December 11, 5:30 P.M.—Slept late this morning. Did not get up until 5 A.M. Bob and I rode bullocks to the hunting area. We found them to be fair mounts but they have only two speeds: slow and stop. Steering is by a small rope attached to a ring in the nose. For straight ahead, the rope lies between the horns and one does nothing to start the trip except heel him in the flank. For a turn, the rope is flipped off the horns and the nose is pointed in the direction one wishes to go.

Bob and I rode bullocks to the hunting area.

We used the horse saddles on the bullocks. These are specially made here in Brazil. Narrow and high. In place of the pommel on a Western saddle, these peak high, resembling a kind of gondola. For roping, a lariat of beautiful, hand-twisted cowhide is tied to a ring under the skirt at the rear side. Stirrups are only about two inches wide—just big enough to accommodate the first two toes of a bare foot. No one wears shoes here but our saddles have wider stirrups to accommodate boots.

All of the island horses are small.

All of the island horses are small. They can traverse this mud and water remarkably well. Only once did mine bog down and Bob was thrown when his cinch broke in a floundering effort. They are never shod, as there is not a rock on the whole island. Bridles are not used. Just a halter with rope reins. They neck rein very well.

We rode bullocks today because the horses needed a rest and because we went south to a new area and the going was too rough for a horse. Bullocks, with their split hooves, seem to have better balance. Much of the way was through belly-deep mud which they negotiate without much difficulty. We rode about two miles, mostly through open marsh country and then into the jungle where we tied our mounts and proceeded to track again.

There were big buffalo tracks all over. We routed two herds without seeing a hair, however. It was oppressively hot and I reached the conclusion that this was not for me—that trying to get a buffalo by this tracking business was too difficult with bow and arrow.

» «

We have built another platform at a wallow and hope for a rain to wash our man scent away. From here on we will hunt from these platforms. Plans are to get up there about 4 P.M. and stay through the night. The buffaloes come out of the forest in late evening to feed in the open marshes and go back in about day-light, visiting these wallows on the way to the bedding grounds deep in the jungle.

I have not hunted anything more wary than these buffaloes. The ranchers don't want them here and their cowboys shoot at them on sight. We are told that just about all of the bulls have bullets in them and thereby have developed a hatred for man. Cowboys being killed or gored by these heavy beasts is not uncommon. They charge their horses from thick bush at close range.

I wonder if some of this hatred doesn't come from the fact that these cowboys, to supplement their one to four dollars a month income, lasso younger animals in the evening or on moonlight nights. And that takes some doing in this mud. They have to get them to market alive as the meat would spoil quickly in the heat and humidity.

Thursday, December 12, 8 A.M.—Slept until six this morning. We start night-hunting tonight. This is the first day that we have seen sunrise here in camp. Bob got up early and shot fourteen parrots for dinner today. If we shoot a buffalo, we will have fresh meat for only a day and a half. There is no refrigeration and the meat will not keep beyond that point. After that, it will be heavily salted and dried.

We have no butter here, no bread, nor any but canned vegetables. Breakfast consists of Kellogg's corn flakes and powdered milk, plus very black coffee. We do not carry lunch with us on the hunt, but upon getting back sometimes in late

Raimundo returns from the hunt packing a monkey and wild fruit.

afternoon, we eat cheese and a canned pudding made from goiabada fruit that tastes something like figs.

Dinner, about 9 P.M., is whatever can be scrounged up in the way of meat (Raimundo left at daylight today with the shotgun to hunt monkeys), potatoes or rice, canned peas, and coffee. There is usually a can of fruit for dessert. We sometimes have an audience at dinner. Our cook, several children, the trackers, and visitors stand about and watch.

Bob and I have a fine bugproof tent. Mason's Plott hounds, which he uses for

We sometimes have an audience for dinner.

We have a bugproof tent.

jaguar hunts, are tied up nearby. Seven native dogs, owned by the cowboys, run loose, but are used to round up the cattle and pigs on occasion. There are many pigs of all sizes—also chickens, turkeys, and ducks. The natives do not eat eggs. Eggs are saved for hatching.

At the ranch where we landed, flying in from Belém, the kitchen was a sort of porchlike affair with an open cooking fire on a waist-high, earth-covered table. Beside the fire was a pen with a pig in it. The pig hung out over the top rail and squealed whenever the woman came near the stove. He was being fattened for the pot.

*Beside the fire was a
pen with a pig in it.*

Nearby, in a box, a turkey sat on eggs, a chicken had chicks in a box, and a duck had ducklings in a basket. Outside, just a short distance away, two vultures perched on the outhouse.

There was one exception to not eating eggs. Beniditto brought four children here to visit recently—ages about three to seven. Each carried a gift of a turkey egg in a small hand which was shyly presented to us and then, even more shyly, offered their hands in sort of a greeting. The custom is, Beniditto told us, for them to present gifts in exchange for the blessing we must pronounce as we shook their hands. It was hard to determine which was more meaningful to them: the blessing or the candy we gave them. There is no furniture in their houses, except a table and boxes to sit on. They sleep in hammocks.

Brazil won its independence from Portugal a hundred years ago, but the ties are friendly. The language is Portuguese and the population numbers around ninety million.

Tarantulas are numerous and widespread. We have seen some big ones. There are scorpions here also, but we have not seen them, although we check our boots every morning. There are other insects, of course, of which the fire ants are the worst. One does not sit down without carefully examining the ground first. Insects have not been a great problem, however, as we have good repellent.

Friday, December 13, 5 P.M.—Things look somewhat discouraging. In six days of hunting we have not seen one of these elusive buffaloes, although fresh tracks are numerous all around the area. I have always said that the white-tailed deer is the wariest animal I have hunted but this experience may change that opinion.

Yesterday afternoon we had a hard rain. There was thunder and heavy black clouds. About a half inch fell in a half hour. At two-thirty the storm had passed over and we left for the first platform. Rode through a light shower and spent the night overlooking the wallows.

On the way in, we flushed a deer and saw five coatimundi, but saw nothing else all night. We heard a buffalo walk by, about a hundred yards away; and some kind of small animal was scurrying around beneath us, but we could not see it as the moon came up late.

On the way back to camp this morning, we followed fresh tracks for about two hours. They circled and crossed our path as we made our way back to camp in time for lunch. After lunch, a bath and a nap and it is cool now sitting in the thatched hut. A thunderstorm is going through just west of us and a good breeze always accompanies rain.

Saturday, December 14, 12 Noon—Just got back from a buffalo roundup. Last evening Dick came up with a master plan and this morning he, Bob and I rode north 1½ hours, on bullocks, to a predetermined spot between the swamp and the forest. Four cowboys, including Raimundo and Beniditto, had gone ahead to either push a buffalo by us or possibly to bring a bull to bay in the thick swamp. Nothing happened again and we returned to camp empty-handed. This afternoon we will go to the second platform to spend the night.

Sunday, December 15, 11 A.M.—We went to the second platform yesterday afternoon as planned but it was a great disappointment. Not a single buffalo had been through there since we built it three days ago.

Raimundo now had a plan. He suggested that we go to an abandoned farm house about a mile away, spend the night there, and get up early to be at a big wallow near there by daylight the next morning.

This we did and as we came out of the forest at the break of day, there were a dozen buffaloes, all bulls, Dick said, in the open. Our first sight of them in eight days of beating the bush and sloshing in mud and water. None of them were of any great size, however. The largest, with horns of about four-foot spread, was out of bow range. Two smaller bulls were staging a mock fight about sixty yards from the last bit of cover we had and that was scanty. The others were scattered around at greater distances.

We were in deep mud and somebody's foot made a smacking sound as it was withdrawn from the mire. This alerted the herd which looked our way and three of them advanced cautiously to within forty-five yards, where they stopped, shoulder to shoulder, and stared with great curiosity. Our targets were only heads, horns, and legs, however, and we stood fast waiting hopefully for a better opportunity. Caution overcame their interest in us finally and they wheeled in a dash for the forest beyond and our arrows fell short seventy yards away.

We reached camp at 9:30 A.M., had a bath, breakfast, and a bull session over the usual gin and water flavored with lime juice, during which we came to some conclusions. One was that these buffaloes, with the rainy season on, present the toughest hunting there is. We agreed also that before the rains, when they were limited to only a few water holes and wallows, one could travel with greater ease and the problem of bagging a good one would be much less. Right now abundant food and water is everywhere and the area is big and the cover thick.

We all agreed that with elevated platforms at strategic places, all-night vigils would bring results, but the platforms should be built at least a week before they are used. The scent from the track of man or horse upsets them badly.

It was agreed also that since we were hunting Asiatic buffaloes and in Asia the elevated platforms erected for tiger hunting are called machans, we would call our platforms machans. The machans we have built are made from a type of palm that sends up a long slender trunk, forty to sixty feet high, reaching through the forest canopy to expose its umbrellalike top to the sun. The butt end is four or five inches in diameter, tapering to two or three inches at the top. This top, the last two feet of it, contains a snow-white core about an inch in diameter that makes a delicious salad. We ate them raw, on the spot. The monkeys feed on this also.

These palms are easily cut with a machete, a tool the cowboys are never without. A living tree is used for one of the four corners. The other three corner posts are built from the butt ends of palms, imbedded in a hole dug with a machete. The floor of the machan is constructed of palm poles laid tightly together and lashed in place, either with palm leaves, a hanging vine, or bark from trees. Our mattresses, half an inch thick, fell somewhat short of leveling off the rounded poles.

During an all-night stand, we stayed awake in shifts, to listen for animals approaching and to awaken anyone who started snoring. Last night, as we slept in the abandoned farm house, Dick advised us to keep our boots on. One's feet are a prime target for large vampire bats that suck blood from humans and animals.

Today we received an invitation, by word of mouth, from a passing cowboy, to be guests at an annual cowboy roundup at a ranch five hours away by horseback. This was to be a special occasion as it was the two hundredth anniversary of ownership by this ranch family. Telling ourselves that we have been pushing too hard and being somewhat broken to the saddle, we've decided to saddle up tomorrow morning and attend the affair.

The ranch owners live in Belém. They visit the ranches only about twice a year and then only briefly. They are not particularly concerned about the people who run their places. Their main interest is checking in the cattle that are shipped by sailboat from the ranches to Belém.

Tuesday, December 17, 5 P.M.—No opportunity to write yesterday. In the saddle five hours, reaching our destination at noon. We were greeted graciously by the owner and host who spoke no English.

The ranch house was enormous. Eight large bedrooms upstairs, each with two beds and any number of hammocks one might wish to string on the many hooks on the corner walls. Downstairs, a wide porch ran along three sides, and speakers were mounted at various places to send out music from a record player.

A much larger building still, off to the side, contained a great many rooms to house the celebrators who slept in tiers of hammocks on three levels and at all sorts of odd angles. The guests numbered about three hundred, mostly young people who had traveled for miles by horse and bullock to attend the celebration.

We had a late lunch, our party of three plus the owner and a man from the bank who was checking on collateral. Five cows had been slaughtered for the occasion plus turkeys, pigs, and chickens.

At about 3 P.M. someone cranked up a generator and music blasted from the speakers with all the volume possible, shaking the very supporting posts that held the house above the mud.

In the beginning, people just sat on benches and looked self-consciously at each other. But after an hour, a few girls started dancing together and an hour later the most daring of the boys joined them. By 10 P.M. when we went to bed, the hardwood boards of the floor were being polished by the shuffling of some five hundred feet. Sleep was nearly impossible. A speaker, mounted on the ceiling beneath the floor of our room, rattled glasses on a shelf and the teeth in our heads.

Daylight finally came, but nothing had changed except that the number of revelers was reduced to about half. We left immediately to go back to camp, experiencing great relief when the noisy din faded as we rode off into the jungle.

It was a blistering day. The temperature stood at about 110 degrees, or so it seemed. We hunted some on the way back, but mostly tried to stay in the forest to escape the heat. Our horses became very tired during the long ride.

» «

There is not the great assortment of bird life here that we saw in Africa. Parrots are the most numerous and the noisiest. The toucan is the most exotic. He has a ponderous bright blue, yellow, and brown bill, seven or eight inches long, and beautiful plumage. Hummingbirds are plentiful and we saw the familiar house wren.

Floral varieties have been a disappointment. Perhaps they have not had time to bloom since the heavy rain or the season is reversed, or late. Raimundo says this is the first time in twenty-three years that they have had rain before the middle of January. Once, while riding through the forest, however, we passed under a mammoth tree that had shed tiny blue flowers completely covering the ground like blue snow.

This is another delightful evening. I am writing on our dining table which is made of palm slats held together with bindings of palm leaves. I level it off with our total library, a copy of *Playboy* that was bootlegged into Brazil and which cost Dick three dollars plus a Latin-American edition of *Time* magazine. I can tell, as I sit here, that I am not as saddle-seasoned as I thought I was.

Our dining table is made of palm slats.

Tomorrow will be another early rise. Raimundo suggests that we visit a wallow he knows about. Just a few miles from camp. We must be there at the break of day. It is in the general direction of machan ⅝2. We will carry a lunch and spend the night in the machan. Raimundo will return to camp as there is barely room for three of us on the platform. We will walk again this time. Our beasts of burden need a day of rest.

Thursday, December 19—The hunt yesterday was fruitless. We reached the machan at 5 P.M. There had been a few buffaloes through the area the night before, but otherwise only hummingbirds looked us over before the bats and fireflies came in as dusk melted into night.

The night was uneventful except for smaller animals rustling through the bushes. The moon had failed us and the very first signs of day unveiled a mist that reduced visibility to a hundred yards. But suddenly we heard the sound of splashing hooves. It could only be buffaloes and they were coming our way. We quickly got ourselves into position as the splashing died into the beat of hooves as they came onto the hard ground near the wallow.

They came out of the mist like gray ghosts. Two ponderous bulls with massive horns that swept back like the wings of a jet. Their crafty caution was thrown to the wind as they lumbered to our ambush, interested, it seemed, only in submerging themselves in the yellow mud ahead.

We had approached our machan from the rear and there was no scent in their path. The situation was perfect except that they were about forty yards apart and

Our machan at the yellow mudhole.

it might be difficult to get two bow shots. Bob sensed this and quickly exchanged his bow for Dick's rifle. This left me with no problem and I could choose the timing of my shot. I let the first bull go by slightly before putting my arrow deep in his lung area from about fifteen yards.

The twang of my bowstring was consumed by the roar of the gun. The 400-grain bullet seemed to have no effect on the second bull. At the next shot he

Buffaloes like this thick cover.

Bob's bull had long swept-back horns.

These Asiatic buffaloes are tremendous beasts!

stumbled and a third seemed unnecessary. He piled up near some ground palms, about sixty yards away.

My buffalo had disappeared in the forest. We waited for an hour, drank a toast to our good luck from the last of our canteens, ate candy bars, and looked over Bob's big bull before taking the trail of the one I had shot.

It was easy to follow. The Razorhead hit resulted in excellent tracking signs. We walked a short way into the forest to find my trophy—a magnificent bull, lying majestically on our path. His horns swept back in a wide arc that spread five and a half feet. The front hooves were seven inches wide and his total weight must certainly have been eighteen hundred pounds. We waited an hour until the light was good enough for pictures and it was 2 P.M. before we got back to camp.

Raimundo and Beniditto and two cowboys went in with horses and four bullocks to bring back the horns and meat. It will be late tonight when they arrive with the first load. They will be busy the rest of the night getting it all in to camp.

We had our last parrot-dove shoot this evening. If we are lucky we might get to Belém tomorrow evening and catch a plane for home the next day.

As always, when a trophy is bagged the hardships of the hunt are forgotten. It is good that the hunter's mind can filter out the arduous and retain only the pleasant memories of such a trip. Our greatest problem was those early rains which made hunting so difficult. If this had not occurred, I am sure we would have had success much earlier and with much less effort. We were extremely fortunate in finally bagging such magnificent bulls. Dick says they are the largest he has seen. Raimundo says, however, that he has seen bigger bulls, one of which he swears has ten-foot horns. I am not sure whether he means ten-foot spread or ten feet measuring around the horns. In either case he would be a whopper with feet, Raimundo insists, that are eight inches wide when not splayed out!

This is the only place in the world where Asiatic buffaloes can be hunted legally. They were imported from Asia, in the dim, forgotten past, and have done well in spite of harassment by the ranchers. Those that survive impart their cunning wisdom to the next generation.

We had a round table discussion this evening, Dick, Bob, and I, and reached certain conclusions in terms of improving the hunting conditions. There was no doubt in anyone's mind that successful hunts could be conducted during October, November, December, and early January, providing early rains did not set in. Dick felt that the machan method would provide trophies for those who wished to hunt this way. As I have said, before the wet season, the buffaloes would not have the unlimited range they now have and a half dozen machans, erected well in advance of the hunt, in the most likely spots, should bring results and allow for a selection of trophies.

It would simply boil down to the business of rotating watches and it would be no chore to go to the machans in early evening and return next morning. Thicker mattresses would ease discomfort and insect repellent keeps the pests away. All one would forgo is the evening dove and parrot shoot but those parrots, living to the ripe old age of thirty to forty years, are no delicacy anyway.

It was agreed also that refrigeration is a must. There is a certain satisfaction in the tinkle of ice when the temperature is in the one hundred zone and a freezing compartment would keep meat for almost any length of time. Dick's water filter works fine but water-purifying pills should go into every batch.

Dick has built an airstrip right near camp and in the dry season it would be no problem to bring equipment in. Hunters could fly to within walking distance and avoid our three-hour ride.

Some memories, I am sure, will remain sharply with us from this hunt. The two buffaloes emerging from the early morning mist and those wonderful evenings sitting under our thatched dining-room roof. There was always a gentle breeze as the heat tapered off to a very comfortable temperature. We talked over events of the day as the clattering of parrots and the howling of monkeys gave way to the frogs and other night sounds of Marajó Island.

Chapter 16

REFLECTIONS

Field notes provide an opportunity to relive, time and again, the experiences of each trip. Without exception, the highlights fall into a pattern.

Hardships are quickly forgotten. Intense heat, bitter cold, rain and snow, fatigue and luckless hunting fade quickly into memories of great fellowship, thoughts of beautiful country, pleasant camps, and happy campfires. Trophies are not really important and have a low priority on the list.

A downed animal is most certainly the object of a hunting trip, but it becomes an anticlimax when compared to the many other pleasures of the hunt. A period of remorse is in order. Perhaps a few words of forgiveness for having taken a life. After this there is a self-satisfaction for having accomplished a successful stalk and made a good shot.

But a hunt based only on trophies taken falls far short of what the ultimate goal should be. I have known many hunters who, returning empty-handed, have had nothing to say of the enjoyment of time spent in nature's outdoors.

I like to think that an expedition be looked upon, whether it be an evening hunt nearby or a prolonged trip to some far-off place, as a venture into an unspoiled area. With time to commune with your inner soul as you share the outdoors with the birds, animals, and fish that live there. And, in another vein, if it is a lengthy trip, select your companions well. A hunting camp is a great place to test the mettle of your friends.

Then there are the horses one gets to know. A mountain horse is a marvel to observe and a pleasure to ride and be associated with. They are, in most cases, the outfitters only means of transportation and they are accepted as part of the family and cared for in the same way.

On two different hunts with Bob Buzby on Dry Creek, Alaska (trips not included in this book), I had a horse named Flicker. He had an insatiable appetite and I condoned the unpardonable by allowing him to munch his way along. As a result, we did not get to our destination in record time, but it did provide the opportunity to see the country in more detail.

In spite of the fact that I always provided him with breakfast leftovers, for which he would nuzzle through my pockets, he was not against heading toward camp if left with only the reins down. He had a clever way of holding his head sideways to keep from stepping on the reins.

On another hunt, a glacier had filled a valley floor with immense boulders. We dismounted and the horses crawled, bellies dragging the rocks, through this spillage for several hundred yards.

Horses have a pecking order also. They are clannish as a group and it is exceedingly interesting to watch their behavior in this respect.

At the top of the list of hunt bonuses, however, are the outfitters and guides who can make or break a trip. When one is lucky enough to draw the old-timers, a hunt can be outstanding.

I speak of woodsmen. Those who have spent most of their lives in the bush. Trappers, prospectors, homesteaders, and sometimes commercial fishermen. These men are homespun philosophers who can judge one's worth in a few hours. To survive in their chosen profession they have to be resourceful to the ultimate degree. Their judgment of a situation does not come quickly, except in emergency, but is well thought out with reference to weather, time of day, and all other factors bearing on the subject. They have a vast amount of experience to draw upon, otherwise they might have perished long ago.

It behooves the hunter to observe and listen to these men. I have sat by many a campfire enriching my knowledge of the wild, and enjoying their spinning of yarns. Many of them true tales of narrow escapes. Some tailored to bewilder the tenderfoot. All highly entertaining.

I feel like one of God's chosen people, having had the opportunity to share, with many fine companions, these varied and lovely realms of our natural world.